SAYFO – AN ACCOUNT OF THE ASSYRIAN GENOCIDE

Alternative Histories: Narratives from the Middle East and Mediterranean

Series Editor: Sargon Donabed

This series provides a forum for exchange on a myriad of alternative histories of marginalised communities and individuals in the Near and Middle East and Mediterranean, and those of Middle Eastern or Mediterranean heritage. It also highlights thematic issues relating to various native peoples and their narratives and – with particular contemporary relevance – explore encounters with the notion of 'other' within societies. Often moving beyond the conventional state-centred and dominant monolithic approach, or reinterpreting previously accepted stories, books in the series examine and explain themes from inter-communal relations, environment, health and society, and explore ethnic, communal, racial, linguistic and religious developments, in addition to geopolitics.

Books in the Series (Published and Forthcoming)

Sayfo – An Account of the Assyrian Genocide
Abed Mshiho Neman of Qarabash
translated and annotated by Michael Abdalla and Łukasz Kiczko

Tunisia's Andalusians: The Cultural Identity of a North African Minority
Marta Dominguez Diaz

Palestinian Citizens of Israel: A History Through Fiction, 1948–2010
Manar Makhoul

Armenians Beyond Diaspora: Making Lebanon their Own
Tsolin Nalbantian

Conflict on Mount Lebanon: The Druze, the Maronites and Collective Memory
Makram Rabah

The Art of Minorities: Cultural Representation in Museums of the Middle East and North Africa
Edited by Virginie Rey

Shi'a Minorities in the Contemporary World: Migration, Transnationalism and Multilocality
Edited by Oliver Scharbrodt and Yafa Shanneik

Protestants, Gender and the Arab Renaissance in Late Ottoman Syria
Deanna Ferree Womack

edinburghuniversitypress.com/series/ahnme

SAYFO
AN ACCOUNT OF THE ASSYRIAN GENOCIDE

ABED MSHIHO NEMAN OF QARABASH

Translated with an Introduction and Notes by Michael Abdalla and Łukasz Kiczko

EDINBURGH
University Press

Edinburgh University Press is one of the leading university presses in the UK. We publish academic books and journals in our selected subject areas across the humanities and social sciences, combining cutting-edge scholarship with high editorial and production values to produce academic works of lasting importance. For more information visit our website: edinburghuniversitypress.com

Edinburgh University Press Ltd
The Tun – Holyrood Road
12 (2f) Jackson's Entry
Edinburgh EH8 8PJ

First published in hardback by Edinburgh University Press 2021

Typeset in 11/15 Adobe Garamond by
Servis Filmsetting Ltd, Stockport, Cheshire

A CIP record for this book is available from the British Library

ISBN 978 1 4744 4750 8 (hardback)
ISBN 978 1 4744 4751 5 (paperback)
ISBN 978 1 4744 4752 2 (webready PDF)
ISBN 978 1 4744 4753 9 (epub)

Published with the support of the University of Edinburgh Scholarly Publishing Initiatives Fund.

CONTENTS

Acknowledgements vii
List of Figures ix
Preface xi
About the Diary and its Author xv
Background of the Region xxiii

Spilt Blood, or the Tragedy of the Lambs of Christ
Diary of a Seminarian
1 From the Author 3
2 The Emergence and Spread of Christianity 8
3 Difficult Times – Persecution Suffered by Christianity in Various Periods of History 18
4 Persecution in the Most Recent Times – the End of the Nineteenth Century 39
5 The Year 1914 – the Beginning of World War I 51
6 My Diary 63
7 Eyewitness Reports – the Story of a Road Worker named Abed Mshiho, who Saw the Most 77

8 The Christians of the City of Amida and its Subordinate Villages – Executions and the Exodus of 1915 98
9 Extermination of Christians in the Villages of the District of Mardin in 1914 118
10 The Sinjar Mountains Suffer on Behalf of Christians 135
11 The Fate of Christian Inhabitants of Other Localities 146
12 Positive and Negative Attitudes of Some Participants in the Exterminations 168

Bibliography 177
Annex 1 187
Annex 2 192
Annex 3 209
Index 212

ACKNOWLEDGEMENTS

I am grateful to many people for the opportunity to translate and publish the work of Abed Mshiho Neman of Qarabash. First of all I owe thanks to my colleague, ʿĪsā Ḥannā of Augsburg, Germany, for providing me with a photocopy of the original Syriac manuscript owned and published (1997) by the Assyrian Democratic Organisation and for his enduring faith that the Polish translation of the work of my teacher (and Mr Hanna's) shall see the light of day. Second, I would like to express my gratitude to Jan Beṯ-Ṣawoce of Södertälje, Sweden, the founder and head of the Mesopotamian Library located at the Södertörn University, Huddinge-Stockholm, Sweden, for his support and patience during this project. Thanks to his comprehensive knowledge of the subject and his excellent orientation in the local geography of the region with which the manuscript deals, and in which he was raised, I was able to make use of his knowledge and of the rich library that he had collected over the last twenty five years. In a joint and intense effort over three days at the Mesopotamian Library, we were able to verify many of the names and the people that are found in the manuscript.

The Polish version of the book was published in 2013 by the UNUM publishing house in Kraków, and later republished and properly marketed in 2015 by the Agape publishing house in Poznań. Thanks also to Professor

Mirosław Rucki, who provided much input and assistance in the course of this endeavour. Additionally, to Łukasz Kiczko, who suggested we also translate an English version for wider readership, I am most appreciative.

Thanks, are also due to the Assyrian Youth Association of Sweden, in particular Mr Johannes Beth Gabriel and Mr Hanibal Romanos for their support. Also, to my colleague Abdulmesih BarAbraham, a native of Ṭūr 'Abdīn, Turkey, who provided useful comments and footnotes, for which I am most grateful. Much appreciation to all.

Michael Abdalla
Poznań, Poland, June 2019

The Assyrian Studies Association helped make this translation possible.

FIGURES

Maps

1 General map of the region xxiv
2 Inset of Ṭūr ʻAbdīn and its environs xxiv

Figures

1 Yusuf Akbulut, the sole priest in Diyarbakır at the Assyrian cemetery in the centre of the town xxxii
2 The ruins of one of the ancient temples in the village of Ḥāḥ xxxv
3 The remains of cells, monasteries and churches on a high mountain to the east of the monastery of Zaʻfarān xl
4 The ruins of an Assyrian farm in the village of Badebe xliv
5 The remains of cells, monasteries and churches on a high mountain to the east of the monastery of Zaʻfarān 64
6 The bishop of the Mor Gabriel monastery with three monks from Damascus and the author of the photographs 156
7 The village of ʻAyn Wardo 200
8 The fortified church of ʻAyn Wardo 200
9 Abandoned graves – the village of ʻAyn Wardo 201

10 The ruins of Ḥesnō d-Kīfō (the rock fortress) at the Tigris, northern borders of Ṭūr 'Abdīn 201
11 Ḥesnō d-Kīfō – the remains of a house 205
12 Title page of *Al-Jihād*, 1915 211

PREFACE

Note on the Transliteration and Editing Symbols

While working on this text, apart from numerous necessary clarifications and comments given in footnotes, it was necessary to use the following symbols to clarify amendments of the original text:

> [ ] reconstructed text, supplementary terms, marginalia, certain dates or clarification of passages, as well as the manuscript's original page numbers
> { } different versions or translations of the name of the described locality or concept, or passages shifted in location from one place in the manuscript to another place in the edited translation in order to uphold and maintain the sequence of events recollected.

Notes on General Translation and Editing

The task of determining the geographic location of many of the settlements the author describes has proven to be quite a challenge; some of these towns and villages in particular bear other names today than those that were known when the text was created. It is known that Kemal Atatürk ordered the *Turkification* of not only Assyrian personal names but also names of places (toponyms), in a process of 'cultural genocide'. Personal names and place names that were participles or nouns in Syriac (which is quite common among Semitic peoples) were directly translated into Turkish, while others were granted entirely unrelated names from a list drawn up by Turkish officials.

In fact, the author himself uses on more than one occasion various names or notations differing from those used earlier on to describe a specific locality or uses respective parallel declination as compared to forms mentioned previously. Apart from this, the author often provides names of ancient localities, used in Syriac texts, in most cases in the way they were rendered in Greek, which on modern Turkish maps are recorded in altered forms or plainly sound different. Despite tedious searches on available official and unofficial maps, as well as searching various sketches and descriptions, including those drawn up by travellers and missionaries, it was impossible to determine the modern equivalents of names of many localities and, accordingly, to describe their locations on maps of what today is the Republic of Turkey. A great help in this regard was provided by the work of Helga Anschütz (1985).[1] One cannot exclude the possibility that certain localities ceased to exist after the slaughters of Christians. The same locality has been recorded with different names, most probably depending on the nationality of the local informant, from whom the cartographer, missionary or traveller had heard it. The adaptation, modification or transformation of place names into the language or dialect of a specific ethnic group, irrespective of those who would live or had lived in it, is a normal phenomenon. For instance, only very few Syrians would name the capital of their country as 'Dimashq' (the official name) but would rather use the name 'Shām'.

During editing of the translated text, names used by the author were assumed. Other versions, both ancient (Assyrian, Greek) as well as modern

[1] Helga Anschütz was a German scholar and linguist from Hamburg (1928–2006). She had devoted most of her adult life to Assyrians of Iran and Ṭūr 'Abdīn and was the author and producer of many works, unique photographs and films. At her request, she was buried in the cemetery by the St Ephrem monastery belonging to the Syrian Orthodox Church. Ms Anschütz transferred all of her inheritance, together with her rich archive, to an Assyrian foundation that had set up an international award in her name, awarded to extraordinary Assyrian scholars.

(Arabic, Turkish), along with their diverse local varieties, are provided in the footnotes. The issue of the proper name of this or that locality, where the atrocities took place, seems to be of limited importance in the face of the tragedy that befell their inhabitants. Hundreds of villages and cities, inhabited for centuries by Armenians or Assyrians, became, after World War I, places that were exclusively or almost exclusively inhabited by Kurds and some Turks.

As a final remark, the editors attempted the translation to be as close to the original as possible. However, the author expands upon certain topics, even if they are few, using large numbers of comparisons. Such an approach, even if commonplace and typical for narrative literature and art, is practiced and accepted among societies of the Near East; however, the European reader perceives this style of writing as melancholic. The contents of such passages were akin to laments or religious litanies and referred in no direct way to the described events. The reduction of the number of such words used, leading to a more precise wording of a specific fragment, was undertaken solely and exclusively where the original intent of the author could be preserved with ease. Such interventions were unavoidable, particularly in the final chapter.

The text contains many Turkish honorifics and titles of nobility popular at the time it was written down, such as Pasha, Agha, Beg (or Bey), Efendi, Hajji, Sheikh. These were used by members of the military as well as civilian or religious figures, persons 'well born', affluent, having authentic or alleged social stances, and tribal leaders. These titles continue to be used in Arabic countries, particularly in dialects and television series.

The author describes exclusively the fate of the inhabitants of those localities that he had known, or those about whom he had heard from eyewitnesses. However, the atrocities took place everywhere Christians lived in Turkey. In this regard, the author's revelations were amended by two annexes, describing the fate of inhabitants of a few other Assyrian villages, just a few among many. The first annex concerns the events of the year 1895, the second one deals with the effects of the subsequent wave of terror, to which victims from almost all of the same villages fell prey in the years 1914–15. These annexes are a very modest addendum covering but a small portion of the image of destruction orchestrated in one of many regions. After reading this testimony, many readers may come to the conclusion that each Armenian, Armenian-Assyrian or Assyrian locality deserves to be spoken of individually, not only based on the available sources but also with the use of stories of those witnesses or heirs of witnesses that are still alive. At this point, we must say that numerous Assyrian intellectuals should be praised for working over the years quite vigorously on preserving for future generations the memories of older people, witnesses to these massacres, who are now scattered across many countries. The stories told by each individual narrator can only be treated as a small part of the events that transpired; it shall only be their merger, analysis and verification that shall enable us to picture the actual scale of this tragedy. For any researcher dealing with this period of history, which is shrouded in uncertainty and a sense of loss, the occasional discovery of new documents and writings, of whose existence nobody, not even closest family members, was aware, are very valuable. Elegies drawn up in a particular style by eyewitnesses, mainly in Syriac, are a separate source of information about the fates of particular localities and their inhabitants. Much of this body of work remains unstudied.

Michael Abdalla and Łukasz Kiczko
Poznań, Poland, 27 March 2018

ABOUT THE DIARY AND ITS AUTHOR[1]

The book, originally titled in Syriac *Dmō zlīḥō* [Bloodshed], was published first in Germany by the Assyrian Democratic Organization (1997), and shortly after that in the Netherlands by Bar Hebraeus Verlag (1999/2002).[2] In 2002, Bar Hebraeus Verlag published its German translation *Vergossenes blut*, as well as the Dutch version *Vergoten Bloed.* In 2005, Bishop Mor Thawfilos George Ṣalībā translated the work into Arabic and it was published in Beirut under the title *Ad-Dam al-masfūk*. Unfortunately, none of those versions was revised and equipped with a scientific apparatus, and the Arabic edition may have contained printing errors. Michael Abdalla published an edition with a critical apparatus in Poland, Poznań, in 2015 in cooperation with Agape Publishers.

The present edition is based on the manuscript belonging to Mr ʻĪsā

[1] Based on the biography authored by Barṣōm, A. M., *Aḍwā' ʻalā adabina as-suriānī al-ḥadīṯ* [On Our contemporary Assyrian Literature], pp. 85–92.

[2] Abed Mshiho Naʻman Qarabāš, *Dmo zlīḥō awkīṯ nekesto d-ʻōne da-mšīḥo* [Bloodshed, or the catastrophe of Christ's lambs] (1997); Abed Mshiho Naʻman Qarabashi, *Dmo Zliho: Vergoten Bloed: Verhalen over de gruweldaden jegens Christenen in Turkije en over het leed dat hun in 1895 en in 1914-1918 is aangedaan*, George Toro and Amil Gorgis trans. (Glanerbrug, the Netherlands: Bar Hebraeus, 2002).

Ḥannā, an Assyrian immigrant in Augsburg. It was written in the liturgical tongue of Syriac but needed appropriate commentary and references to explain and contextualise its narrative. Various available sources were confronted in order to correct some inaccurate data and statements. The author, Abed Mshiho of Qarabash, wrote his work in very difficult and unstable circumstances. He was forced to leave one country after another and lived in what became modern Turkey as well as what was once known as Greater Syria (Jordan, Palestine, Syria and Lebanon).[3]

In the book, Abed Mshiho presented the story of the persecutions of Christian people in the region in which he lived, from ancient times up to his own present day, beginning with the very first confrontation with Judaism, then with the Roman Empire, the persecutions performed by Persians in the fourth century of the Common Era, which are still little known in Europe, and so on. A large part of the work is dedicated to the forgotten massacres in the period from 1895 to 1918 that took place in the southeastern regions of Turkey.

The value of the book is great because it contains the authentic accounts made by witnesses and a few survivors, interviewed by him in the historical monastery Dayr az-Zaʿfarān (near Mardin), which had been a patriarchal seat for centuries. It was one of several monasteries left unharmed in the region, while tens of others were completely destroyed. Abed Mshiho at the time was a young student in the monastery's seminary, where as an orphan he found shelter at the tender age of eight. Here in the monastery he found a diary written by Fr Laḥdō, martyred by Kurds, who witnessed the massacres in 1895. Abed Mshiho used this diary in one of chapters in his book. In addition, he included stories related by people, both Armenian and Assyrian, who survived the massacres of 1914–18. Thus, the present book is a valuable first-hand account on the terrible fate of Assyrian and Armenian Christians in the region of southern Turkey.

Despite of his own difficulties, Abed Mshiho of Qarabash managed to educate a generation of Assyrians. Many of his students achieved high posi-

[3] The name is most often rendered in Arabic: ʿAbd al-Masīḥ Nuʿmān Qarabāshī. The author spent most of his life in Arab countries once known as Greater Syria. Masters, B., *Christians and Jews in the Ottoman Arab World: The Roots of Sectarianism*, p. xii

tions as scholars, teachers or writers and continue his educational mission both in Middle East and in diaspora. Apart from the current work *Dmō zlīḥō*, he wrote primary school Syriac textbooks and treatises on Syriac grammar. He wrote also tales and poems published in Syria and Lebanon, as well as some plays dedicated to the history of Assyrians.

Moreover, Abed Mshiho translated numerous books from Arabic into Syriac, among them historical books written by the martyred Bishop Adday Sher. Most importantly, he undertook his efforts completely voluntarily. Usually, his books were published by general donations and he himself took care of the orphans and victims of the various persecutions. In many circles he is seen as the most well versed author of Syriac in the twentieth century.

Abed Mshiho Neman of Qarabash was born in 1903 in the village of Qarabash (from which stems his regional name, Qarabashi), not far from the city of Amida[4] in southeastern Turkey, to John and his wife Manush. At the age of six he lost his father. Two years later, encouraged by the bishop of the Syrian Orthodox Church[5], Elias Shakir,[6] he entered the Zaʿfarān monastery.[7] The monastery cook cared for the eight-year-old boy, treating him as if he were her son. It is here that young Abed Mshiho studied Syriac, Arabic and Turkish under three famed monks and demanding teachers: Elias Malke Qōrō,[8] Tūmā Yaʿqūb and Yūḥānōn Dolabani,[9] the latter being Bishop

4 Diyarbakır, the current official name of city Āmid or Amida, was created in the tenth century before the Common Era (BCE).

5 The church was originally known in English as the Assyrian Orthodox Church according to Akdemir, S., *The Syrian Orthodox Community in the Mosaic of Istanbul.*

6 He later became the patriarch of this church and died in Malabar, India in 1932; it is where his mausoleum is located, a pilgrimage site visited by the faithful.

7 The Assyrian name of the monastery is Dayro d-Kurkmo (from *kurkmo* – curcuma), and the Arabic name is Dayr az-Zaʿfarān (from *zaʿfarān* – saffron).

8 This man became a bishop and patriarchal vicar in India (1881–1962).

9 Mr Dolabani lived from 1885 to 1969, serving as the bishop of Mardin, Turkey, from 1947. He was one of the great Assyrians of the twentieth century, a mentor, scholar, lover of language and history, and author and translator of numerous works. He led the life of a hermit that could be compared to the life of the first 'fathers of the desert'. He is buried at the Zaʿfarān monastery. His funeral was a grand event. Thousands of Assyrians from Syria took part, as thanks to the agreement of officials from both border regions they were liberated from the duty of needing to obtain visas. Butros, P., Mor Filoksinos Yuhanon Dolabani: A Man of God & Assyria (https://bethnahrin.de/2007/08/19/a-man-of-god-and-assyria/ [translated by Tomas Isik]).

Philoxenos of Mardin. Dolabani had a particularly broad knowledge, which he taught with exceptional dedication to his seminarians However, in 1921, the ambitious and gifted Abed Mshiho had a conflict with the prior, Ḥannā Ghandūr.[10] The boy abandoned the monastery and travelled to Amida. These were particularly difficult times for Christians. Fearing for the boy's life, under threat of inevitable service in the Turkish military from which very few Christians returned home, the contemporary bishop of Amida, Dionosiyyos 'Abd an-Nūr sent the boy secretly to Beirut. In 1926, and again 1935–6, Abed Mshiho taught Syriac at the Assyrian orphanage established in the city, following an assignment on an invitation as a teacher, first to Bethlehem for two years (1937–8), and then to Jerusalem, spending twelve years in Palestine. In 1951 he travelled to Qamishli,[11] Syria, where for seventeen years he taught the Syriac language in various Assyrian schools until they were closed by a governmental order in 1967.[12] After this venture he again returned to Beirut, where from 1972 to 1975 he found employment as a language teacher at St Ephrem seminary.[13] He died in Beirut in 1983.

Working under markedly unfavourable conditions, Abed Mshiho of Qarabash was able to educate people who are today known and respected as teachers and writers within the Assyrian community. All of them recall their teacher and mentor with sympathy and treat the continuation of his work as

[10] This man was said, as the bishop of Beirut and Damascus, to have joined into union with the Roman Catholic Church.

[11] Qamishli is a large city in northeastern Syria close to the Turkish border, founded in 1925 by Assyrian survivors of the genocide from the Ṭūr 'Abdīn region in southeastern Turkey. The city counted until recently close to 300,000 inhabitants: Assyrians, Arabs, Armenians, Kurds and others. Until 1974, it also had a Jewish settlement. On the Assyrian community in this city, see Abdalla, M., 'The Assyrian Community of Qamishli in North-Eastern Syria in the Years 1925–1970', pp. 87–103.

[12] The translator and editor of this book was a basic level pupil at an Assyrian private school in Qamishli (1958–64). He found himself in the group of pupils that decided in the summer of 1967 to see their professor (*malfōnō*) off before his departure to Beirut. The professor lived in a mud house to the south of the city centre. There was no Assyrian in the city who would not have known the professor.

[13] Abūnā, A., *Adab al-lugha al-ārāmiyya*, pp. 567–9, gives other biographical details: 'The boy was sent to the monastery at the age of 10 by his uncle, the priest Faulos (Paul), son of priest 'Ablaḥad Gabriel, and had left it in the year 1922, after the school closed down. As his village was already empty, he set off for Diyarbakır. A year later he found himself in Aleppo, and from there he travelled to Beirut'.

a mission, both in the countries of the Near East as well as in the diaspora. Beside his work as a teacher, Abed Mshiho of Qarabash left behind a rich literary heritage.

About the Manuscript

The manuscript is composed of 104 sheets, bound together in smooth cardboard, numbered using numerals commonly referred to as 'Hindu' (or Arabic), whereby the first four pages are designated to be an 'Introduction'[14] and bear numbers 222–225, the title page, composed of half a sheet, bears the number 221, and the final sheet of the manuscript bears the number 177. Such a numbering scheme might suggest that the text is not complete, and that it is missing close to fifty pages. The question also arises as to why the title page bears the number 221 instead of 1? One may surmise that this part of the manuscript was written down last, and it is so numbered because the pages 177–220 missing from the manuscript contained – perhaps – a different text, such as homework being part of the studies at the monastery school, where the author was a pupil. It is almost certain that during those difficult times, the pupils had only one notebook each.[15] Furthermore, the numbering system used by the author attracts attention, as it is only rarely seen in monastery schools; the letters of the Aramaic alphabet were more commonly used, and they are still used for the purpose of pagination and dating by writers in this language.

The top left corner of page one of the manuscript contains the author's dedication which reads: 'Offered sincerely to student of the clerical school, 'Abd al-Aḥad Gallō Ṣṭayfō'. Under the dedication, there is the signature: 'The Syriac letters 'ayn (an abbreviation of Abed) and M (abbreviation of Mshiho) of Qarabash, (26.03.1974)'.[16] It is also difficult to understand why the author uses in the text itself another system for dates based on Arabic numerals, but at certain places, such as in subheadings, he uses Aramaic letters.[17]

[14] In the translation, this heading was changed to *From the author*.

[15] This was the case in Assyrian private schools in Qamishli in the 1950s and 1960s as well.

[16] 'Abd al-Aḥad Gallō Ṣṭayfō was a seminarian at a clerical school in Beirut in 1974. He confirmed having given a photocopy of the manuscript to his colleague, 'Īsā Ḥannā.

[17] The letters of the Aramaic alphabet, and their corresponding numeral values, continue to be used for dates.

Despite inconsistent pagination of the manuscript, the text is a comprehensive whole.[18] Using his own pagination, the author arrived at the correct number of 203 pages, which make up the manuscript. And this is the continuous numbering that he used, entering the new numbers at the page centre in the footer.

The paper, on which the author had written down his diary, was a lined notebook. The pages have the dimensions 14.5 by 20.5 centimetres and hold 22 rows with six to eight words each, with an average character count of 25 to 40 per line. The author most probably used a pen and black ink. The writing is clear and careful; the writing style is uniform, with adherence to an even right margin; the sentences are correctly punctuated; and the first words of paragraphs are shifted slightly to the left.

There are numerous words corrected by the author, and the text often also includes an 'x' mark, included in a fashion similar to footnotes located at the bottom of the page or along the margin – in most cases, the right margin – and provided with one or more sentences that should be found where the mark is placed in the text, as an amendment to the text. There are also other remarks – found on margins in most cases – along the general lines of 'move to such and such page'.[19] In addition, the paragraphs of page 222 (numbering five) and all three paragraphs making up page 223, are provided

[18] In the manuscript, the sequence of page numbers is confusing. Following uninterrupted numbering from page 3 to 30 (the author had also entitled this chapter 'Introduction'), there are pages 36–43 (without pages 31–5) and 45–80 (without pages 36–44), and after page 80, there begins a new, albeit discontinuous numeration, from 49 to 176. The sheet with page numbers 106 and 107 is seen twice, and its contents are the same; however, the sheet with numbers 128 and 129 is bound only after sheet 130–1. The sheet with numbers 162–3 is also missing. A. G. Ṣṭayfō confessed during a conversation to the editor that he personally photocopied the original of the manuscript and bound its sheets, and that he numbered the sheets that had no numbers assigned by the author himself, adding that he executed all of this only imprecisely.

[19] For instance, page 176 in its entirety should be moved to page 80, and the margin of page 80 reads 'see page 176'! During the translation, these specific 'footnotes' and remarks were introduced into the text, as they are its integral and logical parts. The procedure was the same when transferring fragments of the text from one page to another, as indicated by the author. It remains unclear, however, why the author had crossed through several pages of the text using one diagonal line or two lines intersecting at the centre, spanning the entire page (such is the case with pages 222, 74–5, the final paragraph of pages 104, 105–6, 108–9, 114–16, 118–22, 137–9, 146–58, 164–73, four lines on pages 174 and 176).

with frames. Upon an analysis of the text, the editor arrived at the conclusion that these fragments formed an inherent and inseparable part of the topic. They were accordingly treated as such. The text also had certain words or sentences marked with a felt pen in yellow, bright green and bright pink. This 'retouching' is most probably the work of persons who have read the text or had transcribed it on computers or translated it into other languages; such pens were unknown at the beginning of the previous century.

Doubtless the manuscript had passed through many hands. Pages 221, 71, 80 and 177 hold stamp imprints saying 'Īsā Yēshū' Ḥannā. Bē̱t Erke d-Ninos'. The same name – with a full address and phone and fax numbers – is found in a stamp affixed at the lower part of page 221 and both internal covers. Page 67 in turn bears the framed date of 03.07.90, with a hardly legible signature of a person of European ancestry, most probably a German scholar in Syriac studies, to whom the manuscript was lent out. The same date and signature is found on page 49 as well, but they are not placed in a frame, and on page 74, with the date 04.07.90.[20]

The title of the manuscript provided by the author is *Dmō zlīḥō awkīth nekstō d-'ōnō da-Mshīḥō – Spilt blood, or the tragedy of the lambs of Christ.* However, the second part was omitted from all five past editions.

The editor and translator decided to subtitle this book 'Sayfo – 'An Account of the Assyrian Genocide', in order to convey its subject matter to prospective readers today and in the future. Over the past two decades, in particular, books and documentary films use the term 'Sayfo' or 'Year of the Sayfo' to refer to the massacre, often by sword, of the Assyrians of the Hakkari, Diyarbakır, Harput, Marash, Urfa and Si'irt (Seert) regions in the Ottoman Empire and in Ottoman-occupied northeastern Persia, including Urmia.[21]

20 'Īsā Yēshū' Ḥannā confirmed that he had made his copy of the manuscript available to many people and that the passages in the text were underlined by them. The stamp found on pages 221, 71, 80 and 177 is his.

21 Barryakoub, A., 'Academic Conference on Seyfo Held in Sweden', *Zinda Magazine* (19 November 2005), http://www.zindamagazine.com/; Bē̱t-Ṣāwōᶜe, J., *Sayfo b Ṭurcabdin 1914–1915*; Gaunt, D., *Seyfo: Folkmordet på assyrierna: När-var-hur*; Shirinian, G., 'Background to the Late Ottoman Genocides', *Genocide in the Ottoman Empire: Armenians, Assyrians, Greeks*, pp. 19–81; Talay S. & Barthoma, S. O. (eds), *Sayfo 1915: An Anthology of Essays on the Genocide of Assyrians/Arameans during the First World War;* Yohannan, A., *The Death of a Nation: Or the Ever Persecuted Nestorians or Assyrian Christians*, p. 149.

Besides the modern Assyrian term *Seyfo/Sayfo* (*Seypa/Saypa* in the eastern dialect) for 'sword', they also use the term *firman* (decree, edict or ruling) and *qaflat* (the forming of caravans, flight or forced march) and further to the east, in Urmia, the native phrase/word *raqa raqa* (flight) to recall the events of the early twentieth century.[22] Frequently there is a question of why 'sword' specifically is utilised and the simplest answer is that is appears frequently in organic responses to the events. For example, a poet who experienced the attack on Āzah by the Kurds and the Turks and during World War I wrote:

> When they enslaved us by violence,
> They were mercilessly planning
> To slay all of us by the sword . . .
> Having unsheathed [their] swords
> They sorely oppressed them.
> They led them before the horses.
> They had no pity for their plight.[23]

Similarly, another resident wrote of the events of 1914–15 that:

> A shining sword separated the faithful from their priests.
> Some they dispersed, others they killed, they perpetrated a massacre.[24]

[22] Abdalla, M., 'The Term *Seyfo* in Historical Perspective', *The Assyrian Genocide: Cultural and Political Legacies*, p. 92.

[23] The translator of this volume also translated this poem from the original in Syriac. Abdalla, M., 'The Term *Seyfo*', p. 100. For information on the original source of the passage, see Beṯ-Ṣawoce, J. (ed.), *Beth-Zabday Azech. Vad hände 1915?*, pp. 280, 285.

[24] The translator of this volume also translated this passage from the original in Syriac, Ibid., p. 101. For information on the original source, see Çiçek, Y. Y. (ed), *Memre de-al sajfe da-sbaln mšīḥaje be-Turkaja men šat 1714–1914 de-sīmīn be-jad ktube surjaje de-Ṭur abdīn*, pp. 89–90.

BACKGROUND OF THE REGION

The area known as Ṭūr ʿAbdīn is located in the south of present-day Turkey, near the Syrian border. It is a plateau covering an area of approximately 9,000 square kilometres between the city of Cizre (Gzirto) in the east and Mardin in the west. On its southern border lies the city of Nusaybin (Ṣōbā, Nisibis), famous for its academy that significantly contributed to the early history of Oriental Christianity. The northernmost edges of this region, where the city of Hasankef on the river Tigris stands today, used to be marked by the splendid Ḥesnō d-Kīfā castle.[1] In medieval works by Arab geographers modern Assyrian place names, together with descriptions of churches and monasteries, can be found.[2] In time, however, most of these names had been replaced with Arabic,

[1] At some point a city grew around Ḥesnō d-Kīfo, becoming periodically the capital of Ṭūr ʿAbdīn and the Assyrian province of Gharzān. Immediately before the pacification on 5 June 1915, the city was administered by Assyrians, only one of whom managed to escape. The massacre of more than 500 Assyrian families of the city is described in a poem by Asmar el-Khūrī. Ḥennō, S., *Gunḥē d-Suryōyē d-Ṭūr ʿAbdīn*, pp.153–4; Gōrgīs, A. K. al-Q, *Ğirāḥ fī tārīkh as-Syriān* pp. 15–20, 83–93.

[2] They are widely quoted by the Syrian Orthodox patriarch Ighnāṭiyyos Aphrem I Barṣōm, *Maktḇōnūṯō d-ʿāl aṯrō d-Ṭūr ʿAbdīn*, pp. 198–9.

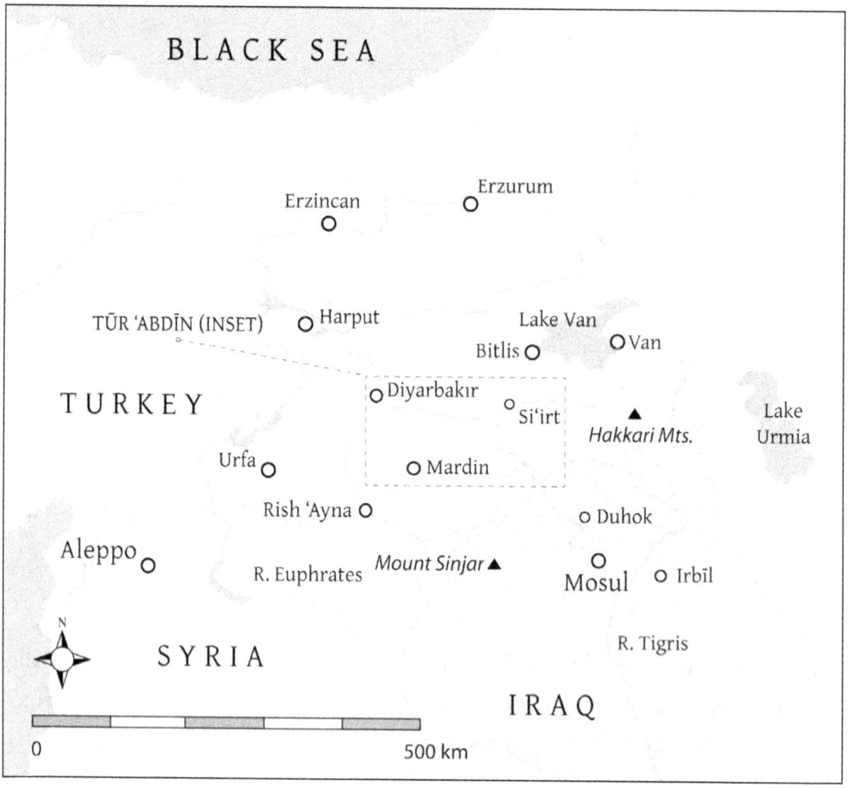

Map 1 General Map of the region

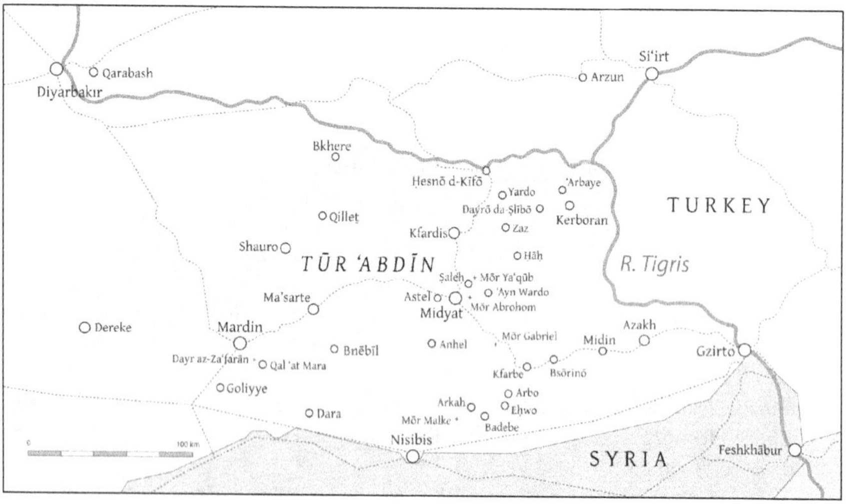

Map 2 Inset of Ṭūr ʻAbdīn and its environs

Turkish or Kurdish toponyms, occasionally preserving the original Assyrian root.[3]

Located on the border between Persia and the Byzantine Empire, Ṭūr ʿAbdīn changed hands often. Its inhabitants started converting to Christianity as early as the first century. The region is said to have been on the route of the Magi (the Three Wise Men/Kings of Orient), who presented gifts to Jesus, and in the village of Ḥāḥ, where they stopped, according to the tradition, the first church in Ṭūr ʿAbdīn was built.[4] The Gospel was also preached here by Mōr Adday (St Thaddeus). By the year 120 of the Common Era (CE) an Assyrian bishop named Mazra resided in the village of Azakh/Bēṯ Zabdāy (Turkish, İdil).[5]

Mōr Yaʿqūb (died 338 CE) worked in Ṭūr ʿAbdīn at the turn of the 4th century CE and funded the above-mentioned theological school in Nisibis, transformed by his disciple St Ephrem (died 373 CE) into the first Christian academy.[6] Mōr Yaʿqūb took part in the First Ecumenical Council in Nicaea in 325 CE. He loved Nisibis so ardently that before his death he asked for his remains to be placed in the city walls. After the city was transferred from the Byzantine Empire to Persia in 363 CE, St Ephrem moved his academy to Urhoy (Edessa, Urfa), devoting to Nisibis seventy-seven homilies full of love and concern. Urhoy is also where the Western Aramaic script was developed and the final revision was made of the Assyrian New Testament, first translated as early as the 1st century CE. This translation, known as Peshitta, is still

[3] Changes of toponyms are a common practice in the Middle East, especially in Turkey and Syria. It is worth noting that Atatürk's "Surname Law" (*Soyadı Kanunu*) of 1934 forced Assyrians (together with other ethnic minorities) to change their surnames to Turkish ones.

[4] For information about the origins of the Magi (*Mghūshē* in Syriac) and their role and place in Assyrian religious tradition see Abdalla, M., 'Z kręgu folkloru chrześcijańskich Asyryjczyków'(*Literatura Ludowa*, 1988); Kałużyński, S., *Tradycje i legendy ludów tureckich* (Warsaw: Iskry, 1986). Written Assyrian sources mention the church in Ḥāḥ from the 5th century. The village was the seat of bishops between 1050 and 1660. Keser-Kayaalp, E., 'Church Building in the Ṭūr ʿAbdīn in the First Centuries of Islamic Rule,' in *Authority and Control in the Countryside: From Antiquity to Islam in the Mediterranean and Near East (Sixth-Tenth Century),* (Leiden: Brill, 2018).

[5] Barṣōm, A., *Makṯbōnūṯō*, p. 200.

[6] Atiya, A., *Historia Kościołów Wschodnich*, pp. 213–15; Pigulewska, N., *Kultura syryjska we wczesnym średniowieczu*, pp. 66–101; Szymusiak, J. M. and Starowieyski, M., *Słownik wczesnochrześcijańskiego piśmiennictwa*, pp. 86, 128–9, 634.

considered a model of accuracy and reliability. Also here the first illustrated Gospels were written in the sixth century, now kept in Florence, Italy.[7] The Greeks, however, were not favourably disposed towards the development of the school in Urhoy, leading to its closure in 489 CE and displacement back to Nisibis, where it functioned almost until the end of the ninth century. It was called 'Mother of Scholars' or 'Mother of Wisdom' and the city of Nisibis referred to as 'Mother of Science' or 'Mother of Cities'. The statutes of the academy have been conserved as a magnificent relic of educational history, the oldest regulations governing higher education in the early Middle Ages.[8]

In the middle of the 4th century CE Mār Augin (St Eugene) arrived in Ṭūr 'Abdīn from the Monastery of St Pachomius in Egypt. He bolstered the ascetic movement in the region, gaining many followers[9] who played an important role in spreading Christianity and the construction of new temples. In 397 CE his disciples, Mōr Shmouwel and Mōr Shem'un Qartmīnōyō, built near the city of Midyat an enormous monastery known as Dayro d-Qartmīnōyō (after its founder) or Dayro d-Mōr Gabriel (after the successor of the founder). In the description of the altar of the monastery's church, which survives to this day, we can read:

> It was 37 metres long and 25 metres wide. It had three aisles: the central one was six metres wide, while the others were four and a half metres wide each. The walls were covered with paintings showing heads of lions, bulls, eagles and human faces. On the miraculous stone, left in the middle of the altar, they put a large vessel of gold, surrounded with silver wreaths and decorated with three hundred precious stones, in which were carved scenes from the earthly life of the Saviour. Above the altar a copper dome was made, sup-

[7] Atiya, A., *Historia Kościołów Wschodnich*, p. 201.

[8] The statutes of this academy have been translated into English, German, Russian and Polish (in Polish see Pigulewska, N., *Kultura Syryjska Wewczesnym średniowieczu*, pp. 101–19; in English see Vööbus, A., *History of the School of Nisibis*).

[9] Arthur Vööbus, a specialist in history and culture of Assyrian Christians, claims that the ideas of monasticism had been brought from Mesopotamia to Egypt and Greece. For example, in Egypt monks are addressed as *Abba* (meaning 'father' in Syriac), and in Greece they are referred to as *ihidaya* (meaning 'a loner'). The first signs of asceticism are said to have appeared around Nisibis, therefore in Ṭūr 'Abdīn. Vööbus, A., 'The Contribution of Ancient Syrian Christianity to the West European Culture', pp. 8–14.

> ported by four marble pillars. In the dome there hung a big golden lamp. The floor of the altar was entirely covered with black, white, red, blue and green marble. On both sides of the aisle, in front of the altar, were two copper trees, thirty metres high, with 180 leaves serving as torches. Fifty silver chains hung on their branches together with animal, mostly bird figures, crosses and tiny wreathes.[10]

Although the monastery is still in use, none of these elements remain.

In the year 446 CE there were already 483 skulls of deceased monks in the crypts; by 590 CE there were 802 of them. By the end of the fifth century 1,800 monks lived in the monastery; by the year 734 CE twelve of them had become saints. The monastery was the source of thirteen patriarchs, the first of whom died in 755 and the last in 1662 (four of them died tragically), one *māfiriono* (catholicos, corresponding to a cardinal in the Roman Catholic Church) and seventy-nine bishops. The well-known Assyrian historian Mōr Mīkhōyel Rābō (Michael the Great), living in the twelfth century, listed the names of forty-seven bishops consecrated in the monastery between 793 and 1199, including one consecrated as patriarch in 723.[11]

Unlike the inhabitants of Urhoy, who converted to Christianity en masse through the efforts of their king Abgar V Ukama[12], the people of Ṭūr ʻAbdīn converted gradually. In the fifth century a monk named Ishāy mentioned 632 people baptised in one day in the village of Anhel and the conversion of 3,600 people in Warde near Nisibis. In the same century

[10] Barṣōm, A., *Maktbōnūṯō*, p. 221.

[11] Ibid., pp. 223–40.

[12] Tradition has it that it was the first city whose inhabitants were baptised in the first century by order of their king. The historians of the Oriental Church had been writing about a mission from Edessa to Christ, a member of which, a painter named Ḥanānia, was said to have perpetuated his image on canvas. At the turn of the fourth century there were allegedly around 300 monasteries in this area (Sākā, I., *Kanīsatī as-Suriāniyya*, p. 58). In a poem about the massacre of Christians in Urhoy in 1895, written by the priest Ḥannō Aynwardoyo, we can read that 'on the first day of the New Year the Muslims killed in Urhoy more than 30 thousand people. First, they surrounded the city so that nobody could leave it. They ordered all inhabitants to gather in churches and monasteries, which then they set on fire together with the crowds gathered inside. Others searched all the houses, taking the prettier women and children and killing the rest. The milk of breastfeeding mothers mixed in their babies' mouths with their blood. Even Nebuchadnezzar was more civilized than the Ottomans when he entered Jerusalem.' (Gōrgīs, *Ǧirāḥ fī tārīkh as-Syriān*, pp. 15–21.)

a certain Mōr Āhō supposedly brought here a piece of the Cross from Constantinople.[13] It was only in the sixth century that the entire population of Ṭūr ʻAbdīn accepted Christianity.[14] By then the Assyrians inhabited five cities and more than 150 towns and villages. Almost all of them had a church. The number of monks and hermits was exceptionally high, reaching nearly 600,000.[15] Their hermitages were spread all over the region and the sound of recited psalms came from all directions all night long. They also lived in twenty-five monasteries, located in Ṭūr ʻAbdīn at the time, eight of which were classified as 'big', that is, self-sufficient both educationally and economically.

St Āḥō was born in the city of Rish ʻAyna (today Ra's al-ʻAyn in Syria). While he was a Persian prisoner, he was baptised by St Mīkhōyel of Nineveh. Following their release, they both made their way to Ṭūr ʻAbdīn, where they began broad educational activities. Among his closest friends was the Armenian St Mesrop Mashtots, translator of the Gospel and many liturgical books from Syriac into Armenian. St Āḥō founded five monasteries in his lifetime, of which only one is active, dedicated to the Holy Cross, close to the village of the same name in Ṭūr ʻAbdīn. Another monastery of St Āḥō (in the Gharzān region) was entirely devastated. Among the famous pilgrimage sites in northeastern Syria there is the church of St Āḥō built in 1942 in the village of Damkhiyya (eight kilometres to the west of Qamishli) by Gawriyye Shmouni, a famous Assyrian activist of that time. The foundations of the church, refurbished in 1963, are stone blocks from the monastery of the Holy Cross. The day of St Āḥō is celebrated twice a year: on the second Monday following Easter and on 14 September. In 2007, an indulgence pilgrimage to the Damkhiyya church consisted of 3,000 people. Profiting from the presence of a translator in the area in the summer of 2010, the local clergy asked

[13] Isḥāq, L. and Asmar, J., *Sīrat ḥayāt Mār Āḥō*, p. 46. St Helen, the mother of Emperor Constantine the Great, who is said to have recovered the Cross of Christ, according to Philip de Terrazzi, was Assyrian, together with Theodora, wife of Emperor Justinian I. (de Terrazzi, P. de, *ʻAṣr as-Syriān aḏ-Ḏahabī*, p. 27). The circumstances of the recovery of this relic, which was transported to Constantinople, are visibly reflected in the popular forms of celebration of the Assyrian Feast of the Cross (14 September).

[14] Barṣōm, A., *Makṯbōnūṯō*, pp. 200–1.

[15] Ighnāṭiyyos Yaʻqūb III, 'The Syrian Orthodox Church', a lecture given on 8 October 1985, in Göttingen, p. 7.

for a translation of the contents of the informational brochure from Arabic into Polish, explaining that there is a significant number of Poles visiting the church.

In the middle of the fifth century a monastery was founded by and named after Bār Ṣaumā (died 457). It was the main residence of the patriarchs under Arab rule and it is here that the greatest literary monuments of ecclesiastical history saw the light of day: the famous *Chronicles* by Mōr Mīkhōyel Rābō (died 1199), the anonymous *Chronography* of 1234 and most of the *History*, written in turbulent times by Bār ʻEbrāyā (Bar Hebraeus) (died 1286). The monastery boasted an enormous library and among its residents 21 became patriarchs, 9 *māfirions* and 110 bishops. At the end of the 13th century the monastery was burned down by Kurds. After its destruction the patriarchs moved in 1293 to the az-Zaʻfarān monastery, built in 472–9 CE.

Assyrian schools in Ṭūr ʻAbdīn between the third and thirteenth centuries were renowned centres of science, both religious and secular. Greek philosophical and medical treatises were translated here, and clergymen, doctors and artisans who were educated here were among the first to become missionaries in India, Mongolia and China.[16] Thanks to these centres of learning the Assyrians continued to build schools and hospitals, leaving their mark in the worlds of education and discovery.

After the great massacres of Christians in Turkey at the beginning of the twentieth century the patriarchy was moved in 1924 to Homs in Syria, at the time under French mandate, and in 1959 further west to Damascus. Nowadays almost half of the Syriac-speaking bishops of the Assyrian Orthodox Church originate from Ṭūr ʻAbdīn. The seminaries of the two still functional monasteries of Ṭūr ʻAbdīn (Mōr Gabriel and az-Zaʻfarān) have less than a hundred students today –a pitiful image compared to ancient times.

The scale of the fall of Ṭūr ʻAbdīn can be illustrated with one more fact. At different times there were more than a dozen bishops residing in the region, while other bishops originating from the area served numerous Christian communities in countries such as Afghanistan (seventh century), India and Cyprus. Today the whole area of Ṭūr ʻAbdīn is under jurisdiction of just one bishop, while more than ninety per cent of the indigenous Assyrian

[16] Abdalla, M., ʻŚladami asyryjskich misjonarzy', *Przegląd Prawosławny*, pp. 86–90.

population live as political refugees in Western Europe, the Americas and Australia.[17]

Some Important Locations in Ṭūr ʿAbdīn

Edessa, today Urfa (Assyrian Urhoy, Arabic Ar-Ruhā) in southern Turkey, in Upper Mesopotamia. In the period from 132 BCE to 244 CE it was the capital of the Assyrian kingdom of Osroene. Some people believe that it was Ananias, the court painter of King Abgar and one of his emissaries to Christ, who painted the portrait of Christ on a cloth forwarded to Abgar (on the fate of the mandylion).[18] The description of travels across the lands of the Orient in the mid-seventeenth century by a discalced Carmelite Vincenzo Maria di S. Caterina da Siena lists the city of Edessa, through which he passed:

> The Edessians say that these houses are the remains of the palace of Abgar, who lived in times of Christ, and who was worthy of acquiring this holy likeness, I speak here of this wonderful painting that is kept in our homeland of Italy.[19]

It is in Edessa that the Christian academy, where St Ephrem taught, functioned.[20] The city had its monographic history written by J. B. Segal[21], spanning the period until 1146, when a great tragedy befell the Christian inhabitants, decimated by both the Turks and Crusaders. The final years of Assyrian presence in the city, and the circumstances of the journey to Aleppo in Syria (1924) are described by Yūsuf Nāmiq.[22]

St Sharbel was not the bishop of Edessa but a pagan archpriest who converted to Christianity while making sacrifices to deities, thanks to a bishop of Edessa named Bār Samia.[23] St Sharbel is the patron of many churches in the Near East. One of them is found in the city of Midyat in Ṭūr ʿAbdīn. The name Sharbel is particularly popular among the Maronites of Lebanon. Much

[17] Abdalla, M., 'Asyryjska diaspora', *Sprawy narodowościowe*, pp. 55–75.

[18] Atiya, A., *Historia Kościołów*, pp. 211–12.

[19] Binyamen Ḥaddād, 'Riḥlat al-abb Vincenzo ilā al-ʿIrāq' (*Magallat Magmaʿ al-Lugha as-Surianiyya*, 1975).

[20] Pigulewska, N., *Kultura Syryjska*, pp. 101–19.

[21] Segal, J. B., *Ar-Ruhā – al-madīna al-mubaraka* [Edessa – the Blessed City].

[22] Nāmiq, Y., *Al-Qāfila al-akhīra* [The Last Caravan].

[23] Abūnā, A., *Shuhadāʾ al-mashriq* [Martyrs of the East].

more is known about the Lebanese hermit St Sharbel Makhlouf (1828–98), beatified by Pope Paul VI in 1965 and canonised and declared a saint in October 1977. His grave is found at a monastery in the locality of ʻAnnāyā and is now a pilgrimage site.

St Mārūṯā was a graduate of the Edessian School founded after the Persian victory against Julian the Apostate in 363 CE and the resulting takeover of the city of Nisibis. He was a member of three Roman emissary missions to Persia, always welcomed warmly by Yazdegerd I, the successor to Shapur II, and oversaw the reconstruction of the Assyrian Church in Persia. In 410 he summoned a synod of forty bishops to Seleucia, the decisions of which have survived, and installed bishops in Bahrain and Khorasan (Central Asia), thus beginning the famed march of the Assyrian ('Nestorian') Church all the way to China.[24] Many hymns of praise to martyrs authored by St Mārūṯā were made part of liturgy.[25] The history of the Church in the Near East also knows a different Mārūṯā, a catholicos residing in Tikrit (628–39 CE). His jurisdiction encompassed a broad part of Asia.

According to a report by Edward Lewes Cutts[26], in 1876 the city counted 29,210 inhabitants, including 15,400 Muslims, 13,500 Christians (Orthodox Armenians – 11,600, Assyrians – 1,520, Protestant Armenians – 380) and 310 Jews. The Assyrians had a bishop and school, attended by about one hundred pupils up to twelve years of age, with a single teacher. The author describes the architecture of the Assyrian church, internal decorations, liturgical items and a copy of the Gospel from the mid-fifteenth century, beautifully written in two columns per page, one in Assyrian, the other in Arabic using Assyrian letters (the Garshuni system).

Amida. The current official name of this city, Diyarbakır, created in the tenth century, is well known partly thanks to the usage of Amida by the Arab historian Aṭ-Ṭabarī (died 923).[27] It is believed that the city began to gradually lose its Assyrian character after 502 CE, when the Persians conquered it and slaughtered several thousands of its inhabitants.

[24] Young, J. M. L., *By Foot to China.*

[25] Atiya, A., *Historia Kościołów*, pp. 211–12.

[26] Cutts, E. L., *The Assyrian Christians. Report of the Journey, Undertaken by Desire of His Grace the Archbishop of Canterbury and His Grace the Archbishop of York*, pp. 4–6.

[27] Ṭabarī (aṭ-), *Tārīkh al-umam wa-l-mulūk.*

Figure 1 Yusuf Akbulut, the sole priest in Diyarbakır at the Assyrian cemetery in the centre of the town, a large part of which was turned into a rubbish dump (photograph by J. Kaczmarek, 2003)

American missionary Horatio Southgate in his study[28] indicates that 'Diarbekir' counted close to 2.7 thousand families, including 1.5 thousand Muslim families (Turks, Kurds, Arabs), 650 Armenian families, 425 Assyrian families, 50 Jewish families and 20 Greek families. George Percy Badger in turn provides the following statistics:[29]

> The population of the place is more than half Moslem, including Turks, Arabs, and Coords [. . .] the Armenians of Diarbekir number 1700 families, with two churches, a bishop, and thirty priests [. . .] Bishop Egop. [. . .] Until lately the papal Armenians worshipped with the Chaldeans, but they have now built a splendid church. They number about seventy-five families with two resident priests, and their numbers are said to be on the increase.

[28] Horatio Southgate, H., *Narrative of a Tour through Armenia, Kurdistan, Persia and Mesopotamia, with an Introduction and Occasional Observations upon the Condition of Mohammedianism and Christianity in those Countries*, pp. 298–9.

[29] Badger, G. P., *The Nestorians and their Rituals; With the Narratives of a Mission to Mesopotamia and Coordistan in 1842–1844*, pp. 41–5.

> [. . .] The Greeks have a small church in the town [. . .] only fifteen members of this rite left [. . .]. The Chaldeans of Diarbekir number 120 families, with a bishop and three priests [. . .]. The old church, which was rebuilt twelve years ago [. . .] is a good substantial building. [. . .] Mutran Botros, the Chaldean bishop [. . .] Mutran Abdool-Messiah, generally known to us as Athanasius [. . .] had gone over to the Romanists and returned again to his own community, [. . .] Diarbekir is not the seat of a Jacobite bishop, but is under the immediate control of the patriarch, who occasionally sends a bishop to act as his delegate. There are about 250 Jacobite families in the city; the papal Syrians number forty families with two priests, who are under the jurisdiction of Mutran Antoore of Mardeen.

If one assumes that a family numbered on average seven people at that time, then the number of Armenians would be around twelve thousand and Assyrians approximately three thousand. Taking into account the high natural growth rate throughout the nineteenth century, as well as migration from rural areas to cities, it is easy to count that after fifty years the number of inhabitants could have at least tripled. The official census conducted in 1881–2 indicated that the Diyarbakır province was inhabited by 328,644 Muslims, 132,549 Christians and 9,000 Yazidis. However, in their reports, European missionaries indicated a higher number of Christians: 176,570 Armenians and Assyrians, including a subdivision by individual churches.[30] Thus, Christians accounted for a third of the population. It should be added that in 1879 a lay mid-level Assyrian school with a relatively rich curriculum was founded here. Beside the main language (Syriac), Arabic, Turkish and French were also taught. The school played an important role in spreading knowledge – its graduates were almost all Assyrian intellectuals from Greece. In 1895, the Ottoman government closed the school down and its head, Ḥannā Syrri Jaqqi, had to flee.[31]

[30] De Courtois, S., *The Forgotten Genocide of Eastern Christians. The Last Arameans*, p. 61.

[31] As of early 2015, Diyarbakır is home to but a few dozen Assyrian and Armenian families. They follow various denominations and are provided with services by the sole Assyrian priest, Yusuf Akbulut. His name became widely known in 2000/2001, when his actions were reported in the press – information on this cleric can be found online in various languages. The city has numerous old churches, most of them closed, some turned into mosques or warehouses. The Assyrian cemetery in the city centre is a particularly gruesome

Mardin is a city located approximately eighty kilometres to the southeast of Diyarbakır. It is located on a rock plateau and a large part of the houses on the mountainside are built in a cascading manner, the mountain itself being 1,100 metres high. Due to its topography and number of churches, it was referred to as the 'second Jerusalem'. In 1839, the population numbered around 3,000 families (c. 21,000 people), including 500 Armenian and 700 Assyrian families. The remainder comprised Jews and Muslims.[32] In 1882, in turn, 20,000 inhabitants were recorded, of which almost half were Christian, mainly Assyrians.[33] Presently Mardin has about 100,000 inhabitants, including around 70 Assyrian families. They use a particular dialect of Arabic. The locality of Al-Hasakah in northeastern Syria is home to a larger group of former inhabitants of Mardin referred to as the *Merdalliyye*. They are also part of a scattered diaspora.

Azakh (presently İdil in southeastern Turkey, about ten kilometres to the east of the Tigris River and twenty-five kilometres north of the Syrian border) is an ancient locality that was home to a bishop as early as 120 CE. Until World War I Azakh was inhabited solely by Assyrians. Their heroic and well-documented defence of the town against Turkish troops and Kurds was provided with descriptions and studies based on testimony of the participants.[34] The inhabitants, surrounded from all sides by Kurds, had to leave their houses in most cases and travel to Syria, where they built a new town close to the Turkish-Syrian-Iraqi border, called Dērīk (presently Al-Malikiyye). The Hazkhōyē use a characteristic subdialect of the Arabic language.[35]

Nisibis, today Nusaybin, is a city in southeastern Turkey close to the Syrian border, once a grand node of culture and science of Assyrian Christians. It was here that the famed St Ephrem was born and taught (until 363 CE). 'In the year 1839, Nisibis was a village with thirty houses and a

picture: crosses and holy images destroyed, gravestones covered in excrement and a part of the cemetery used as a rubbish dump by the nearby Kurdish inhabitants and shop-owners.

32 Southgate, H., *Narrative*, p. 277.

33 Courtois, S. de, *The Forgotten Genocide*, pp. 66–71.

34 Michael Abdalla, M., 'The Fate of Āzakh: An Assyrian Town in Ṭūr 'Abdīn, Turkey', pp. 59–77; Ibid., 'Jihad in Practice. The Assyrians of Azakh in Upper Mesopotamia during World War I: Resistance, Agreement, Demilitarization, and Exodus', pp. 141–86.

35 Isḥāq, L., *Amṯāl ša'biyye min Bāzebde* [Sayings from Bāzebde].

Figure 2 The ruins of one of the ancient temples in the village of Ḥāḥ where, according to folk tales, the Assyrian Magi passed from Mesopotamia to Bethlehem (photograph by M. Abdallla, 1999)

settlement of barracks housing five or six hundred Turkish soldiers.'[36] 'In the year 1915, the village counted about two thousand people, including 460 Assyrians (200 Uniate Christians, 200 Orthodox, 60 Protestants), 600 Jews, 940 Muslims.'[37]

Ḥāḥ village. The legend, famous among Assyrians of Ṭūr 'Abdīn, speaks of twelve Magi who came from Mesopotamia and whose route to Palestine ran through the locality of Ḥāḥ, which they liked so much that nine of them decided to suspend their journey and remain there. The remaining three, having returned from Bethlehem, told about the miraculous birth of Christ. At the spot where they allegedly visited the humble stall and manger a church was erected. The inhabitants of Ḥāḥ are convinced that it was actually their ancestors who provided the Magi with the gifts they gave to the Christ child. The legend of the twelve Magi divided into three groups is particularly strong

[36] Southgate, *Narrative*, pp. 272-273.
[37] De Courtois, *The Forgotten Genocide*, p. 72.

in the Assyrian Church of the East (sometimes referred to as the 'Nestorian' Church), and they are considered the first followers of Christ.

Presently, the village of Ḥāḥ, once a large and important locality and in addition the seat of the bishop, is home to some thirty Assyrian families. It hosts a historic church dedicated to the Holy Mother, the architecture of which awes visitors. On the feast day of the Holy Mother pilgrims from the entire region come to the church for indulgence. The Swedish city of Västerås is home to several times more families stemming from Ḥāḥ, who have established their own church and a large club.

Kerboran. Asmar al-Qass Gōrgīs refers to Kerboran as a city.[38] In 1915, about seven hundred Assyrian families lived there, including five Catholic and twenty Protestant ones. Beside the above-mentioned bishop, Gōrgīs names seven priests: Ephrem, Sisan, Ya'qūb, 'Īsā, Murad, Karīm, Laḥdō, and a monk, also named Laḥdō. He also provides descriptions of four other active churches: of St Shmouni and her seven sons (constructed in the seventh century out of enormous stones on a hill, destroyed by Tatars in 1395 and now marked by a large tree in the courtyard), of the Holy Mother (on the west side of the town, with the central cemetery), of St George (by the river in the northern part of town, its structure similar to the church of St Shmouni), St Quriaqos the Martyr, St Marqus (Mark) the Martyr and his mother Yulītā (built in the nineteenth century with a short tower and a crypt to the north side, where Bishops 'Abd al-Aḥad and Ya'qūb are buried; the upper floor served as accommodation for the priest and offices for the bishop).

Gōrgīs also describes the reasons for Mustafa 'Ali Rammo's dislike towards the bishop: on the feast of the Magi, amid heavy snow, Christian homes burned wood in their furnaces and smoke came out of their chimneys of Christian homes. It would seem that the holiday atmosphere did not appeal to Agha Mustafa. He turned, via his messengers, to the bishop, who was to order each family to bring him a pile of wood that same day. The bishop replied: 'Let us postpone it until tomorrow. It is Sunday today, the snow hinders efficient movement, and your Agha lives in a different village.' The messengers conveyed to the Agha not only the bishop's decline, but also some fabricated curses abhorrent to Muslims alleged to be the words of the

[38] *Ǧirāḥ fī tārīkh as-Syriān*, pp. 30–3.

bishop. Mustafa decided to take revenge. He gathered the military, besieged the town, cut off the water supply and, three days later, he attacked, burning down houses (their roofs were primarily made of wood) and murdering people. He subsequently turned to the governor so that he would capture the bishop and hand him over. The governor promised to do this but, having no intention of killing the bishop he intended to announce to the populace that the bishop had converted to Islam, which would to sow chaos. However Mustafa was steadfast and insisted on killing the bishop with his own hands. Shmouni, Yūḥānōn Gawriyye's daughter, said: 'I have seen him leading the bishop away. He held his head high and spoke loudly of the treachery of the Agha.' The Agha released him to his servants, who took him to the roof of the Agha's house and threw him to the ground, abandoning his dead body in a field. After a few days the city's inhabitants obtained permission to take the body and he was buried in the crypt of the St Quriaqos church. Following these massacres, the city was left with only sixty families. In 1926 close to 150 Christian families from various villages came to live in the town. The last major exodus occurred in the 1960s.

Shauro. An ancient locality in the region of Mḥalmaytō (southwestern part of Ṭūr 'Abdīn). Ighnāṭiyyos Aphrem I Barṣōm[39] gives the names of a few localities in the Mḥalmaytō region, including the village of Shur (nowadays most probably Şuri, twenty kilometres to the northeast of Mardin). The name in classic (literary) Syriac means 'neck', as the houses are built on a high mountain slope. A river, named Kadiş in Turkish, flows through the town. The largest mosque in the city was once a church dedicated to St Thomas. The walls, built of large stones, are covered with inscriptions in Syriac.

Astal (Astil, Estel and Estil) is a city not far from Midyat, on the west side inhabited mostly by the Mḥalmōyē (the name comes from the region name: Mḥalmaytō). The Assyrian-Christian population of the region occupy around fifty villages converted to Islam at the beginning of the seventeenth century under unclear conditions. Ighnāṭiyyos Aphrem I Barṣōm writes:

> In the year 1609 (another possible date: 1583) the misdeeds orchestrated against Christians and limitations of their rights by despotic Turkish rulers

[39] Barṣōm, *Maktbōnūṯō*, p. 252.

> climaxed, which consequently forced representatives of the Mḥalmōyē tribes, including Astal, Raşidi, Muhaşni, Sura, Ahmadi, Reshmel, Kabalah and Lashtiyye, to convert to Islam. It was their only recourse.[40]

The folk customs of the Mḥalmōyē retained many Christian components and, without knowledge of Syriac, it is not possible to understand their subdialect of Arabic. The villages they inhabit still bear Assyrian names and remains of monasteries and churches can be seen. Their leader, Sheikh Sa'īd (as of 1999) resides in the village of Kafr Ḥwārā (official name: Gelinkaya), meaning 'White Village'.

Qilleṯ is a village approximately thirty-eight kilometres to the northeast of Mardin by the main road from Midyat to Savur, and about seven kilometres east of Savur. In 1842 it was home to approximately 120 Assyrian families[41] and by the beginning of the twentieth century its population was around 1,000 (600 orthodox Assyrians, 100 Protestants, 100 Uniates, with the rest being Muslims).[42] Currently, only a handful of Assyrians remain, most having emigrated in the 1980s, mainly to Germany and Sweden. In the northern part of the village one can find the ruins of two ancient monasteries.

Ḥesnō d-Atṯō (Turkish Eskikale). As already mentioned, the inhabitants of Mardin and the nearby villages speak Arabic. This village is located five kilometres south of Mardin, halfway to the az-Za'farān monastery. In the sixteeenth century it was inhabited by about 900 Assyrian families (about 6,300 people). Following the massacres of 1895, this number dropped to 1,500 people (including 1,320 Orthodox Christians with three priests, two churches and a school, 100 Uniates with a priest, a church, a school, and 80 Protestants). The last Assyrian family left the village in 1994 following the kidnapping of the sole young girl of the village by a Kurd and the fruitless efforts of the parents to retrieve her.

The village **Kafarbe** is found on a hill on the southwestern side of the Mōr Gabriel monastery. In the summer of 1999 it was visited by the editor of this book accompanied by several seminarians from the monastery. Each year, on the feast of St Sṭēfānos (Stephen), the seminarians celebrate a short

40 Ibid. p. 252.
41 Ibid. p. 54.
42 Badger, *The Nestorians*, p. 48.

mass at the local church, which is otherwise is empty and run-down and its keys are kept by a Kurdish village elder.

The village of **Qarabash** is where the author was born. During the period of genocide, the last Assyrian to die for refusing to leave his cell was a monk by the name of John. The area surrounding his cell is supposed to still bear the name Bustān ar-Rāhib ('Garden of the Monk'). The four final Assyrian families left their homes in 1948, making their way to the city of Qamishli in Syria.

Mōr Gabriel monastery. Among the forty-nine Assyrian monasteries founded since the sixth century, only five survive to this day, the two largest being Mōr Gabriel and Dayr az-Za'farān. The former (older) monastery is located on a hill, twenty-four kilometres from Midyat, surrounded by a dense oak forest. A road three kilometres northeast leads to the village of Qartmin, birthplace of one of the monastery's founders, and northwest to Kafarbe. Both are now populated by Muslims and have purely Turkish names, assigned to them during the reign of Kemal (Pasha) Atatürk.

Mōr Gabriel monastery was founded in 397 CE. Between 625 and 1049 it was the residence of the archbishop; subsequently and until 1915 it constituted a separate diocese. Its construction is attributed to Shmouwel Sauroyo and his disciple Shem'un Qartmīnōyō, sponsored by two sons of Emperor Theodosius I the Great. Until 668 the monastery was known as Dayro d-Qartmīnōyō, later as Dayro d-Mōr Gabriel, after a bishop to whom many miracles are attributed. In the early years of functioning of the monastery 400 monks lived there, who had previously prayed in nearby hermitages.

In the summer of 1997 planned celebrations (1,600 years of the monastery), with a number of diaspora Assyrians willing to participate, were cancelled. Several fundamentalist groups in the area, both Turkish and Kurdish, promised to organise a massacre of the pilgrims, claiming this land as theirs. A sad fate was met by three Assyrians who went to Turkey earlier to ask the authorities for permission to organise the celebrations and discuss the details. The car in which they travelled to the monastery was showered with bullets; nobody survived. They were shot at from the roadside ditch. The massacred bodies were transported to Augsburg, Germany, where the three victims had been living for twenty years with their families.

In 2005 attempts were made by surrounding villages to occupy some of

Figure 3 The remains of cells, monasteries and churches on a high mountain to the east of the monastery of Zaʿfarān. Guide: the monk Malke (photograph by M. Abdalla, 1999)

the lands of the Mōr Gabriel Monastery. Following the intense pressure that came from Europe and with the support of the Turkish government, the occupation attempt was stopped, but the cadastral land registry works were not finished. In addition to the unfounded claims raised by Eğlence village, Yayvantepe (previously known as Qartmin, until 1915 a purely Assyrian village) is also causing concern with its boundary dispute against Mōr Gabriel Monastery. Intimidation and false accusations continue to this day.[43]

Dayr az-Zaʿfarān monastery. The Assyrian name of the monastery is Dayro d-Kurkmo (from *kurkmo* – curcuma), and the Arab name is Dayr az-Zaʿfarān (from *zaʿfarān* – saffron); both of these take on the yellow colour of the walls, from the dye used in the mortar during construction. In this text the shortened name Zaʿfarān will be used. In the years 1293–1932 the

[43] A detailed account of the ongoing situation is presented in the *Report* by Metropolitan of Ṭūr ʿAbdīn, bishop Timotheos Samuel Aktas, available at <http://www.aina.org/reports/rotipftsmomg.pdf> (last accessed 21 September 2018).

monastery was the seat of the patriarch of the Syriac Orthodox Church. In 2013 the monastery was home to a bishop, two monks and seminarians. The building was erected in the 4th century CE, it is believed, on the foundations of a Hittite temple and is visited by both domestic and foreign tourists, particularly in summer. On the western side of the monastery there rises a mountain massif hiding the remains of numerous hermitages and churches carved into rocks, which could hold hundreds of monks. Even in the 1950s some of them were home to hermits, among them the famous Bishop Dolabani.

The inhabitants of **Bnēbīl** village were traditionally the ones to participate in the congregation events of the next patriarch residing in the Zaʿfarān monastery in greatest numbers. Only they had the privilege of carrying the patriarch sitting in an armchair to the altar, and a selected group of men would protect him during every trip. One more story survives concerning them recorded by Asmar al-Qass Gōrgīs:[44]

> In the year 1910, the inhabitants of the village of Reshmel, who converted to Islam in the year 1595, built a small mosque for themselves, not on the territory belonging to their village, but on the shores of the river Nahrasa, close to Bnēbīl. Each Friday, their *mullah* would arrive with the required number of forty Muslims to carry out prayers. Not knowing about this, a certain Christian woman from Bnēbīl travelled to the river to fetch some water. There, she noticed the Muslims ritually cleansing themselves, in that they sprayed their intimate body parts with water in quite a wild and brave manner. As a result, the woman failed to fetch the water, but returned to the village distressed. She noticed a group of other villagers at the closest house, sitting by a wall and chatting away. She paused and broke an empty vase by their side, shouting: 'You are not men! You have no honour! The Muslims from the mosque dirty our water with their excrement, and you just sit quietly!' One of the present, named Josef Baroke, took this in heavily, and just as loud as the woman spoke, ordered her: 'Go home, and do not tell anybody anything!' That evening he discretely organised a few strong men. They travelled with pickaxes and shovels to the spot

[44] Gorgīs, *Ğirāḥ fī tārīkh as-Syriān*, pp. 33, 94–8.

where the mosque stood. They took the entire building apart, down to its foundations, whereafter they ploughed the soil, sown barley and irrigated the area with water taken from the river using a quickly built duct. On the next Friday, the same *mullah* arrived as was customary with a group of Muslims, but found no trace of the mosque; barley was growing where it once stood. Turning to the inhabitants of Bnēbīl with threats, he heard: 'You must have seen this mosque in your dream. There never were and there are no Muslims in our village. So, who would have built such a mosque, and for whom?' The *mullah* did not give up, however. He complained with the Pasha of Mardin, who arrived at Bnēbīl with a committee and inspector 'Abde Chalabi. The committee determined that the village is entirely Christian, and that barley is growing at the spot indicated by the accusers. They considered the complaint to be groundless.

Some Dates of Tragic Events[45]

On the maps of ancient and contemporary Turkey it is not possible to find even one Assyrian village that has not been attacked and destroyed multiple times, first by Persians, later by Kurds and Turks. In these towns and villages with their rich history there is little or no trace of Assyrians or Christianity.

Mōr Gabriel monastery suffered numerous attacks. The first tragedy befell on it in 581 CE, when, together with its entire library, it was burned down by the Persians. Subsequently it was incessantly attacked by the Kurds, who ruined the monastery, killed the monks and burned priceless manuscripts. Villages became empty after their inhabitants were barbarically murdered and all goods were stolen. A poem describing the results of looting in 1100, which lasted for fourteen days, survive to this day: 'The pages of torn books from Mōr Gabriel monastery were blown away by the wind all the way until the city of Nisibis.' These books included, among others, seventy volumes written in 988 on parchment in *estrangelo* (Syriac script) by the best calligraphers. This alphabet, after 100 years of neglect, was restored again by survivors who hid in the Rock Castle – the bishops who had escaped alive recreated from memory several liturgical and historical books. A similar tragedy happened

[45] This part is mostly based on the book by Patriarch Ighnāṭiyyos Aphrem I Barṣōm, *Maktbōnūtō*.

again in 1146, when the Turks completely destroyed Midyat. Ṭūr ʿAbdīn was again pacified by the Kurds in 1185 and 1286, when a man appeared among them who declared himself the 'awaited al-Mahdi'. The Bēṯ Risha province suffered the most at the time.

The inhabitants of Ṭūr ʿAbdīn suffered tremendous loss during the Mongolian conquests. In 1296 the reconstructed Mōr Gabriel was set on fire, which destroyed the precious items gathered therein. The walls and ceiling still bear the marks of molten gold. Acts of vandalism were equally committed by Tamerlane's hordes. In 1394 more than 500 people died of smoke inhalation after having hidden in a grotto at the feet of the monastery. Among them were four priests, forty monks and a bishop. Kurds, who supported the attackers, occupied the monastery over the next four months, transforming it into a stable.

The traditional Kurdish intolerance towards Assyrians intensified after the Crusades. The Seljuk Turks joined them and a destructive wave of fanaticism flooded the whole of Ṭūr ʿAbdīn. Between 1416 and 1426 churches and homes were pillaged. In the Mōr Gabriel monastery a chest was destroyed, containing a fifth-century relic – the arm of Mōr Gabriel himself. In the village of Kafarzo(e) the oldest and most worshipped sixth-century icon was burned. Over the next five years Assyrians were forced to pay high taxes. Famine, illnesses and epidemics decimated the population to such an extent that in several villages no one survived. In the village of Basebrino (Bsōrīnō) alone more than 500 people died. Vineyards were devastated as well, while cattle and agricultural produce got confiscated. Twenty years later the Kurds captured Assyrian women and children from ten villages. During the Great Lent in 1446 they attacked Basebrino (Bsōrīnō), killing all men who refused apostasy and capturing children and women to take to their harems; several of them were sold in the slave market. In 1493, Kurds looted many churches and monasteries, including Mōr Yaʿqūb monastery in Ṣaleḥ, founded in the fifth century, where the patriarch was residing at the time, together with the Mōr Yaʿqūb monastery in Nisibis, which dates from 707. In 1506 Kurds smoked out 312 people, including 32 monks and the *mafiriono* of Ṭūr ʿAbdīn. The assassins also reached the inhabitants of nearby villages, hiding in the village fortress of Bēṯ-Isḥōq. Men were murdered, and the children and women sent to harems.

Figure 4 The ruins of an Assyrian farm in the village of Badebe (photograph by M. Abdalla, 1999)

In 1727 the Kurdish Agha Ḥamza took an army of 7,000 against Assyrian villages. They captured Basebrino and stole more than 14,000 sheep and 3,000 goats. More than 20 Assyrian villages were burned down, and farmhouses were levelled with all their defenders murdered; 350 people died in Badebe.

On 15 May 1801 Kurds attacked the village of Arbo, killing thirteen priests, most of the men and women and taking away all the cattle. Those who remained suffered from famine and died of cholera. In the nearby village of Ehwo (Ḥabāb) nobody survived; the bodies of the victims lay without burial. In November 1829 Kurds, under the command of Sayfuddin and Badr Khan, attacked Arbo and destroyed the castle. The bodies resting in the crypts of the churches (Holy Mother and Mōr Ḍīmat) were set on fire and both churches destroyed. Next, all inhabitants together with priests and altar boys were murdered. The culmination of this ethnocide was the dragging of 60 men, only 20 of whom survived, by horses all the way to Diyarbakır. For the next two years the inhabitants of Diyarbakır had to pay ransom in wheat, the amount corresponding to the weight of each taxpayer.

The pages of monastery manuscripts were used by the attackers as wads for their rifles.[46]

Badr Khan was especially cruel and went down in Assyrian history as an exceptional butcher.[47] The year 1855 was marked with another conquest of Assyrian villages by Kurds, this time commanded by ʿIzzaddin Sher and Masʿoud Beg, who burned crops, stole cattle, destroyed temples and raped women and girls in full view of their fathers and husbands. Dozens of Assyrian villages turned to ruins, but this time – for the first time ever – Turkey sent to Ṭūr ʿAbdīn a punitive expedition against Kurds under the command of Korekli Pasha. The captured Kurdish leaders were brought to trial in Istanbul.

The interventions of Turkish forces against ungoverned tribal attacks were sporadic. The gendarmerie, which was supposed to protect Assyrians in 1895 from Kurds, cooperated with them to ensure their own part in dividing the bounty. It was almost a rule that the prettiest Assyrian women were given

[46] Priest Giwargis Bēṯ-Zabdōyō (Gorgīs el-Āzakhī) wrote a poem about the Assyrian tragedy of 1829. He says that 'the Emir of Rawandez like a bloodthirsty wolf invaded the Christ's flocks / On the first day of October Mayor Sayfuddin joined the forces of the evil / They created a satanic alliance / They turned houses serving love into butcheries /. . ./ They gored bellies of pregnant women with spikes / They carried babies away from their mothers' breasts and stepped on their pert bodies /. . ./ They turned the Church of the Holy Mother into a public house /. . ./ Church and monastery bells became silent, voices of playing children and music in the wedding house disappeared /. . ./ How many times has the Kurdish Herod organized a massacre of Christ's children? / How many times the Kurdish Kain kills Abel?'. This and similar poetry of facts has been collected and published by the metropolitan Yulius Yēshūʿ Çiçek in the volume *Mimrē d-ʿāl sayfē dasbāl mshīḥōyē d-Turkia mēn shnāṯ 1714–1914*, containing twelve poems describing Assyrian villages stricken by massacres in 1714, 1829, 1891, 1895, 1914–20 and 1941–6.

[47] Badr Khan also attacked Assyrians living in the region of Hakkari, to the east of Ṭūr ʿAbdīn, which had been inhabited by Assyrians since antiquity and now is part of Kurdistan. Only ruins are left of monasteries and churches there. Popko, M., *Turcja*, p. 302. The tragedy of Assyrians, which took place in Hakkari 170 years ago, has also been described by the English archaeologist Henry Austen Layard, *W poszukiwaniu Niniwy*, pp. 137–99. On 4 November 1993 the inhabitants of Hassana were forced by the Turkish authorities to leave their historical place of residence (Thiry, A., *Mechelen aan de Tigris*, Brussels 2001). This event has received widespread public attention in the west, for instance by Ward Bosmans and Sven Van Haezendonck, 'Melikan Kucam als held onthaald met groots feest na negen maanden cel', *Gazet van Antwerpen,* Mar. 10, 2019, 20:24, https://www.gva.be/cnt/dmf20191003_04643337/melikan-kucam-als-held-onthaald-met-groots-feest-na-negen-maanden-cel. Badr Khan has become a Kurdish national hero.

to the gendarmes. In Assyrian history there are many cases of mass suicides by captured women, who thus protected themselves from the upcoming humiliations. Some of these events grew into legends, always with a motive of treason by even the best, non-Christian friends, who informed the enemy about the location of hiding places of the persecuted.

Gabrielle Yonan devoted her book *A Forgotten Holocaust* to the history of massacres in Ṭūr ʻAbdīn in 1895 and 1914–18 and later, proved the participation of Germany, allied with Turkey, in the genocide.[48] The Turkish armies attacking Christian cities such as Urhoy were often led by German generals.[49] Nazi Germany also supported the anti-Assyrian policies of the Iraqi government in 1933.[50] In the report presented to the Peace Conference in Paris (1919) a member of the Assyrian delegation, Bishop Aphrem Barṣōm (who later became patriarch) counted 90,313 Assyrians murdered during World War I in Ṭūr ʻAbdīn alone by Kurds and Turks. About 345 villages were completely ruined, 156 churches were destroyed, 156 priests and 6 bishops were killed.[51] The massacres and destructions meant the end to all five Assyrian newspapers, printed between 1906 and 1915 in Diyarbakır and Mardin.[52]

[48] Yonan, G., *Ein vergessener Holocaust: die Vernichtung der christlichen Assyrer in der Türkei.*

[49] Gōrgīs, A., *Ğirāḥ fi tārīkh as-Syriān*, p. 21.

[50] Odisho, W., ‘Mawqif almānia an-nāziyya min al-mas’ala al-ashūriyya’, *Beth-Nahrain Star, Journal of Assyrian Cultural Centre*, pp. 19–21.

[51] Yaʻqūb, S. T., *Tārīkh al-kanīsa as-suriāniyya al-anṭākiyya*, pp. 23–5.

[52] In books written at that time the fate of the Assyrians is compared to that of Incas and Aztecs, and some texts have received the title ‘Death of a Nation’; see Abdalla, M., ‘Losy Asyryjczyków’ [Fate of the Assyrians], *Sprawy Narodowościowe 2*, pp. 67–82.

To the Assyrians, dispossessed of their ancestral lands, and the dispersed daughters and sons of Ṭūr ʻAbdīn

SPILT BLOOD, OR THE TRAGEDY OF THE LAMBS OF CHRIST

[Diary of a seminarian, covering the genocide of Armenians and Assyrians in the year 1895 and during World War I]

Abed Mshiho Neman of Qarabash

1

FROM THE AUTHOR

This handwritten diary constitutes a recollection about times of disquiet, suffering, pain and tragedies. It presents shattering practices of violation of the name and dignity of man. It describes immeasurable acts of hate, aggression and abuse, as well as persecution and destruction that have ended with a genocide perpetrated in 1915 without any cause or guilt, to which the Christian people[1] and particularly Assyrians fell victim. The instigators and executors of this genocide – Ottomans and Kurds – were not men, but degenerated abominations of the humankind. They presented wildness, primitivism, betrayal, inhumanity and barbarism. Their obsession was hate towards Christians. Over the course of at least four years,[2] they hunted their victims with savagery, preying on and murdering them. The territory of their activity was the Mesopotamian soil, in particular provinces found in the north [Upper Mesopotamia] and the west [Western Mesopotamia].

My notes are not chronologically ordered. I am also far from claiming that they cover all the events that shook this region. Acts of individual and mass murders, together with pillage, theft and takeover of possessions, on

[1] Armenians and Pontic Greeks were victims of the genocide as well.

[2] The massacres commenced in 1914 and continued for several years with varying intensity.

a scale hitherto unknown, took place everywhere in Upper Mesopotamia. It is probably not possible for anyone to count these acts. The swords of tyranny cut away the heads of innocent lambs of Christ without any mercy, not making any distinction between man and woman, young, old or infant, village and city – leaving decaying bodies everywhere, and the ones left alive had only loneliness, fear, regret and tears. Cries and lamentations could be heard from every home.

My notes are based on the testimony of eyewitnesses. Some of them stem from the lips of those that have survived the massacres. Their stories, as well as the entire manuscript, are but a minuscule fragment of what occurred; most probably it is a fraction of the complete story [2 – page number of original manuscript]. I also have to mention that the issue least important for me was the beauty of the language that I use to describe these tragedies. I do not consider myself educated, and I have no experience in writing.[3] I am but a pupil of the spiritual seminary at the monastery of Zaʿfarān, the seat of the patriarch of the Syriac Orthodox Church. I am not even fifteen years of age yet.

I have commenced writing this diary from the beginning of 1915 until the year 1918, when the swords were laid back to their sheaths, when the persecutions and slaughter ceased, the streams of human blood dried, and hunger and epidemics were conquered. Many people that survived extermination fell to the hunger and epidemics. Among the hungry and naked, only those with toughest body and strongest spirit survived. The bodies of many are marked by traces of bullets and swords. Having lost everything and everyone, they hid away in secluded spots, with nobody to care for them.

I did not come to the thought of writing this diary following a plea of any official, i.e. for statistical reasons, and not to disclose anyone's actions, and also not for reasons of a disgruntled rebel. My goal was to convey to the world the landscape of barbarism, to which probably only wild beasts of the jungle are capable. I am aware that time is deceitful, that it is friend to tyrants, that

[3] The European reader is more subtle and dislikes repetitions, from which the author could not liberate himself. One needs to remember, however, that he had lived in an atmosphere of tragedy, describing every case separately, living and reliving it. Despite his young age, he used elegant language and had a 'cultivated' and legible writing style, typical for monastery seminarians.

it hurts the poor and the weak, that it holds neither place nor compassion for the frail, the suffering and the orphaned. Justice does not care about the fate of the injured [3] and it does not rush to help those, whose wings were broken, and who were robbed of their physical strength.[4] I am haunted by the bitter impression that the civilisation of the twentieth century requires and wants exactly such a policy, in which evil, in all its colours and tones, surpasses the good. This is a false civilisation and one that is doomed to fail.[5]

What can we say besides this? God remains our only shelter and support. God, praised be His name, whose boundless patience and gentleness helps the depressed and hopeless people.[6]

I stress that I have written down this diary with all my efforts in order that these events reverberate in the ears of generations to come; in order that the ears of thoughtful people open up, when they hear the cries and moans of those hurt, powerless and defeated, and when their eyes and minds open up to these scenes of barbarism as if they had played out before their own eyes, they shall touch them and remember them. The suffering of all mankind had focused in the hearts of my people, who constantly need to give testimony of their faith. They are an innocent victim, a martyr, due to their faith and their mission based on love and which is foreign to others. They have been hurt and betrayed because they had never done any sort of harm to anyone – near or far. They are not even capable to do so.

4 Regret with respect to 'time' and 'justice' are frequent motifs in contemporary Assyrian literature with a self-reflective and pessimistic tone.

5 The author's regrets should be viewed in the context of the tragedy that his people suffered, as well as that of the Armenians, in which certain European countries, particularly Germany, played a dissapointing role. A light was shed on a similar policy practiced by Britain with respect to Assyrians in Iraq a few years later, directly referred to as treacherous: Wigram, W., *Our Smallest Ally: A Brief Account of the Assyrian Nation in the Great War*; Naayem, J., *Shall this Nation Die?*; Yohannan, A., *The Death of a Nation, or, the ever-persecuted Nestorians or Assyrian Christians*; Stafford, R. S., *The Tragedy of the Assyrians.*

6 As Christians, Assyrians were considered for the most part pious religious people, who even considered the greatest of tragedies they faced as ascribed to their weak faith and considered them punishment by God. There were exceptions, however – some, in hopeless moments of history, did not hide their regret of God, others still looked for the causes of their poverty and in general many considered lack of attention by international policy. The representatives of this second belief justified themselves with a particular mode of thought expressed using the motto: 'God says: "If you get up, I shall support you; if you continue in your laziness, count only on yourself!" '.

There are with certainty societies that we do not know of, perhaps living in unknown lands at the time. When they hear of the massacres that have decimated us and turned us into beggars, and when they confront this with the historic achievements of our ancestors, they shall with certainty feel our pain, cry over the injustice that had befallen us. Was it not our ancestors who gave the world the permanent and eternal values in terms of law and faith?![7] When the world is ruled by peace and freedom, the survivors of the slaughter, among them the children of the genocide victims, shall come to weep over their fate, to speak of the bitter message concerning the animal-like actions of people who have murdered their fathers and mothers with inhuman bestiality. For me, in turn, these notes are something uncommonly important. They are first of all a memory. Every time I read them, I see these terrible atrocities come alive anew before my eyes, I am pierced by the pain, overwhelmed by sadness, and I experience insurmountable bitterness and regret. It is often so that the only way to experience relief is tears and tears again. How much pain and how much suffering were inflicted upon our fathers and mothers? They died under indescribable torture. The raping, instigated in groups and with criminal intent, that was orchestrated against our mothers, immature sisters, before the eyes of our fathers and brothers, awaken the greatest regret and rebellion in me. Indeed, these rapists were devoid of any human values, shameless, with beast-like instincts, born out of hell itself [4]. I am not able to stop the stream of feelings about this great tragedy that befell us, but also about the pride because of the heroism of our fathers and relatives.

I believe that time shall regain balance and memory, and that it shall become aware of the scale of the tragedy that it allowed to pass.[8] It is then that it shall examine its conscience and it is then that it shall give testimony and account of the macabre deeds of the bandits, that it shall feel regret and that it shall compensate those who survived the flood of blood, show mercy, replace suffering with peace, transform sadness into joy, and threat into safety, and that it shall let the dried eyes see the light of life, and that it shall let wounded hearts feel the taste of freedom. {At this time, those reading these notes shall

[7] The author is here referencing the famous Code of Hammurabi, and the mythology of Mesopotamia, his heritage.

[8] Here, for a second time, we see the author personifying time.

pay tribute to the murdered, their fathers and mothers, their brothers and sisters, led to the slaughter like lambs.} Let us turn to God for mercy for the martyrs. Divine providence is not indifferent to the cries of the poor and the harmed [5].

Abed Mshiho Neman of Qarabash
Monastery of Za'farān
5 September 1918

2

THE EMERGENCE AND SPREAD OF CHRISTIANITY

Before I describe the distressing events that took place in the years 1895 and 1915[1] I want to concisely present the beginnings of Christianity and the circumstances of its spread in the countries of the East, particularly in Mesopotamia. Following this, I shall describe the painful events, more or less tragic, that befell the local Christians at various points in time. Finally, I shall present the material that I was able to collect about the latest, it would seem, most gruesome persecution and atrocities {which fell upon us in present times}.

The Christian faith first appeared in Jerusalem. The voice of our Teacher, Saviour and Lord, Jesus Christ, sounded in this city, and it was here that His eternally pure blood was spilt for the redemption and salvation of humankind. In Jerusalem, the Holy Spirit descended upon the holy Apostles, filling

[1] To prior persecution of Assyrians by Kurds, under the leadership of Badr Khan in the Hakkari mountains (northeastern Turkey) in the 1840s, the English archaeologist Austen Henry Layard devoted a chapter in his book *Nineveh and Its Remains* (pp. 137–99). Due to the uniqueness of the story (we know the history of archaeological discovery in Mesopotamia from many sources), this chapter was translated into Arabic, and published as a series in the magazine *Hujådå*, vols 5–12, 1990, and in 1994 it was published as a book by the Swedish publishing house Dar Sargon.

them with strength and wisdom, and from [there] they set out to preach the Gospel, baptise Jews and representatives of other nations. Thanks to the Apostles and [other] preachers, Christianity arrived from Jerusalem in Judea, Samaria and Galilee. Together with the constant growth of the numbers of the faithful, the number of churches in all of Palestine and in countries on the shores of the Mediterranean Sea also rose. The preachers carried [the Word] from Caesarea, Tyre, Sidon and Beirut, to countries in the north, including to two great cities: Damascus and Antioch, indicating to their inhabitants the road to salvation, and including them into the flock of those believing in Christ [6].

Damascus was particularly honoured and distinguished with the Christian faith. It happened just a few months following the descent of the Holy Spirit on the holy Apostles. The preacher Ananias[2] travelled to the city. He taught and Christianised many people who have accepted the teachings of the Gospel. However, the rising number of the faithful in this city made the Jews uneasy, as they took a disfavourable stance towards the Christians. In the year 34 CE Saul [of Tarsus], having obtained letters from spiritual leaders, set out to journey to the city to organise a slaughter of the local Christians.[3] On his way, he received an epiphany; Our Lord had shown himself to him, blessed him with faith and sent him to the mentioned Ananias in Damascus, in order for Saul to learn from him the rules and sacraments of the [Christian] faith. After being baptised, [Saul] immediately started preaching in public gathering places and in synagogues, about Christ the God, explaining, particularly to Jews, that Christ is the awaited Messiah. In this way, Christianity gained strong ground both in Damascus as well as in other Syrian cities, covering with its influence the territory from the shores of the Mediterranean all the way to Aleppo and Mabbug.[4]

[2] Acts 9:10. Ananias was one of the seventy-two students of Christ to have left for Damascus after Pentecost.

[3] Paul the Apostle converted in 38 CE, but the first Christian commune of Damascus was formed in the year 37 CE. Daniélou, J. and Marrou, H, I., *Historia Kościoła*, p. 35.

[4] Presently Manbij (Gr. Hierapolis), a city in northwestern Syria, built on the ruins of a locality very well known in the early medieval period. Its famous bishops include St Philoxenus of Mabbug, a martyr (d. 522). This is where empress Theodora, wife to Justinian the Great (527–65) hailed from; according to Assyrian sources, she was born the daughter of an Assyrian priest, married the emperor in the year he ascended to the throne (527), and died

In Antioch the oldest Christian church, after that in Jerusalem, was created. From Antioch stems the name of Christianity,[5] and it is the mother of Christianity in the East.

The Church of Jerusalem was created in 34 CE, during a period of persecution. After the stoning of Mōr Ṣṭēfānos (St Stephen), the martyr, the preachers scattered. Some had made it to Antioch and began preaching the Gospel, calling only upon Jews to accept the Christian faith. Students from Cyprus [7] and Cyrene[6] were among those that came; they converted and baptised Greeks and people from other nations.[7] In 37 CE, Mo Feṭrus (St Peter) travelled to Antioch to visit his brothers, the Apostles.[8] He preached the Word of God, baptised many people and founded his apostolic seat here, creating the foundation and the primary of all the great apostolic seats. {And St Peter, being the 'head of the choir of apostles'} remains until this day the first patriarch among Assyrian patriarchs keeping to the simple [Orthodox] faith.[9]

Edessa[10] and Mesopotamia

Before the preacher Mōr Adday (St Thaddeus) was sent to Edessa, according to the will of our Lord Jesus Christ, all of Mesopotamia, including Media and Persia, were prepared to accept the Christian faith.[11] When our Lord

in the year 548. She is included among grand defenders of pre-Chalcedonic churches, which were viewed by Byzantines with abhorrence. Thanks to her efforts, Mor Ya'qūb Bured'ōnō (Jacob Baradeus) could be consecrated as a bishop of the Syrian Orthodox Church (543) and the Christianisation of Ethiopia could be concluded.

5 Acts 11:35.

6 Cyrene was an ancient Greek colony in what is now Libya.

7 Referred to here are the Hellenists of Cyprus and of Cyrene, who arrived in Antioch from Jerusalem.

8 Atiya, A., *Historia Kościołów Wschodnich* p. 149, believes that, according to tradition, St Peter managed the newly created Church of Antioch for seven years (33–40). This is attested by Pope Gregory I (the Great) (590–604). St Peter organised the Christian communes existing in Antioch and ordained Evodius as bishop and his successor. Ighnāṭiyyos of Antioch (d. 107) was in turn the third bishop of this city, which can be inferred as well from the contents of his letters written en route to his martyrdom in the Roman arena.

9 In the year the diary was concluded (1918), the patriarch of the Syrian Orthodox Church was Mor Elias III Shakir, the 118th patriarch, counting from St Peter.

10 Today Edessa is Urfa in southern Turkey, in Upper Mesopotamia.

11 It is not known on which grounds the author makes this highly doubtful hypothesis.

Jesus Christ was born in Bethlehem, he was visited by the Magi of the East, led by the star. Upon their arrival, they offered Him gifts: gold, myrrh and frankincense. It is also known that many Jews, inhabitants of Media, Persia, Parthia, Alania [Sarmatia] and Mesopotamia, stayed in Jerusalem during Pentecost in the year 34 CE. They were reached by the news of the descent of the Holy Spirit upon the Apostles, and they had heard the famous lecture of Peter, while they saw the crowds that believed in and accepted baptism. The news of these wondrous events were spread by the Magi upon their return to their home countries.[12]

Tūmā (Thomas) the Apostle

On his way to India, Thomas the Apostle made a pause in Mesopotamia. Here, he taught and had baptised people from many lands[13] [8]. He had particular success in Edessa, the Assyrian city being the cradle of all cities of Mesopotamia and the small capital of kings of the Abgar dynasty. It was a subject of the Roman Empire. When its king, Abgar V, named Ukāmā [the Black], found out about the Lord Jesus Christ and about the signs and miracles that He had made on the Earth as part of his plan of salvation, he sent his emissaries to Jerusalem with the suggestion that Christ come to Edessa and cure him of leprosy, which the king suffered from. The letter sent to Christ had the following content:

> From Abgar Ukāmā, king of Urhoy,[14] to Jesus Christ, the Saviour, who had emerged in Jerusalem. Peace [be with You]. I have heard of you and of the signs and miracles that you conjure without medications and [long term]

The subsequent sentence suggests that a reference is rather made to the sky-gazing Magi. However, their profession had little to do with faith in God. They constituted but a fraction of the multi-ethnic society of Mesopotamia, and even less in terms of Media and Persia.

12 The legend, famous among Assyrian Christians of Ṭūr ʻAbdīn, speaks of twelve Magi.

13 Mesopotamia was and is inhabited by many ethnic and religious groups. In the time of Christ, the southeastern part was under Persian rule, while the northwestern part was under the governance of Romans and Greeks. Tradition has it that after his mission at Osroene, St Thomas returned to Jerusalem towards the end of the forties and then moved on to India. His remains were transported from Indian Malabar to Edessa in the year 412, in a time when Abraham was its bishop. A cathedral dedicated to this saint was built at the spot where the remains were buried.

14 The Syriac name of Edessa.

> treatment. I therefore ask you to be so kind and undertake the effort of visiting me, to come to cure me of the disease that saps me. I have also heard that Jews insult you, and that they even want to harm you. I am the king of a small and appealing city, which will be enough for both of us.

In order to stress his faith in Jesus, King Abgar ordered the delegation as follows: 'If Jesus would not wish to come with you, then bring me his likeness so that I could see him.' [9]

When the emissaries reached Jerusalem and passed the letter on to Christ, Christ read it and replied to Abgar as follows:

> Blessed are they that have not seen, and yet have believed.[15] If you ask me to come to you and see you, I inform you that precisely here [where I am] I should conclude all my efforts and make my way to the One that had sent me. After my ascension into Heaven I shall send to you one of my pupils. He will cure you of your disease, bring life to you and shall bless your province, which shall not be ruled by Parthians.[16]

Lord Jesus, who knew of things hidden and unseen, asked to be handed some water and he washed his face. Then he took a cloth, on which, when he wiped his face, his image was imprinted. He handed the cloth, along with the reply to the letter, to the emissaries of Abgar, who returned [with this gift] to Edessa.[17]

Thomas was the one to fulfil the promise of our Lord, who sent his brother Thaddeus[18] to Edessa. [Thaddeus] had cured the king of his disease and led him to the path of salvation, whereafter he had baptised him and his court along with important dignitaries of the town. This happened in the year 50 CE. Subsequently, Thaddeus began to teach freely in Edessa, after which he

[15] John 20:29.

[16] The alleged letters contain words allowing one to doubt their authenticity and are rather considered apocrypha. The first Greek translation was published by Eusebius of Caesaria (4th century) in his famous work *Ecclesiastical History*. See also Eusebius of Caesaria, *Church History, Life of Constantine the Great, and Oration in Praise of Constantine.*

[17] One can come across information that it was Ananias, the court painter of Abgar and a member of this party of emissaries to Christ, who had painted the portrait of Christ on a cloth.

[18] Thomas and Thaddeus were twins.

moved on to other cities and towns of Mesopotamia, including Amida. He travelled and taught in lands to the north of Arzun,[19] in the eastern valley of the Tigris, in the region of Adiabene,[20] in Bēṯ Zabdāy[21] and the neighbouring provinces [10]. Afterwards [Thaddeus] returned to Edessa, where he built a church and a clerical school and became its first bishop. He departed from this world in this city.

Aggai, a student of Thaddeus, was his successor; he was sent earlier both to Assyria as well as to Bēṯ Zabdāy.[22] In this way, Christianity spread and solidified in all lands of the [Near] East.

The Lands of Kush [Abyssinia]

In 316 CE, Meropius arrived from Tyre on the shores of Abyssinia. He was accompanied by two brothers of a young age: Edesius and Frumentius. The Abyssinians attacked their ship, killing all [passengers] except these two brothers, whom they kidnapped and gave to their king. The king appointed Frumentius to the post of his secretary, and on his deathbed, he asked him to care for his son, a minor, his successor.[23]

[19] This region most probably bears today the name Garzan, approximately fifteen kilometres to the west of the city of Si'irt. Its Turkish name is Kortalan. The Assyrian village of Buknad, one of many like it in the region, was the location of a monastery dedicated to St Yūḥānōn Naḥlōyō.

[20] Adiabene's capital was the city of Arbela (the current name is Irbil, an ancient Assyrian city in northern Iraq). Here and there one can come across the view that the name initially had the form Arba-Ille, meaning city of 'four deities'. 'In the time of the Parthians, a part of Nineveh was settled again, even the former temple of Nabu was reconstructed. In the first century BC, the city became an administrative centre, with its own mint and administrative structure, with *epistrategos* Apollonios, listed in two inscriptions from approximately 31–2. Kalchu and Ashur as well as Arbela also lying in the valley of the Tigris became cities. Assyrian religious customs flourished anew, with the same gods, which is proof of the extraordinary endurance of tradition, lively enough to survive several centuries. In the Parthian kingdom, Assyria was a separate province, Adiabene, its area close to that of Assyria from the first millenium BC.' Joannès, F., *La Mésopotamie au 1er millénaire avant J.-C.*,pp. 161–2.

[21] Azakh, presently İdil in southeastern Turkey, is located about ten kilometres to the east of the Tigris and twenty-five kilometres to the north of the Syrian border.

[22] These two lands, due to their distances from Edessa, should be named in the opposite order.

[23] Atiya, A., *Historia Kościołów Wschodnich*, p. 45, writes: 'The ship sailed from Tyre to India and broke up in the Red Sea on the borders of Ethiopia. The survivors were rescued by men of the king of Ethiopia, who had taken them on as his servants, bestowing Frumentius with

[These] two brothers began to preach the Christian faith in these lands. After a while, Edesius returned to Tyre, where he was ordained a priest. Frumentius in turn travelled to Alexandria [of Egypt], to St Aṯanāsiyyos the Great,[24] whom he foretold that these lands [of Abyssinia] were ready to accept the Christian faith and asked him to send a bishop to them.

[Hearing these stories] St Aṯanāsiyyos told him: {'Who is more worthy of this blessing and this grace than the one who preached to these peoples Christianity and had led them to the holy flock!}' and consecrated him as bishop [11] around the year 341, after which he sent him back to Abyssinia. [The latter] was greeted enthusiastically and with honours, both by the king as well as the people of Kush, who declared the will to accept Christ. In this way, Abyssinia became a Christian kingdom, and remains so until today.[25]

the task of educating the young successor, with Edesius to become cup-bearer.' On this story, Wipszycka, E., *Kościół w świecie późnego antyku*, pp. 91–2 writes, quoting Rufin of Aquilea (345–40/411): 'A certain inhabitant of the Phoenician city of Tyre, the philosopher Metrodorus . . . travelled to India to get to know this land. He was accompanied by two boys, his relatives, Frumentius and Edesius. On the return trip, close to African shores, the crew of the ship on which they were travelling was massacred by barbarians, with only Frumentius and Edesius surviving.' A similar recollection may be found in the story by Mōr Mīkhōyel Rābo (d. 1199), *Tārīkh*, pp. 182–3, calling Ethiopia 'Inner India', as opposed to 'Outer India' where St Thomas preached. He stresses that those indicated were able to win such respect in Ethiopia as the biblical Joseph did in Egypt.

24 St Aṯanāsiyyos (295–373), Archbishop of Alexandria from 328, was a participant of the first general council of Nice (325). During the invasion of Egypt by Arabs, the venerable relics of this saint were moved to Constantinople and placed in the orthodox church of Holy Wisdom. After the takeover of the city by the Crusaders, King Baldwin gave an arm of the saint to Monte Cassino and moved the body to the Benedictine church in Venice. In 1806 they were moved to the church of St Zakharias, where they remain today (source: <www.cerkiew.pl> last accessed 21 September 2018).

25 Beginning with the council of Chalcedon (451), the Ethiopians have joined the Coptic Church. In 1968 the Empire of Ethiopia became a republic. Presently, Ethiopia is a country with the majority of the population being Christian, belonging to the orthodox church of the rite of Alexandria (the Coptic Church). It is noteworthy that the Acts of the Apostles speak of an apostle Philip, who introduced Christianity in Ethiopia earlier, in the first century. In the first century of Christianity, Ethiopia was a flourishing and independent kingdom called Aksum (from the name of the capital). It spanned the territory of today's Ethiopia and Somalia as well as the territory of present-day southwestern Yemen. According to various traditions, Apostle Matthew also preached the Gospel in Ethiopia.

Iberia [Georgia]

In the first half of the fourth century, a certain girl came to the capital of Iberia, a hostage by the name of Nino,[26] who employed herself in the services of Midian,[27] the ruler of the region. It happened that the son of the ruler fell ill. Nina turned to God, praying for the boy to get well. The boy did. The same happened with the king's wife,[28] who [thanks to the prayers of Nino] regained her health. When asked about her faith, she replied that she was Christian, and she began talking about her faith. The king sensed a liking of Christianity and, encouraged by Nina, invited clerics from the territory of the Roman Empire. He also wrote to Emperor Constantine [the Great], who sent emissaries and representatives to the king of Iberia; they taught the Iberians the Christian faith and baptised everyone, including the king and the queen. In this way, Iberia became a Christian land.[29]

The land of Saba': Yemen

Halfway through the fourth century, a group of [Christian] missionaries arrived in the land of Saba'; they preached the Gospel to the people and they had brought them to the Christian faith.[30] At this time, Christianity developed dynamically in the land of Hirah[31] and [the southern valley of

[26] The person referred to here is St Nina, the patron of Georgia. She originally came from Cappadocia. For more on her mission in Iberia see Lang, D. M., *Dawna Gruzja*, p. 72. One can find here and there information, among Georgians as well, indicating Assyrian roots of this holy woman.

[27] The name of the king of Iberia was Mirian. In Assyrian ((Syriac script), the letters 'r' and 'd' are differentiated by the location of a dot.

[28] Her name was Nana.

[29] This happened around 330 CE, seventeen years following the edict of Milan. 'The Emperor, having sent priests there, rejoiced about this fact more than he would have, had he conquered foreign peoples and unknown kingdoms' – Wipszycka, E., *Kościół w świecie późnego antyku*, p. 91.

[30] Missionaries arrived in Yemen from Mesopotamia, Egypt, Syria and Persia. It is thought that in the time of Mohammad, every tenth inhabitant of Yemen was Christian. The most broadly known is the mission by Emperor Constantine II to the Arabian Himayrites of Yemen, which included Theophilus of India, consecrated bishop by Eusebius of Nicomedia, an Aryan. Having accepted the Christian faith, the ruler of Yemen ordered the construction of churches in Aden and in the capital, Zafar.

[31] In Arabic, Al-Ḥīra. This was once a large city and important Christian centre in the south

the] Euphrates, as an extension of the work of the preacher Thaddeus and his student, Aggai. Churches were built, schools were opened, and an elite was formed, among them holy bishops and great scholars, who had elevated the ranks of the Christian faith to a very high level [12]. However, the greatest flourishing of Christianity in the East was the result of the development of monasticism; many monasteries were formed, which were famed for their science and knowledge. They had brought about the end to pagan temples, on the ruins of which churches for Christ were built. Many church writers recorded testimony that Christianity spread across all of Mesopotamia, and developed since the beginning of the second half of the second century from the birth of Christ.[32] Bardaiṣān, comprehensively educated and very well known, who died in the year 222, wrote in his *Book of the Laws of the Countries* as follows: 'What can we say about our new Christian people, the foundations of which were laid, for the whole world, by our Lord Jesus Christ, a people who filled particularly well Mesopotamia, Persia, Media and Edessa.'[33]

of today's Iraq, inhabited mostly by Arabs from the Lakhmid tribe. In executing the last will of Mohammed, second caliph Omar deported close to 50,000 Christians to this city from Najran in Yemen for refusing to convert to Islam. On the circumstances of the deportations and on the fate of the deported, see Abdalla, M., 'Losy chrześcijan himjaryckich jemeńskiego miasta Nadżran (VI-X w.) w źródłach arabskich i asyryjskich', in *Arabowie-Islam-Świat.*

32 The monastic movement in Mesopotamia was markedly reinforced upon the arrival of St Eugene the Great of Klizma and his company from Egypt in the 4th century. Most of the monasteries of Ṭūr 'Abdīn, now in ruins, were built in this time; some of them are devoted to Egyptian patrons.

33 Edessa is located within Mesopotamia, unless the author of the diary was thinking of the kingdom of Osroene, of which Edessa – as already mentioned – was the capital. The above quote is an abbreviation of a paragraph from the book by Bardaiṣān, which speaks of changes to pagan practices following the acceptance of Christianity not only in the indicated countries. It reads: 'What can we say of our new generation, a generation of Christians living in different countries? Wherever we are, we call ourselves Christians and we meet on Sunday, and we fast on specific days of the week. Our brothers in Gilan (northwestern Iran) do not marry boys any more, those living in Parthia do not take two wives, those from Judea have stopped circumcisions, our sisters in Gali and the land of Kashan (?) have stopped fornicating with foreigners, those from Persia do not take their daughters for wives, in Media they do not reject the dead, they do not bury their sick before death and they do not let them be eaten by dogs, the Edessians do not kill their wives and daughters if they pursue magic, and they do not abandon them, but they submit them to divine judgement. Those living in cities do not stone thieves. In no land, where Christians live, may the law of the

This information is confirmed by the educated Tertullian, who remarks:[34]

> All the peoples living in Mesopotamia, as well as Persians, Medians and Elamites believed in Christ and accepted Him, {similarly in Egypt and towards the west, in the region of Rome, thanks to the holy Apostles. In Egypt in turn, it came about through actions of Marqus the Evangelist already in the first half of the first century, whereby in the province of Rome, the Apostles Peter and Paul contributed to this}. However, Rome came after Damascus, Antioch and Alexandria.[35] {The Patriarchate of Alexandria was formed in the year 61, and that of Rome in the year 68}[36] [13].

earth supersede the laws set out by Christ, Christians may also not be bound to undertake practices based on the belief in magical powers. Magic makes their lives impure'. Based on Ishō, S. Y., *Bardaiṣon: Kṯōbō d-nōmūsē d-aṯrāwōṯō*, p. 67.

34 Tertullian (born 150–60, d. 230–40), one of the greatest Latin writers and apologetics of North Africa. He was born in Carthage (present-day Tunisia). He is the author of the famous quote: 'Every time you reap us, we multiply; the Christian blood is the seed'. On Tertullian and his numerous works, see Szymusiak, J. M. and Starowieyski, M., *Słownik wczesnochrześcijańskiego piśmiennictwa*, pp. 377–81.

35 The life of St Peter does not list Damascus as a further place of his activity. We know, however, that he had travelled throughout the Near East for many years.

36 The Patriarchate of Rome was founded in the year of the martyrdom of Apostles Peter and Paul, in the years 66 or 67. From the chronological point of view, it is the fourth patriarchate, after Jerusalem, Antioch and Alexandria.

3

DIFFICULT TIMES: PERSECUTION SUFFERED BY CHRISTIANITY IN VARIOUS PERIODS OF HISTORY

Persecution by Jews[1]

The year 34 was a breakthrough year in the spread of Christianity. In this particular year, [the Apostles] added [to their divine services] seven students.[2] [Jewish] clergy were also among the converted. This intensified the dislike by Jews, the council of which sentenced St Stephen to death by stoning. The wave of persecution that began at this time covered almost all

[1] The author is most probably referring to leaders of Judaism and not ethnic Israelites, despite the fact that in the minds of contemporary Eastern peoples one's nationality tied very closely together with one's religion. It is worthwhile to consider what guided the author to describe, over several pages, the earlier (however, not all) instances of persecution of Christians in various countries in chronological order. He laments their fate no less than he does the fate of his relatives and countrymen. This approach by a young man from the Near East shows the role of religion in the life of an individual at the beginning of the twentieth century and the way faith was lived. He treats all Christians equally.

[2] The author neither explains this thread nor does he say who he is referring to. We know that St Peter summoned in the year 35 (or 36) the Twelve in Jerusalem, so that they 'select seven men enjoying good opinion, full of Spirit and wisdom', to serve as deacons. One of these was the great preacher, St Stephen. See Rufin, B., *Apostołowie po Kalwarii*, p. 41.

followers of Christ known in Jerusalem, and the result of which was their scattering across Judea and Samaria.

It is solely through divine providence that the still young Christian community was not wiped out completely. In the year 70, when Emperor Titus[3] destroyed Jerusalem, almost 600,000 people died of hunger, not to mention those that perished in dungeons, wells and on roads, and there was nobody to bury them.[4] Was it divine punishment or the fulfilment of a curse? Similarly, hundreds died from swords, and almost 100,000 were resettled and spread out across the Roman Empire. The few remaining in Jerusalem were destined to live as if they were slaves. Jerusalem turned into ruins covering hills, and prophecies were fulfilled, in particular that of the Lord of the Prophets: 'And shall lay thee even with the ground, and thy children within thee; and they shall not leave in thee one stone upon another'.[5]

When those few Christians of Jerusalem saw the signs of the destruction of the town at a difficult moment for them, they knew that this happened according to the word of Jesus. They decided to abandon the city before it succumbed to a complete downfall. They moved to the nearby village of Pella, found on the left bank[6] of the river Jordan. There they lived off their small supply of food and off that which the earth provided for them.

[3] Titus (Emperor of Rome 69–79 CE), son of Vespasian. This is actually incorrect; Titus reigned in the years 79–81 and destroyed Jerusalem; the indicated reign is that of his father, Vespasian.

[4] These numbers are definitely inflated. In the years 66–73, a Jewish uprising in Judea against the Romans took place; it was described by Josephus Flavius in his famous work *The Jewish War*.

[5] Luke 19: 44.

[6] Pella was a city located on the west side of the river Jordan. It was on the left side of the river with respect to the place where the author was. In order to save the Church from destruction in 70 CE, when Jerusalem was destroyed and its inhabitants massacred by Romans, St Simeon of Jerusalem, son of Clopas, brother to Apostle James the Less and St Matthew, cousin of Christ, made bishop of Jerusalem in 62 CE, moved the seat of the Church of Pella – Rufin, B., *Apostołowie po Kalwarii*, p. 72. Judeo-Christians escaped to the mountains of Pella after Galilee fell and when the Romans were closing in on the city. By word of a certain oracle – as reported by Eusebius – they fled there about 67–8 CE (archaeological findings seem to indicate this date). St Simeon was the second bishop of Jerusalem, successor to James the Just. He was crucified when he was 120 years old.

Roman Persecution of the Church of Christ

Not only Jews gave the Church proof of their dislike with respect to the faithful: pagans also took a hostile stance. In this they differed from Jews in that the persecution instigated by them was broad in its geographical reach. Among the many periods of persecution, one can name the ten most gruesome, conducted by Romans throughout the first three centuries and in the beginning of the fourth century. When it comes to the reasons for these persecutions, one can list those that have personal grounds, ethical grounds and social grounds, as well as others of political and moral nature.

Personal, ethical and social grounds:[7]

1. Bad conduct of pagans and lack of ethics in their actions. There is nothing curious that they were opposed to the Christian faith that binds the faithful to love one's neighbour, obey rules of good conduct and act with simplicity and honesty.
2. A threat to priests and temple assistants from Christians, who wished to introduce a new social order, as well as for sculptors of monuments of gods and for those trading in these goods. The spread of Christianity would limit their profits and even rob many of them of the means to live altogether. It is precisely these alleged disadvantages that incited society, antagonised it and mobilised it against Christians.

Political and moral grounds:

1. Fear of pagan rulers and pagan nobility against sects and divisions that could have threatened the unity of the country as a result of religious differences and practices.
2. Failure of Christians to submit to absolute rule of the emperors, who would on many occasions force the people to treat them as if they were gods and to worship them, a notion completely unacceptable to a Christian; they only bow before one God, and not this or that random idol. This could not appeal to the rulers.

[7] In line with the subsequent words of the author, one could add 'ambition and economic grounds'.

3. Slave trade, practiced widely at that time, was contrary to the Christian doctrine, which teaches that all people are equal and that everyone has the right to call God their father.

The first [wave] of persecution [years 64–68][8]

The first wave of persecution was initiated by the brutal Roman emperor Nero on 19 July 64, who set the city of Rome on fire. He hated Christians so much that, perhaps following suggestions from those Jews that favoured him,[9] he accused the Christians of this act and issued an order requiring their complete extermination. The persecutors thought up complicated torture methods and new ways of killing. They dressed some victims in animal fur and fed them to dogs, others were crucified. They covered the bodies of some of them with asphalt and lit them so that they burned in the night bright as torches. The number of those that fell in such abhorrent ordeals is hard to estimate.[10] The prime martyrs were the leaders of the Apostles: Peter and Paul.[11] The persecutions stopped only after the death of Nero in 68 CE.

The second [wave] of persecutions [years 94–96]

The persecutions were initiated by the Emperor Domitian, son of Vespasian, brother to Titus. The direct cause of these persecutions was the lack of consent to consider the emperor as a God. Among the many that were slain were St Dionysius the Areopagite,[12] the bishop of Athens, as well as St

[8] The description of both this 'wave of persecution' as well as subsequent waves lack time periods. However, the periods are indicated in the text and have been distinguished in the subheadings by the editor.

[9] It is likely that there were no Jews in Rome at this time. The edict of Claudius (emperor between 41–54) required them to leave the city in 49 CE.

[10] Both Roman as well as Christian historians speak of 'great numbers'. There could have been hundreds, thousands or (which is less probable), tens of thousands of victims. Rufin, B., *Apostołowie po Kalwarii*, p. 52.

[11] Paul, born in Tarsus, was beheaded in the year 66. Such punishment was destined for Roman citizens.

[12] Quite a mysterious person bearing this pseudonym emerges in European sources on church history as a scholar and thinker, a Christian philosopher of Byzantium originating from Gaza, a student of the school of Alexandria, the work of whom profoundly influenced the West during the Middle Ages. Daniélou, J. and Marrou, H. I., *Historia Kościoła*, p. 286. One may infer that he lived between the fifth and sixth centuries. Athens is not named, nor is the

Anthimos[13] and St Barbat(i).[14] St John the Evangelist was thrown into a cauldron full of boiling asphalt. When nothing happened to him, he was banished.[15]

Domitian died in 96 CE, and upon his death Christianity flourished again.[16]

The third [wave] of persecutions [years 100–107]

The initiator of this persecution wave was Emperor Trajan, who believed that the Christian people were hostile towards the Roman civilisation. To the persecutions fell prey, among others, St Phocas[17], burned alive in the year 104, St Sharbel[18] of Edessa, whose head was cut off with a saw in the year 105, and his sister Barbe, as well as St Simeon, the bishop of Jerusalem, crucified in the year 106, and St Ighnāṭiyyos of Antioch, thrown to wild beasts [to be eaten] in the year 107.[19]

martyrdom. It is probable that this scholar could have taken on the name of the bishop of Athens, murdered in the first century, as his patron, as suggested by Szymusiak, J. M. and Starowieyski, M., *Słownik wczesnochrześcijańskiego piśmiennictwa*, p. 341: 'Pseudo-Dionysius, a writer from the fifth and sixth centuries, wanted to be known as the Dionysius converted by St Paul on the Areopagus'. For Eusebius of Caesaria on Dionysius the Aeropagite, the bishop of Athens: Eusebius of Caesarea, *Church History*, pp. 201–2.; Stępień, T., 'Pseudo-Dionizy Areopagita – u źródeł chrześcijańskiego rozumienia symbolu', *in Niemuzułmańskie mniejszości Iraku. Historia – Kultura – Problemy przetrwania*, pp. 209–16.

13 St Anthimos, the Bishop of Nicomedia, was beheaded. Eusebius of Caesaria, *Ecclesiastical History*, 13:1.

14 Barbat(i) – available sources contain no information about a female martyr bearing such or a similar name.

15 On the island of Patmos, St John the Evangelist, suffering 'because of the Word of God and the testimony of Jesus', on one Sunday 'was awed' and received a vision that became the basis for the writing of the book known as the Apocalypse (Revelation).

16 The new emperor, Marcus Cocceius Nerva (96–98) did not persecute the Church and permitted John to return to Ephesus, where he died a natural death of old age.

17 St Phocas, the bishop of Sinope.

18 Sharbel was not the bishop of Edessa but a pagan archpriest who converted to Christianity when making sacrifices to deities.

19 The dates of martyrdom of the last four mentioned fathers of the Church were not arranged chronologically in the manuscript. Assyrian churches celebrate the memory of St Ighnāṭiyyos on 20 December, while on 28 January celebrations commemorate the transfer of his remains from Rome to Antioch, which took place at the beginning of the 5th century. The greatest permanent tribute paid to the saint is the assumption by all patriarchs of churches stemming from the Antiochian tradition of the titular name of Ighnāṭiyyos.

The persecution of Christians continued. When one wave subsided, a different one was instigated with twice the exacerbation.

The fourth [wave] of persecutions [years 124–138]

These were initiated by Emperor Hadrian. Their direct cause was a report sent to the emperor by Licinius Granianus, who was dispatched to Asia. Licynius wrote in the report: 'The Romans inflict pain on the followers of the Christian faith and murder them, and such actions on the part of the Romans are deplorable.'[20] The intent of the delegate was an accusation of the Romans, but it was not understood or interpreted that way by the emperor. Instead of putting an end to the actions of Romans, the emperor began instinctively to persecute Christians, believing that they did not abide by the law. Countless people and many fathers of the Church and bishops died. In 134 CE the rage of the emperor expanded to include Jews and, in addition, he concluded with the destruction of Jerusalem all the way to its foundations, to rebuild it afterwards and naming it Aelia Capitolina.[21] He also destroyed the remains of Solomon's Temple, and built at its site a temple dedicated to Zeus. Close to the cave of Bethlehem, he built a temple dedicated to Adonis. The gate to the burial tomb of Jesus and Golgotha was buried under sand and, at this spot, he built a temple to the goddesses Aphrodite and Ishtar. The persecution subsided only upon Hadrian's death and upon the take over of power by the emperor Antoninus Pius[22] in the year 138.

The fifth [wave] of persecutions [years 162–177]

This wave of persecution began in the reign of Marcus Aurelius.[23] Cataclysms, earthquakes, troubles and hunger, which had plagued the empire in the year

[20] Eusebius of Caesaria, *Church History*, pp. 181–2, describes the author of the letter as 'one of the most outstanding great rulers', referring to him as Serenius Granianus. He also recalls contents of correspondence between himself and Emperor Hadrian.

[21] In the year 130 the Roman emperor Hadrian founded a military colony in Jerusalem, which he named Aelia Capitolina. The author of the diary probably utilised the book named 'Church History' by Eusebius of Caesaria, translated into Assyrian in the fourth century. It was the first translation of this work into a foreign language, based on which the later Armenian version was drawn up. In the work of Eusebius of Caesaria, *Ecclesiastical History*, 4:6 we read that Hadrian had named Jerusalem as Aelia Capitolina. *Church History*, p. 177

[22] Antoninus Pius reigned until the year 161.

162, as well as the acute illness of the emperor were explained by some interpreters with unfavourable attitudes towards Christians as being blameworthy and a response of the gods to sins committed by Christians. Appreciating such an interpretation, the emperor initiated the persecution of Christians in Asia Minor during the year 166. These actions were so violent that the human mind is unable to imagine them and language unable to describe them: some people were flayed through hitting with cord, some were told to walk barefoot on hot iron. These persecutions caused the martyrdom of Polycarp, a beloved student of John the Evangelist, together with five other bishops. In Lyons, in the land of Gauls, Vettius,[24] the first bishop of the city, was killed, as well as all the clergy and the faithful. The ashes remaining after the burning of their bodies were thrown into the Rhine.[25]

The sixth [wave] of persecutions [years 202–211]

This wave spread during the reign of Emperor Septimius,[26] even though it seemed that in the first years of his reign he sympathised with Christians, employing many of them as officials in the imperial court. However when, in the year 202, he noticed that the Christians were better organised, their numbers continued to grow and that they were taking over more and more important positions across the country, he felt threatened. The first step that he took was to forbid conversion to Judaism [21] or to Christianity. A convert faced the possibility of the death penalty.

The emperor announced the obligation of Christians to honour pagan idols and to eat the meat offered to the gods. There was no mercy for those who declined participation in these events. The persecution was particularly harsh in Alexandria. Many people were tortured to death, many churches were razed and the scholar Athenogenes[27] and the bold soldier Basilides[28]

[23] He ruled in the years 161–180.

[24] Error in the manuscript. The first bishop of Lyons, dying as martyr in the year 177 CE, was St Pothinus.

[25] Error of the author. The river flowing through Lyons (Lat. Lugdunum) is the Rhône.

[26] Septimius Severus, emperor during the period 193–211.

[27] The case concerns most probably an apologist from Athens, who wrote to Marcus Aurelius and his son Commodus a letter defending Christianity, in approximately 177 CE. However no information about his martyrdom is available. Simon, M., *Cywilizacja wczesnego chrześcijaństwa*, pp. 142, 397.

together with Leonidas, father to church father Origen,[29] were all burned alive. The persecutions covered all of Asia, Africa and Phrygia.[30] Until the death of the tyrant in 277 Christians of Rome conducted their masses after dark and assembled in catacombs, caves, grottoes, cemeteries and private houses.[31]

The seventh [wave] of persecution [year 235]

The murder of the young Emperor Alexander[32] by the violent Maximinus[33] caused much dismay among Christians. Alexander was a man of peace, full of kindness and tolerance, and most of all he liked Christians and favoured them. Hence, following his murder, Maximinus commenced persecuting Christians. He began with the extermination of those church hierarchy members and representatives of the educated elite who had good relations with the murdered emperor. However, not long afterwards, his anger

28 Eusebius of Caesaria, *Ecclesiastical History*, 5:1–7 included the following information about Basilides: 'Basilides, one of the officers of the army, led her to death. But as the people attempted to annoy and insult her with abusive words, he drove back her insulters, showing her much pity and kindness. And perceiving the man's sympathy for her, she exhorted him to be of good courage, for she would supplicate her Lord for him after her departure, and he would soon receive a reward for the kindness he had shown her. Having said this, she nobly sustained the issue, burning pitch being poured little by little, over various parts of her body, from the sole of her feet to the crown of her head. Such was the conflict endured by this famous maiden. Not long after this Basilides, being asked by his fellow-soldiers to swear for a certain reason, declared that it was not lawful for him to swear at all, for he was a Christian, and he confessed this openly. At first they thought that he was jesting, but when he continued to affirm it, he was led to the judge, and, acknowledging his conviction before him, he was imprisoned. But the brethren in God coming to him and inquiring the reason of this sudden and remarkable resolution, he is reported to have said that Potamiæna, for three days after her martyrdom, stood beside him by night and placed a crown on his head and said that she had besought the Lord for him and had obtained what she asked, and that soon she would take him with her. Thereupon the brethren gave him the seal of the Lord; and on the next day, after giving glorious testimony for the Lord, he was beheaded.' Eusebius of Caesarea, *Church History, Life of Constantine the Great, and Oration in Praise of Constantine*, p. 253.

29 Atiya, *Historia Kościołów Wschodnich*, p. 31, writes about Origen (c. 185–254): 'He was a son of Egypt, a Copt of flesh and blood, the most gifted student of Clement of Alexandria (c. 150–215), brought up in at atmosphere of pain following the martyrdom of his father, suffered by him for his Christian faith'. However, he does not provide the name of Origen's father.

30 Phrygia formed the western part of present-day Turkey and belonged to Asia.

31 The indicated date of death of the emperor is not correct.

32 Severus Alexander, emperor during the years 222–35.

33 Maximinus Thrax, emperor during the years 235–8.

extended to all Christians, without exceptions: churches were burned, and possessions confiscated. The most broadly known martyrs of this time include St Pontian,[34] the bishop of Rome, and Hippolytus of Rome[35] [22]. Both were deported to plague-infested Sardinia, and both died there.

The eighth [wave] of persecution [year 250]

The architect of gruesome, mass persecution, conducted using diverse and extraordinary methods of torture, was the tyrant Emperor Trajan Decius,[36] full of hate for Christians. In 250, by his order, some were thrown into cauldrons of boiling asphalt, others were seared to death using red-hot sharp rods, and still others became food for lions and other wild beasts. A large number of the faithful died in prisons. Even though the persecutions lasted only for a short time they had horrendous results. They covered all of Europe, Africa, Ionia and Asia Minor, including Pontus and other areas. Among the excellent fathers of the Church crowned with martyrdom during this time were: St Fabian,[37] bishop of Rome; the elderly St Alexander,[38] bishop of Jerusalem; St Babylas of Antioch,[39] who was full of apostolic energy and engagement and

[34] Pope of Rome in the years 230–5.

[35] Bishop, priest of the Latin Church, outstanding theologian, writer, wrote in Greek.

[36] Trajan Decius, emperor in the years 249–51.

[37] Pope in the years 236–50.

[38] He was first bishop in Cappadocia and, having moved to Jerusalem, he founded a library there, which was used by many ancient writers. See Szymusiak, J. M. and Starowieyski, M., *Słownik*, pp. 21–2.

[39] St Babylas was the thirteenth patriarch of Antioch. He built a cathedral in Antioch, devoted to the Apostles, later referred to as the great cathedral. It was there that John Chrysostom gave his famous sermons. History recorded that Babylas was so attached to the ethics and rules of the faith that he would not let persons living in sin enter the church. An example of this was Philip, the prefect of Antioch, from the city of Bosra in Syria, who, despite being Christian, had multiple wives. When coming to masses by the patriarch, he had to stand with humility outside of the church walls. Philip advanced to become emperor (244–9), however he was murdered for being Christian along with his son by Trajan Decius, by order of whom patriarch Babylas also suffered martyrdom in prison. An extraordinary cult remained around Babylas in Antioch, which spread to the West in the eighth century. Close to Antioch, ruins of a vast four-nave building were discovered, constructed according to a cross ground plan, surrounding a square sanctuary adorned with a mosaic from the year 387 honouring St Babylas. It was already a famous pilgrimage site in the 4th century. Armala, I., *Tāriḇ al-kanīsa as-suriāniyya*, pp. 60–1; Daniélou, J. and Marrou, H. I., *Historia Kościoła*, pp. 240–1; Atiya, A., *Historia Kościołów Wschodnich*, p. 151.

the patriarch of Antioch; the great teacher and spiritual guide Dionisius,[40] patriarch of Alexandria; St Abion,[41] provost of Smyrna; and St Cyril, bishop of Crete. However, the great scholar Origen was arrested and jailed [23]. It is worth remembering that the famed history of the eight brothers of Ephesus stems from this time; they were said to have escaped and hidden in a cave close to the city and were known as the 'people of the cave'. Having found this out, the emperor ordered the entry to the cave to be sealed. God put them to sleep for 180 years. When they awoke, it was during the reign of Theodosius the Younger.[42]

The ninth [wave] of persecutions [year 257]

The Emperor Valerian[43] also mounted persecutions, encouraged by his advisor Martianus, who made the emperor issue the following two rigorous ordinances:

1. Ban of assemblies of Christians at cemeteries or in catacombs for the purpose of prayer, and enforcement of the duty to make offerings to pagan idols by Christian clerics. Failure to adhere to this led to banishment.

2. Confiscation of mobile and immobile property belonging to Christians, particularly those employed at the emperor's palace and holding official positions, and execution of these along with their relevant priests.

Other Christians were free to choose the idols that they wished for

[40] Dionysius, also referred to as the Great, before he became patriarch of Alexandria (246–64), led the famous local school. He probably suffered martyrdom. During the persecutions mounted by Decius, he hid in the desert (251), and in times of Valerian, he was exiled to Libya (258), from which he returned in the year 262. See Szymusiak, J. M. and Starowieyski, M., *Słownik*, p. 121. In the year 253, Cornelius, bishop of Rome, died while in exile in Centumcellae.

[41] This is most probably St Pionius.

[42] This is a reference to the famous legend of the seven sleepers of Ephesus, which found its way into the Qur'an and forms a part of Surah 18, 9–26, referred to as 'The Cave'. The first version of the legend was written down in Syriac, from which it was translated into Greek (Ighnāṭiyyos Zakkā I ʻĪwāṣ, *Qiṣṣat ahl al-kahf fī al-maṣādir as-suriāniyya*, in *Rā'iḥat al-Masīḥ aḏ-ḏakiyya*, pp. 11–33; Santucci, L. and Klimaszewski, S., *Legendy chrześcijańskie*, pp. 131–5. This legend, having Christian and Muslim roots, was the topic of a diploma thesis (1997) written by Bartłomiej Grysa, who until October 2010 was lecturer in the Department of Arabic Studies at the Adam Mickiewicz University of Poznań, Poland.

[43] Emperor in the years 253–60.

themselves. It was assumed that, if they were left without their clergy and care-givers, ridden of their churches and assets, they would live in chaos and, accordingly, that they would return to organised paganism by themselves.

St Cyprian, bishop of Carthage, was banished in this wave of persecutions.[44] Many other members of the clergy, church assistants and lay people, including bishops, were given sentences of hard labour [24]. In order to distinguish them and prevent them from escaping, their foreheads were marked by burning embers and one side of their heads was shaved.

Valerian was not fully happy [with his violent deeds]. Towards the end of his reign many wars with Persians broke out. Defeated by King Shapur I,[45] he was imprisoned and died in prison in 262, suffering terribly: he was immured in one of the Persian temples after his skin was cut open and smeared with red dye.

However, the persecution of Christians continued and remained in place with varying intensity until the reign of the three subsequent emperors: Gallienus, Claudius Gothicus and Aurelian.[46] The latter conquered the kingdom of Palmyra, took Queen Zenobia and deported her to Rome, having bound her arms with golden chains.[47]

The tenth [wave] of persecution [years 303–313][48]

Of all that occurred, this wave was the largest and most uncompromising in its wildness and tragedy, and lasted the longest, relatively speaking. It consumed the most victims, using new methods of torture.

[44] Cyprian was arrested in the year 257 and sent to the desert for hard labour. In 258, he returned to Carthage where, in the presence of most of the faithful, he was executed. In the same year Sixtus, bishop of Rome, the deacon Lawrence of Rome and Fructuosus, bishop of Tarragona, also suffered martyrdom.

[45] Shapur I of the Sassanid dynasty, which was founded by his father Ardashir I (220–41). He ruled in the years 241–72. He conquered Nisibis, Dura Europos (its ruins are found in present-day Syria), Carrhae (Kirkuk in Iraq) and Antioch (present-day Turkey).

[46] Gallienus (260–8), Claudius Gothicus (268–70) and Aurelian (270–5).

[47] This took place in the year 272. Zenobia was the protector of Paul of Samosata, condemned by the Fathers of the Church.

[48] Father Lisiecki, the translator of *Ecclesiastical History* by Eusebius of Caesaria into Polish, wrongly calls this period the ultimate time of persecution against Christians (1924: XI). Such a statement only pertains to Christians living within the Roman Empire. Christians in fact also resided outside of the Imperium Romanum and they were the subject of no less cruel persecution, this time by Persians, of which the author of the diary writes on subsequent pages.

In 303 CE the terrible and violent Emperor Galerius[49] encouraged Emperor Diocletian[50] to adopt four ordinances substantiating the destruction of Christian churches and homes, the take over of their property and their killing [25] if they did not return to paganism. Following the proclamation of these ordinances, the state administration officials notified the government that the Christians would rather die for their faith than return to paganism. In light of such a reaction the emperor, as well as the court rulers and advisors, legalised the murder of Christians: the murders began, churches began to be destroyed, property was taken over and sacred books and Christian literature were burned. However these actions did not break the Christians; with chants and joy in their hearts they went to their deaths, collectively and bravely. Only a few, of weak faith, broke under fear of capital punishment, thus sentencing themselves to death.

The persecution intensified from day to day, and the instigators became more violent, using new methods of killing. Among their practices were: crucifying the resisting head down in Mesopotamia; burning men alive in Syria; inserting red hot nails under fingernails and pouring boiling lead into the wounds in Pontus; tearing away pieces of skin from the body and inserting pieces of porcelain into the flesh until bones broke in Egypt. Every inhabitant of Phrygia was burned, together with the entire city, as not one pagan was found among them;[51] in other countries, the left leg of a Christian was cut off and a dye was poured into the right eye.

These [persecutions] lasted until the year 306,[52] when Diocletian died, to be replaced in the East by the twenty-year-old Maximinus Daia.[53] He continued the persecution [of Christians] until the year 313, when the governance was taken over by Constantine the Great, who believed in Christ[54] and ele-

[49] Galerius, emperor in the years 305–11.

[50] Diocletian, emperor in the years 285–305.

[51] Eusebius of Caesaria mentions this: *Church History*, pp. 331–2.

[52] Diocletian abdicated in the year 305.

[53] Maximinus II Daia, emperor in the years 311–13.

[54] Among some Christians of the Near East the opinion prevails that Constantine got to know Christianity directly from his mother, Helena, who was supposed to be an Assyrian from Edessa. However, the Assyrian chronicler Bar Hebraeus stresses that Helena only accepted Christianity following the victory of Constantine over Rome. There is a minor mention of the origins of Helena in Daniélou, J. and Marrou, H. I., *Historia Kościoła*, p. 202.

vated the prestige of the Church [26]. Furthermore, he proclaimed the Edict of Milan, in which he ensured the freedom to practice the Christian faith, and declared himself to be a defender of the faith and the faithful, wherever they would reside. He also began to spread Christianity and to strengthen it by building churches, distinguishing the virtuous, releasing church officials from taxation and assigning to them regular wages as a source of sustenance. He also introduced Christians to the staff of his palace and ordered Sunday to be an official day of rest. Out of respect for the cross, he forbade the use of crucifixion, even with respect to the greatest of criminals. Having strengthened his rule, both in the East as well as in the West, he ordered the demolition of pagan temples and chapels for idols and built churches in their places. In this way, Christianity began to flourish.

Persecution Initiated by Emperor Julian [the Apostate], who Ruled in Rome in the Years 361–3

Julian was a stubborn yongster, a Christian who returned to paganism. [Ever since he took on his ruling post], he assumed a stark anti-Christian policy, ordering the dismissal of Christians from the official posts they held, the closure of their schools, the pursuit of hidden clerics and the withholding of their wages. On the other hand, he instigated a programme aimed at increasing the prestige of paganism, adorning the temples and monuments to the gods. These undertakings were executed at the expense of Christians and their property [27]; pagan sites were equipped with items confiscated from Christian places of worship, which led to the emptying of churches and the desecration of graves of saints. By his order, bishops, priests and monks were murdered, along with countless masses of the faithful. The martyrs of this period include Basil, bishop of Ancyra,[55] and the ascetic Domitian.[56] The emperor was so arrogant and vengeful that he decided to rebuild the Temple of Jerusalem solely to create doubt as to the prophecy of our Lord, which said

[55] Of the three religious figures named Basil known in the times of Emperor Julian, Basil the Great (d. 373), bishop Basil of Ancyra (d. 364) and presbyter Basil of Ancyra, only the latter 'was subject to various tortures, whereby he heroically proved his faith'. Sozomen, H., *Historia Kościoła*, pp. 316–17.

[56] In the periods of persecution discussed by the author, many nameless Christians were martyred. The available sources lack information about any Domitian the Ascetic as a martyr.

'. . . they shall not leave in thee one stone upon another . . .'[57] Large sums of money were donated to the reconstruction and a great number of workers and craftsmen were employed. His project was accepted and approved by the Jews. They began to excavate the foundations and erect pillars.

However, after the foundations were ready, a strong earthquake struck: the foundations shattered, the equipment was destroyed and everything was covered in sand; some of the workers died under the rubble. When the decision was finally made to resume work, the soil suddenly tore apart, spewing fireballs and a hot avalanche outside, turning everything into rubble and ash and showering the workers with a deadly storm of stones that had been prepared for the construction work. The people were stunned by this and many Jews turned to believing [in Christ]. In this way, finally, the construction of the Temple was abandoned.

At this time the deceitful Julian was preparing to wage a preventive war against Persians. Hearing about this, St Basil travelled to him in the company of bishops, to admonish him [for his policy with respect to Christians up to that point]. Seeing Basil approaching him, the emperor initiated a mostly tactless discussion:

> 'What do you want?'
>
> 'We want to be governed by a lawful emperor', replied Basil [28].
>
> 'And where did you leave your carpenter?'[58] asked the emperor mockingly.
>
> 'I left him there, where he is preparing a coffin for you!'
>
> This angered Julian, so he turned to the gathered crowd:
>
> 'Arrest him. After I return, I shall show him what torment he will endure until he dies!'
>
> Hearing this, Basil spoke:
>
> 'If you return from the war, I say that the Holy Spirit does not speak through me!'
>
> The prophecy fulfilled. The emperor died in battle hit by an arrow. When dying, he took a handful of soil, soaked it in the blood flowing from the wound and tossed it high up, crying in despair:

[57] Matthew 24:2, Mark 13:2; Luke 19:44.

[58] This is a reference to Christ.

'Nazarene! You have defeated me! Now be king on earth and in heaven!'[59]

In this way, God saved his Church from the plans of the tyrant. In times of the emperors to come, Christians lived in relative peace, and themselves began to persecute pagans, and turn their temples into churches [29].

Forty Years of Persecution (339–79) during the Reign of Shapur II[60] [and After the Emergence of Islam][61]

The scene of this persecution was almost the entire territory of the contemporary Persian Empire, in particular Babylon, Bet Huzaie,[62] Bet Garmaye,[63]

[59] When writing about the death of the emperor, Socrates of Constantinople (1986: 310–12) does not mention such bitterness. However, Sozomen, H., *Historia Kościoła*, p. 356, quotes curious judgments as to the circumstances of this death: 'When the emperor was to depart to commence war against Persians, casting threats that following the war, the churches shall feel his wrath, he at the same time began to mock that nothing shall be able to help the "sons of the carpenter", and so, the cleric replied using these prophetic words: "This carpenter's son is preparing a wooden coffin for your death!". The wounded emperor was said to be in despair about the sun aiding the Persians – or simply not saving him from death, even though, based on some form of astronomical knowledge, it precisely governed the day of his birth – and gesturing with his hand towards the blood, he ejected it out towards the sky.' The recollection of Sozomen allows one to conclude that the spiritual figure was not Basil, but Athanasius of Alexandria. Both Basil as well as Athanasius gained the nicknames 'the Great'; they count among the Fathers and Doctors of the Church. Both were of equal age with Emperor Julian the Apostate; the first died in 379, the second in 373. However, Mikhōyēl Rābō forcibly concludes: 'On one day, Julian came to Antioch. His company, Bianus, a philosopher, asked a Christian wise man: "Where is the son of your carpenter?" The steadfast man replied: "He is preparing a coffin for your king!"'

[60] Shapur II was the Persian Shah (310–79).

[61] The sentence in square brackets is an amendment of the title by the editor of the Polish text. The author also describes this period of time.

[62] Khuzestan (Arabistan, formerly Elam) is a region in southwestern Iran on the Iraqi border, where six Assyrian bishops resided in succession until the eighth century. The largest centre in this region, being at the same time the seat of the Patriarch of the Church of the East, was the city of Bēṯ Lapat (Gundeshapur). The famous Assyrian medical doctor family Bakhtisho, which for three centuries provided services to the Arab caliphs in Baghdad, hailed from this city. Presently, the region is inhabited mostly by an Arabic-speaking community, some activists among which have for years now been revolting against the government of Iran and forming their own structures for the purpose of achieving autonomy.

[63] Bēṯ Garmai is a historical region around the city of Kirkuk in northern Iraq. In the seventh century the region contained six Assyrian bishoprics. The names of the individual bishop

Adiabene[64] and Assyria. An indirect reason for these [persecutions] was the enmity Shapur felt towards Romans. Insofar as numerous groups of Christians lived in the Persian Empire as well, Shapur treated them as enemies and spies for the Romans, and decided to seek revenge upon them because they practiced the same religion.[65] His first move was to double the taxes burdening Christians and to bind the blessed Simon[66] to collect them. Once Simon declined to follow the request, he was sentenced to death along with two assistant bishops.[67] Following this, Shapur issued an order to all satraps and

seats are given by Scher, A., *Tārīkh Kaldo wa Āṯūr*, p. 13. The largest city was Carrhae, today Kirkuk.

64 Adiabene, as the largest Assyrian province, was an ancient kingdom in Assyria. The capital city of the province was the locality of Arbela (modern-day Irbil, Iraq), where Alexander the Great was victorious against Darius in 331 BCE. Until the twelfth century a total of nineteen Assyrian bishops resided here, including in the localities of Bu Nuhadra (recently changed by Kurds to Dohuk) and Zakho. The names of the remaining bishop seats in this province are given by Scher, A., *Tārīkh Kaldo wa Āṯūr*, pp. 12–13. During the reign of Shapur, one satrapy of the Persian Empire, Assyria, with the capital Nineveh, was distinguished. Its satrap was one Sanharib (Sinharib) halfway through the fourth century, whose son Benham and daughter Sarah, along with forty members of his court, took on Christianity and became martyrs on 10 December 352. Assyrian churches honour their memory with a special liturgy. Abūnā, A., *Shuhadā' al-mashriq*, pp. 181–98.

65 A fitting conclusion of the author. Sadly, despite the passage of so many centuries, certain radical groups, Islamic this time, still groundlessly berate the indigenous Christians of the Near East and those living in other Muslim countries to the West, treating them as a so-called fifth pillar. In times of disagreement or conflict between these countries and the West, local Christians become at times the object of fanatic revenge. In reaction to the printing of caricatures of Mohammad by a Danish paper (February 2005), Muslim protesters in many countries set churches on fire, chanted anti-Christian slogans and, in Mosul, they decapitated an Assyrian priest.

66 Simon, or Shem'on bar Sabba'e, occupied the rank of *maphrian* (*catholicos*), known only to the Syrian Orthodox Church. Takahashi, H., 'Maphrian', *in The Oxford Dictionary of Late Antiquity*, p. 957. This post can be compared to a cardinal in the Roman church.

67 Beheaded on 14 April 341, in the Ahwaz region, together with 103 other Christians. Abūnā, A., *Shuhadā' al-mashriq*, pp. 105–37 describes this event in general terms. In response to the order of Shapur, the bishop was supposed to have written: 'The Christians are not bound by this circumstance to pay double the taxes, and I am no tax collector. If you are looking for a pretext to persecute me, then I am readily available: inflict pain on me, flay me, slay me, kill me. Through the love for my people, I do not fear death; for I hold my position for them, and I am bound to care for their well-being and their salvation. If I am required to follow Christ, who offered himself for his lambs, I shall be glorious. My people are also ready to select eternal life through the death of Christ, in the place of earthly life.' Naṣrī, B., *Ḏakhīrat al-aḏhān fi tawārīkh al-mashāriqa wa-l-maghāriba as-Syriān*, p. 71. The same Naṣrī writes

leaders to persecute all Christians and to raze their churches and monasteries; the clergy of Mazdaism, Judaism and Zoroastrianism, filled with rage, also participated in this work.

The persecution was absolute and covered all of Persia.[68] In effect, more than 310,000 people died.[69] Most were killed on Mesopotamian soil: in Babylon, Assyria, Bet Garmaye and elsewhere.[70] Chronicles have recorded the names of many of them [30].

The persecutions ceased only after the establishment of peace between Persians and Romans. A pivotal role in these arrangements was played by St Mārūṯā[71] of Martyropolis, the bishop of Maypherkat,[72] who later became a martyr. His highly delicate diplomacy led to peace between the two powers. One could say that Assyrian Christians fell prey to a conflict between two powers, on the territory of which they lived and with which they had nothing in common. Despite the fact that the church administration of Persia could only be rebuilt during the reign of Yazdegerd I (399–420), the per-

that the bishop, together with five other bishops and a hundred faithful were murdered in 339 on the first Friday following the celebration of the resurrection of Christ, celebrated in Eastern Churches as the day of the faithful.

68 For more on on the persecutions during the reign of Shapur II, see Stewart, J., *Nestorian Missionary Enterprise*, pp. 17–35.

69 Sozomen, H., *Historia Kościoła*, pp. 97–101, and pp. 103–8, gives the number of 16,000 martyrs and describes in particular the martyrdom of *katolikos* Simeon in detail. Syriac sources indicate 160,000 murdered in the southern provinces of Mesopotamia and 130,000 in the northern provinces. al-Qaṣṣāb, Y., 'Al-Iḍṭihād al-arba'īnī wa naṣāra Ḥidyāb: 339-379', *Qāla Suryāya*, p. 131. Muslim sources, in turn, speak of 200,000 murdered. Abūnā, A., *Tārīkh al-kanīsa as-suriāniyya ash-sharqiyya*, pp. 35–9. The violent Persian persecution contributed to large groups of Assyrian Christians emigrating in the fourth century to Malabar in India, with many others looking for safety in Arabia.

70 The author indicates the names of two further lands: Dayro Sumoqo ('The red monastery') as well as Marga/Marge. The former could not be identified, the latter may refer to the city of Maragha (or Maragheh) and its region (formerly Azerbaijan, presently northwestern Iran).

71 St Mārūṯā was a graduate of the Edessian school founded after the take over of the city of Nisibis by Persians in 363.

72 Maypherkat gained its Greek name, Martyropolis, after St Mārūṯā transferred the remains of a great number of martyrs from Persia there. Turkish maps name the city as Silvan, and it is found between two tributaries of the River Tigris, approximately 100 kilometres to the east of Diyarbakır. Close to the city of Diyarbakır used to be a village with the same or a similarly sounding name. The author writes about it on subsequent pages.

secution lasted with varying intensity until the 635 CE, when the Persian Empire collapsed under the attacks of Arab Muslims, who conquered all of Mesopotamia.

{The Christians were not destined to enjoy peace during the times of Islam either. Their desolation and their disappointments were great, even more so as they had helped the Arabs conquer these lands. They were hoping the new rulers would turn out to be more tolerant than the previous ones}. The Arab army, led by caliph ʻUmar ibn al-Khattāb,[73] after the conquest of such cities as Balis,[74] Callinicus,[75] Rish ʻAyna,[76] Gamlin,[77] Kfar Tutha,[78] Dara,[79] Mardin[80] and Tella,[81] forced most of the Christian inhabitants of

[73] ʻUmar ibn al-Khattāb, the second caliph (634–44), was called by Assyrians *fōrūqō, pārūqā* (Arab. Al-Farooq), meaning 'liberator', as they wanted to see in him a liberator of Christians from Persian and Byzantine rule.

[74] Balis is a small town between Aleppo and Ar-Raqqa in Syria, bearing today the name Maskanah (Ancient Greek name: Barbalissus).

[75] Callinicus became known as Ar-Raqqa in southwestern Syria by the Euphrates, before the point where the River Khabur enters the Euphrates, approximately 100 kilometres from the border with Iraq.

[76] Rish ʻAyna (Resaina), Greek Theodosiopolis, is today often called Ra's al-ʻAyn, in the north of Syria on the Khabur river close to the Turkish border; it is the city of Sergius of Rishaina (d. 536), famous physician and philosopher, one of the first translators of Greek works into Syriac. Pigulewska, N., *Kultura syryjska we wczesnym średniowieczu,* pp. 169–90.

[77] The available sources lack indications of such a locality or any locality with a similar name.

[78] Kfar Tutha is the Turkish name of the locality of Kefr Tuth. It is located twenty-five kilometres to the southwest of Mardin.

[79] Dara (Turkish presently Oğuz, Greek: Anastasiopolis) is located approximately twenty-five kilometres to the northwest of the city of Nisibis. Until the mid-eleventh century it was the seat of a bishop, abandoned following the emigration of the remainder of the Assyrian population to Europe. When travelling through this locality en route from Nisibis to Mardin in the summer of 1838, Father Horatio Southgate, author of the *Narrative of a Tour through Armenia, Kurdistan, Persia and Mesopotamia, with an Introduction and Occasional Observations upon the Condition of Mohammedianism and Christianity in those Countries,* remarked that it was inhabited by approximately 100 Muslim and 30 Armenian families (p. 274).

[80] Mardin is a city located approximately eighty kilometres to the southeast of Diyarbakır.

[81] Tella (Turkish: Viranşehir) is the famous Greek city of Goranopolis, about ten kilometres to the east of Edessa, and is also known in Christian literature as Tellu. It is the birthplace of one of the most important figures in Syriac Orthodox Church history, St Jacob Baradeus, in 500 CE, and from here also hailed St John (d. 538), an author of many treatises and letters. Following the massacres of 1895 the city of approximately 7,000 inhabitants was left with just 600 Armenians and 480 Assyrians.

these localities to convert to Islam. In 642 CE, Muslims attacked the locality of Karkaisa, killed all the Christian inhabitants of the city and turned their churches into mosques. The same happened with the cities of Resaina, Kefr Tuth and Mardin; Arsis, the leader of the latter, managed to hide in Harran in time.[82] Almost all of the elite of these cities converted to Islam only to be able to remain the managers of their land [31].

In 692 CE the Muslim emir of occupied Mesopotamia, Muhammad bin Marwan,[83] called on Mawid, the leader of Christian Arabs from the Banu Taghlib tribe, to convert to Islam.[84] When the request was declined, he was thrown into a pit and covered with waste until he died. The same inhuman fate awaited Shmalo, the chieftain of a great tribe of Arab Christians. His decisive role gave rise to the will to execute revenge applying the most barbaric of methods: a piece of his thigh was cut away, which the victim was required to eat after it was fried. This trauma remained with him until the end of his life as a symbol of a specific kind of inter-religious dialogue.[85]

Such policies of Muslims against Christians resulted in the fact that Arab tribes, such as Banu Akil, Banu Tayy, Banu Tanukh, Banu Taghlib

[82] Harran was a famous Bible-era city conquered by a Muslim army in the year 814.

[83] Muhammad bin Marwas was a brother to the Umayyad Caliph, ʻAbd al-Malik ibn Marwān (685–705), and father to the final caliph from this dynasty, Marwān II (744–50).

[84] Christianity was also the religion of many of the Arabs. On the eve of the Muslim conquests, most Arabs living on the territories of present-day Syria and Iraq followed Christianity.

[85] Michael the Syrian writes about both these events. Rābō, M., *Tārīkh*, p. 376. Based on the chronicle of Bar Hebraeus, the chronicle of Pseudo-Dionysus recalls a transcribed fragment of a talk between this Shmalo and caliph Al-Walid. Witakowski, W., *The Syriac Chronicle of Pseudo-Dionysius of Tel-Maḥrē. A Study in the History of Historiography*, p. 41, footnotes 12 and 13. The advice of the caliph was as follows: 'If you are the leader, then you ought not to serve the cross. Fulfil my request and take on Islam.' The opinion prevails that the Banu Taghlib tribe was forcibly converted to Islam in 870. However, the chronological list of the one hundred bishops consecrated by patriarch Dionosiyyos I Telmahroyo (d. 845) covers the names of ten bishops for Arabian churches, including five for Banu Taghlib. Here are the chronological numbers of these bishops: 10. John of the St Zaccheus monastery for Arabia; 12. John of the St Ananias (Zaʻfarān) monastery for the city of Tedmurta (Palmyra in Syria); 35. John of the Karkafta monastery for Banu Taghlib; 44. Thomas from the Bikrom monastery for Banu Taghlib; 53. Abraham of the Tel ʻAda monastery for Arabia; 57. George of Wadi Adam for Bahrain; 59. Joseph (no monastery name given) for Banu Taghlib; 75. Habib of the Knushya monastery for Banu Taghlib; 87. Sabra of the Atu monastery for Arabia; 98. George (no monastery name given) for Banu Taghlib. We should add that the list features forty-four monastery names., M., *Chronique*, pp. 414–18.

and others, that hitherto practiced Christianity, had no choice but to convert to Islam. The greatest intensity of persecutions by Muslims in Upper Mesopotamia occurred in 833 CE, when dauntless and systematic extermination of Assyrians continued in cities such as Dara, Nisibis, Amida, Mardin and Rish 'Ayna. After the murder of the elite of the clergy, teachers, craftsmen and tradesmen, the Muslims turned to plundering churches, monasteries, houses and stores – anything that was valuable. Following this, they burnt most villages subordinate to these cities, raped the women, murdered the youth, and finally turned Christian temples and religious sites into mosques. In light of such violence, Christianity, which reigned and developed in this part of Mesopotamia, began to fade away and decline.

The year 1155 saw a repetition of the previous tragedies. The Assyrian Christian community, reborn in part in Amida and Mardin, experienced further suffering. {The Church of St John in Amida was converted into a mosque, named the Al-Waliyy mosque[86]}, similarly, the great church of the Forty Martyrs of Mardin became a mosque, which was named the Mosque of the Martyr. In 1170, Muslims took over the church of St Thomas; both Bar Hebraeus and the [Edessan] chronicler of Urhoy[87] wrote about this.

The Christians left alive had limited options to cultivate not only their faith and lay culture, but their participation in trade, handicrafts and industry also decreased markedly.

In 1453 Constantinople fell under the fire of Turks led by Mohammed, named Al-Fatih [32]. Sadly, Muslim Turks also proved to be uncompromising towards Christians, many of whom left their land. In 1650 the invaders

[86] The author translates *waliyy* as 'man of God'. It is most probable that Rev. Southgate, *Narrative of a Tour*, p. 298, writes about this mosque as follows: 'The principal mosque of Diarbekir was formerly a Christian church. It is called the Great Mosque and is the finest remnant of antiquity in the place. It has a large square tower which is now used as a minaret. The roof is sloping, and the windows are round at the top. It presents altogether a very singular appearance, being rather European than Oriental in its style. On one side is a spacious court paved with stone and having a large fountain in the middle. Along the lofty walls of this court are rows of columns of various kinds of beautiful marble, and on the four sides of the court are separate places of assembling for the four orders of the Sunnis. On the exterior wall of the church are inscriptions in Cufic, or the old character of the Arabs.'

[87] In the two chronicles available in Arabic by Bar Hebraeus (no date and 1986), however, confirmation of this account is missing. The work of the unknown Edessan chronicler is sadly not available.

initiated, with indescribable fury, persecution aimed against Assyrians that brought with it tens of thousands of victims. Also at this time Islam was forcibly imposed on the inhabitants of villages and small cities in a historically Assyrian region, of which I shall name the city of Shauro[88] and villages around Ahmadi,[89] Astal,[90] Reshmel[91] and Kabala,[92] inhabited by Mḥalmōyē groups: the Rashdiyye,[93] Mghashniyye,[94] Tuk,[95] and Mnizal.[96] Historians estimate that the number of Islamised Assyrians amounted to almost 600,000 in one year alone. Only the inhabitants of the village of Qilleṯ[97] were able to defend themselves effectively and, accordingly, continue practicing the Christian faith.

Summarising, one needs to say that Christianity was treated inhumanely from its cradle. There is probably no other place where such long-time followers of Christ died in such numbers as here. The prophetic statement of Christ found its confirmation in their fates: 'Then shall they deliver you up to be afflicted and shall kill you: and ye shall be hated of all nations for my name's sake . . .'[98] [33].

[88] This is an ancient locality in the region of Mhalmayto (southwestern part of Ṭūr 'Abdīn).

[89] On the maps of Ṭūr 'Abdīn one can see that the locality named Ahmedi is located approximately thirty-two kilometres to the north of Mardin, above the town of Savur.

[90] Astal is city located not far from Midyat, also known as Astil, Estel and Estil.

[91] Reshmel is a locality to the east of Mardin.

[92] Kabala is a locality located to the northwest of Mardin by the road to Midyat, now Kabale.

[93] Rashdiyye (Raşidi) is (or was) a locality northeast of Mardin.

[94] Mghashniyye is a locality northeast of Mardin, now Muhaşni.

[95] Tuk is a locality northeast of Mardin.

[96] The name 'Mnizal' cannot be found on the map. In Semitic languages there exists a problem in terms of the written forms of given names – words that are not vocalised may be transcribed in various ways. An additional difficulty stems from the constant changes of locality of names in the Near East countries and the unstable existence of the populace, who often move from one locality to another. The abandoned locality usually turns to ruin and, with the passage of time, simply gets forgotten. The name Shauro found in the manuscript can be found in the work of Ighnāṭiyyos as Sura. Based on available sources, however, one cannot determine and distinguish geographic from ethnic names, not to mention the determination of the area or the dynastic and tribal differentiation of the Mḥalmōyē people.

[97] A village northeast of Mardin on the main road to Savur.

[98] Matthew 24:9.

4

PERSECUTION IN THE MOST RECENT TIMES – THE END OF THE NINETEENTH CENTURY

Disquiet Experienced by the Inhabitants of the City of Amida[1] and the Surrounding Assyrian Villages in 1895

I have, through complete accident, found a small notebook in the library of Father Paul, son of Father Abed Ḥāḍ b-Shābō from the family of Father Laḥdō.[2] The contents of the notebook are stories written down by Father Abed Ḥāḍ b-Shābō serving the village of Qarabash. He was one of the lucky to survive the massacres of 1895, aimed at Christians living in provinces and cities such as Amida, Edessa, Kartfort,[3] Sibaberk, Melitene,[4] Sasoun[5] and the surrounding villages.

[1] On subsequent pages, the author also writes about the massacres of Christians that took place in this city in 1915.

[2] In Orthodox Churches, priests are able to get married before they are ordained, but, in case of the death of one's wife, they are not able to wed again. Married members of the clergy cannot rise past the rank of provost. Iyawannis of Midyat, who became bishop of Ṭūr 'Abdīn, was married before; higher order clergy were selected from monks.

[3] The name Kartfort, written as it is found in the manuscript, cannot be found on the region's map. It is most probably a name of the city of Harput.

[4] A city located to the northeast of Edessa, once a large and important Christian centre, now called Malatya.

In the notebook we read that at the beginning of 1895, in Amida, the forces of evil and hate gathered in the persons holding the highest administrative, religious and tribal posts. They were headed by the bloodthirsty Djemal Pasha and Bahram Pasha and similar tyrants who set the machine of terror against Christians in motion. Before these noblemen commenced their genocidal acts, they notified the Kurdish Aghas, sending them letters full of agitation and promises.

They encouraged them to participate in the planned murders of Christians, guaranteeing them that they will be able to kill, burn and rob with impunity. The letters to the Kurds also stated that their leaders are supposed to report to Amida to obtain weapons.

During the Friday prayers in the mosques of Amida, the Muslim religious and lay leaders, together with the general populace, assumed the cry to action of 'Muhammad Ṣalawāt'.[6] The exclamation of this phrase was to mark the moment of commencement of pacification of Christians, of plunder and of burning of their homes and stores, churches and monasteries. {The beginning of the action was marked to be Friday, 1 November 1895}[7] [34].

[5] A historic region to the south of the city of Muş, located approximately 80 kilometres to the northwest from the city of Bitlis and approximately 170 kilometres to the northeast of Diyarbakır. Towards the end of the nineteenth century, Muş had one of the largest Christian communities. The number of Armenians alone was close the 25,000.

[6] On the role of the mosque as a place where Friday prayer and preaching, called *khutbah*, is done, see Paolucci, G. and Eid, C., *Islam – sto pytań*, pp. 107–13. 'Muhammad Ṣalawāt' may be translated as 'the prayers of Muhammad' – referring to the prophet of Islam. Its use, in the version 'Salavat Muhammad', is confirmed by Gustave Meyrier, contemporary French vice-consul of Diyarbakır. De Courtois, S., *The Forgotten Genocide*, p. 104. A British consulate, with Hallward serving as vice-consul, was also based in Diyarbakır. Both the above phrases (most probably used locally), as well as the phrase 'Allah Akbar' ('Allah is great'), commonly repeated since Islam began, accompany some military actions by Muslims irrespective of their form and goal, as well as individual executions conducted in cases by decapitation using a sword or *khanjali* (dagger), for instance in recent years in Afghanistan, Iraq, Saudi Arabia, Nigeria, Syria and elsewhere.

[7] This information, as well as the course of the massacre, is confirmed by a report of the above-mentioned French vice-consul in Diyarbakır. Ternon, Y., *Ormianie. Historia zapomnianego ludobójstwa*, pp. 104–5: 'Over the course of three days, five thousand Christians were killed in the city; 95 Muslims also lost their lives, with 70 of them cutting each others' throats during the distribution of the spoils.' In English, this book was published as *The Armenians: History of a Genocide*, pp. 54–108 and pp. 265–6. Telegrams of the French diplomat published by de Courtois leave no trace of doubt that the extermination of Armenians

And so, it happened!

The ranks of the armed Kurds raged. With outstretched swords and with animal-like fury they undertook an attack on Christian districts. The charging Kurds were aided by artillery firing burning balls. Men fell like leaves from trees: bodies of the dead and the wounded littered the streets and corners of the city as well as stores and courtyards of houses. Those that were able to escape hid in churches. The governor[8] of Amida ordered the houses of the ambassador of France to be surrounded by a circle of twenty soldiers.

The barbarians continued to murder Christians, plunder their houses and stores and to burn their property, until Monday morning, 4 November – people were thrown off roofs and from the windows of their houses, with the lifeless falling bodies being shot at; victims lying on the pavement and in the streets were murdered with swords. {Some of the victims were Muslims – those that lived in Christian districts and counted among the wealthier citizens.[9] The governor was not fond of this.}

The governor, together with Bishop Abdeh d-Aloho[10] and the soldiers, attempted to calm the situation down. However, they were not successful. He [the governor] then sent for patriarch Abed Mshiho II,[11] whose seat was in Mardin.

The patriarch, when he arrived, could not believe his eyes.[12] The

and Assyrians was planned ahead of time, substantiated by the fact that the second wave of massacres was initiated in many localities – as we saw – on the same day of 1 November 1895.

8 The person holding this post is referred to in Turkish as the *wālī*. The power of the *wālī* was absolute, and the area he governed was, in Ottoman Turkey, a *vilayet* (district, province). The *wālī* of the province of Diyarbakır in 1895 was Aniz Pasha and counted among Muslim extremists. The Turkish-style administrative division system can still be seen in some Arab countries that were once part of the Ottoman Empire, particularly in North Africa.

9 The fact of more affluent Muslims living in Christian districts (not only in this city) is an interesting sociological phenomenon. The phenomenon may be falsely and groundlessly used to assign some class character to events or for the purpose of political speculation, such as to justify the position of the current Turkish governments that do not acknowledge the genocide and that wish not to hear of it.

10 Bishop Abdeh d-Aloho (1896–1915) originated from the city of Sadad in Syria.

11 Patriarch Ighnāṭiyyos Abed Mshiho II (1895–1905) originated from the village of Qalʿat Mara, which shall be spoken of later. His horseback journey from Mardin to Diyarbakır took one and a half days.

12 Barṣōm, A., in *Makṯbōnūṯō*, p. 316, writes that the patriarch travelled to Diyarbakır on 20

wonderful city was in ruins, along with the churches; bodies lay everywhere in the streets, with cries of the wounded and orphaned heard from all around, mixed with the noise of shots being fired. Seeing the scale of the tragedy, [the patriarch] immediately wrote to the governor. An Assyrian boy was to convey the letter. When the boy turned into a street bearing the name of Al-Malik Ahmad, he was surprised by Muslims, who killed him on the spot. The letter found beside the murdered boy was given by the killers to the governor. Having read the letter, he sent off a division of the army to protect the Assyrian church, where more than 8,000 people from the town and surrounding villages took shelter.[13] Subsequently, the patriarch, together with the representatives of the Assyrian town elite that survived, went on foot to the governor. Their march was long. When they neared the offices of the governor, they noticed a crowd of many thousands of angry Kurds, swords dripping with blood in their hands [35]. Their leaders were in the office of the governor in a conference. In the corridor, walking towards the office, the patriarch heard their loud conversations. These pertained to plans of further extermination of Christians. When [the delegation] crossed the threshold, all Kurds present during the gathering left the place, not even greeting the patriarch. The governor welcomed the guest most kindly and said: 'You should issue an order for the Christians to hand over their weapons.' The patriarch replied: 'I do not believe the Christians had any weapons, but I shall fulfill your request.' When the patriarch returned to the church, the governor asked two officers, Nasif and Bakr, to accompany the patriarch together with a detachment of soldiers, to search the homes of Christians in the city.

October 1895. This proves that preparations for the exterminations of Christians began before 1 November. 'On October 22nd, 1895, the local Muslims stormed the bazaar to buy weapons', Ternon, Y., *Ormianie*, p. 104.

13 There were many churches in the city. The case concerns most probably the church of the Holy Mother of God (alternatively referred to as the Church of the Virgin Mary) called the Mariam Ana in Turkish. It has quite a spacious court, and is surrounded by strong structures that once formed a fixed part of the temple. It is one of the very few surviving churches of this city. There are seven other ancient churches, which are closed, however; some were transformed into mosques, others serve as stores or warehouses. The crypts of the Mariam Ana Church hide the remains of two great men of the Orthodox church: Ya'qūb of Serugh (d. 521) and Dionosiyyos Bar-Salibi (d. 1171). According to calculations for the Diyarbakır province, as a result of the massacres of the Christians in 1895, a total of 105 Christian temples became mosques, see Kucharczyk, G., *Pierwszy holocaust XX wieku*, p. 45.

No weapons were found!

On the way back, these soldiers, together with the Kurds, attacked the houses of the richer Christians, destroying all cabinets and storage spots, shelves, cupboards and boxes, taking anything and everything that was of any value. The march of the thieves lasted three days.

Having found this out, the patriarch returned to the governor with a petition: 'Under the premise of searching for weapons that are not there, your men, including the army, along with the Kurds, plunder the Christians' homes, murder calm people with impunity, and take all of their valued possessions. I demand in the strongest terms the suspension of these acts and the punishment of the guilty.'

{Hearing this, the governor replied: 'I issued an order absolutely forbidding any harassment of Christians and harming them in any way!'

'Perhaps you did so, however, only after the execution of the horrible deeds, for the purpose of which you have created your squadron of death,' the patriarch concluded, observing the attitude of the governor, and then left in great regret and made his way to the church of the Virgin Mary}.[14]

Let us return, however, to the people of Mardin. Many of these, in the face of their doom, fled for Amida and sheltered there in hotels and churches. The patriarch took them all in as guests until the end of the tragic events. The terrible days lasted until 18 December 1895, when the sultan in Istanbul[15] issued the following order: 'We have made certain that the Christians are loyal to the state',[16] which meant that the massacres had

[14] The text in the curly brackets was placed at the bottom of the manuscript, in an opposite direction, from the bottom to the top.

[15] At that time the sultan was Abdul Hamid II (1876–1909). In 1891 he formed an irregular mounted military force referred to as the *Hamidiyye*. It was formed almost exclusively of Kurds and was based on the Kurdish clan system; it counted at least 50,000 soldiers, who were characterised by particular brutality. Mainly these forces executed the massacres of Christians, with or without an order from of the Ottoman government. Travis, H. 'Native Christians Massacred: The Ottoman Genocide of the Assyrians during World War I', *Genocide Studies and Prevention*, pp. 327–71, compares the tasks of these formations to activities loyal to the government of Khartoum of the Arabian *janjaweed*, which for several years have been executing a similar genocidal scenario against the indigenous inhabitants in the Darfur region of western Sudan.

[16] The contents of this letter prove unequivocally that the massacres that were organised were instigated by the sultan himself.

ceased and that those that remained could heal their wounds and live in relative safety[17] [36].

The village of Sa'diyye

Saʿdiyye is located approximately ten kilometres to the southeast of Amida and is inhabited by Assyrians and Armenians, totalling about 300 people. On Friday, 1 November 1895, Kurds attacked the village by surprise and began murdering men and children, taking the women and girls and plundering the houses. [Realising the attack] the Christians hid in the church and closed the gates. However the Kurds and the military accompanying them climbed onto the roof of the church, drilled a hole in it and threw hay inside, poured in crude oil and set it alight. The people were suffocated by the smoke and tried to run out through the gate that they managed to open. However Kurds were waiting at the gate and slaughtered those that escaped. Only three people were saved; they fled to Amida and told the story about what happened.

The village of Qatrabel[18]

This is a village inhabited just by Christians, counting approximately 1,000 people, including Assyrians and Armenians. It lies on the eastern shore of the Tigris, opposite Amida. It was the first village to be attacked by Kurds from the land side (the east), murdering and plundering. Christians hid in the Assyrian church of St Thomas; Father Abd al-Ahad hid with them – he served both the inhabitants of this village as well as those from the village of Qarabash. The priest encouraged those under siege to persevere, attempted to lift their spirits and quoted the words of Christ, afterwards blessing everyone and issuing Holy Communion. When those under siege found out that the Kurds were ready to burn the church down and them along with it, they decided to walk out. However, the attackers locked the gates to the church,

[17] To the massacres of Armenians and Assyrians in Diyarbakır and the surrounding villages, Father Hanno [Yūḥānōn d-Bēṯ Kofar] of ʿAyn Wardo devoted a poem composed of 436 lines. Some poems concerning the genocide period were collected, written in calligraphy and published by Bishop Çiçek.

[18] De Courtois, S., *The Forgotten Genocide*, p. 43, indicates that the village was almost side by side with Diyarbakır from the eastern side, by the bank of the Tigris. The last Assyrians left it in 1928. It was the birthplace of famous poet, Yaʿqūb of Qatrabel (d. 1784).

where [37] many people still remained, climbed the roof, [drilled out a hole], and set [the parisioners] on fire using burning hay. The those that managed to flee the church barricaded themselves along the walls surrounding the village, from where they defended themselves by throwing rocks at the Kurds.

[During the defence] Father Abd al-Ahad sent an Assyrian boy named Simon to Amida. The boy managed to swim across the river, reach the city and notify patriarch Abed Mshiho. He intervened at once and forced the governor to send out the military to return the surviving Christians to Amida. Most were seriously wounded. Father Abd al-Ahad was with them. Here, the patriarch cared for them at all times, and after the situation calmed down, made them return to their village.

The village of Qarabash[19]

Qarabash is a large and populous village once inhabited by more than 1,000 people. It is located approximately ten kilometres to the east of Amida. Most of its inhabitants are Assyrians, with a few Armenian families also in residence. On Friday, 1 November [1895], Kurds attacked it. Over the course of two days, they murdered, burned and pillaged. A large part of the population managed to hide in a tall tower where they had bred pigeons.[20] The birdhouse was located on the eastern side of the village. However, the Kurds entered the tower and commenced murdering those that were inside, destroying the tower completely. The rubble buried those inside. Those who managed to escape [38] were killed by the Kurds that marauded at the door. Nobody from the tower managed to survive.

Only a handful of the inhabitants were able to flee the village. Some of them got through to Amida, others left for the houses of their Muslim friends living in villages close by. Father Abd al-Ahad, including members of his family, hid in the village of Kozan, however his brother, Kaume, who was an altar boy, died, and the daughter of the priest, Hana, a married woman, seeing the attacking Kurds, took her son Zakharias and fled. She was noticed,

[19] In De Courtois, *The Forgotten Genocide*, p. 43, the name is given as Kuabash. Let us remind the reader that this is the village from which the author of the diary originated; hence the regional name Qarabashi – one who is from Qarabash.

[20] The inhabitants of this village were famous throughout the region for their breeding of pigeons. They sold pigeons and pigeon manure in Diyarbakır, earning notable profit.

however, by one of the Kurds who impaled a spear in her back and pierced the belly of her infant child.

After a short while, when the wave of barbarism subsided, some of the surviving inhabitants returned to their village. The damaged houses were reconstructed and life began anew.

The tower, in which and under its rubble so many inhabitants of Qarabash died, was named the 'Tower of Martyrs'. On holidays and on Sunday evenings the faithful and the priests meet there to pray for the souls of the innocent that perished.

Maypherqat

Maypherqat is a city from which the blessed Mārūṯā[21] comes, inhabited by almost 1,000 Assyrians and Armenians [39]. On Friday [1 November 1895] Kurds stormed the village, murdering, plundering and kidnapping the girls. The sole place to hide was the church. However, the Kurds climbed the roof, drilled a hole, poured crude oil inside, and lit it.[22] Of all the city's inhabitants, only twelve men and three women survived.

This is an example of ruthless actions. Having stormed one of the houses, the attackers found a young and beautiful woman inside. Present in the house was also her husband and their infant child. When the aggressors attempted to rape the woman with her husband watching, he took a staff and began defending her, pushing them away. However, they overpowered him and tied him up, thereafter they cut off his hands and feet with an axe and killed him. They did the same with the wife, but they did not kill her. She was not able to feed her infant, however. A good man passing by took her to Amida. She did not live long.[23]

21 St Mārūṯā came from a city bearing the same name, located elsewhere.

22 This was a standard approach; they proceeded exactly as they did in the three previous villages.

23 A work on the genocide (mainly with respect to Ṭūr 'Abdīn) published recently in Sweden, constituting a collection of relations recorded, written down and published in Surayt, the Ṭūr 'Abdīn dialect and the Latin alphabet by Jan Beṯ-Şawoce, *Sayfo b Ṭurcabdin* (Södertälje: Beṯ-Froso Nsibin, 2006), includes the following statement (story no. 19, pp. 250–1): 'The Chaldean bishop Timothy used to come to Midyat from Diyarbakır often. The house, where he stayed at, usually saw many people gather to listen to him. Once he said that during the journey to us a Kurd met him who wanted to talk with him very much. They sat down by the

The village of Alibar

This village is located to the west of Amida, about a half hour's walk away. It is inhabited by [Orthodox] Assyrians, Chaldeans [Uniate] and Armenians. The Muslims that governed the village betrayed their compatriots. They told them: We will take you to Amida [40] and save you from the other tribes from the neighbouring villages. When the inhabitants were walking along the road, the accompanying Muslims began murdering them one after another, and having murdered all of them, they returned to the village and divided among themselves the belongings [of those executed].

Sibaberk (Swirg)[24]

The Christians of Sibaberk were betrayed by Hajji[25] Osman Pasha and his brother, who called and gathered Kurds from nearby villages and incited them

road and the Kurd started talking about Seyfo in this way: "I served in the military at Farkin (i. e. Maypherkat). We shipped another group of Christians, together with their priest, outside the city to shoot them there. When we were nearing the spot of execution, with the bodies lying there not visible yet, the priest felt the stench of blood. He stopped and begged us to agree to a short prayer that he wanted to say with the accompanying crowd. He stood up, began singing something, and everyone that was with him, knelt. After a while he bent over, took a handful of dust, lifted his hand upwards, looked at the sky and spoke as if he was in discussion with someone. The kneeling opened their mouths, and he distributed a little bit of dust to each and everyone's lips. We did not know what was going on. After a while the priest and the accompanying party shouted with one voice: 'We are ready!' We led them to the place where the dead bodies were, and we shot them all. You are dressed different than that priest, but tell me, what did that dust mean?"' An explanation is necessary here. If the ill-fated priest was dressed differently then he was not of the Chaldean Church. After some eastern Assyrians joined the Roman Church, and began to be referred to as 'Chaldeans' from then on, their priests dressed similarly to the clergy of the Roman Church.

24 Beṯ-Şawoce, J., *Sayfo b Ṭurcabdin*, pp. 248–9, records the following about the fate of the inhabitants of this village: 'The Kurds took bishop Danho, who came from the village of Anhel, together with two priests, and subjected them to torture. First they pulled out their teeth and cut the tongues away, and then they killed them with swords, cut up the bodies and abandoned them along roads'. Harris, H. B., in *Letters from the Scenes of the Recent Massacres in Armenia*, pp. 96–102, writes in turn in the sixteenth letter: 'We have reached Severek at 18.00 (on June 1, 1896), and we turned directly to a small damaged protestant church, where we spent the night in one of the classes of the former school. The city suffered a lot; hundreds of widows hunger, they have no clothes and they live in the street. The young priest, Abraham Haratunyan, a graduate of the American Missionary College, described to us the barbaric scenes of the extermination of Christians, including Armenian

to leave no trace of these Christians. The massacre, carried out with swords and spears, continued for two days. Out of more than four thousand inhabitants only four families survived. A similar fate was shared by the Christian inhabitants of most villages in the region of Amida. Here are their names:
{– on the east side: 'Aynshah, Telhas, Ghirnak, Satia, Safna, Kozan[26]};
{– on the west side: Karte, Karakilisa, Kankrat[27]};
{– on the north side: Kadi, Patrakiyye};
{– on the south side: Ka'biyye,[28] Charukiyye, Chan-Aqpenar, Arzu-Oghli, Hulan}.

and Assyrian clergy, who were given the choice: death or Islam. We were suddenly visited by an Assyrian metropolite, an Armenian priest and an Armenian doctor. The doctor informed us with sadness that he is not able to do anything for the wounded and sick, because the Kurds destroyed his surgery together with the equipment and took all medicine. All the walls of the room were covered with a thick layer of dried blood, and behind us hung pieces of brain. It was here that the executions of the more important Christians were carried out, by shots to the head'.

25 *Hajji*, an honorific title stemming from the Arabic word *hajj* (pilgrimage), is given to persons who have completed their pilgrimage to Mecca. It is also used as a greeting for elderly people.

26 The author lists here the village of Sa'diyye as well, which was described earlier.

27 The author also lists the name of the village of Alibar, the fate of the inhabitants of which he described earlier.

28 Harris, H. B., *Letters from the Scenes*, letter XXI, p. 125, provides the following information about this village – its name being recorded as 'Kahby': 'I should say that after crossing the Tigris we passed through a desolated village, by name Kahby. Somehow, I did not at the first moment understand what the silence and desolation meant. We had forgotten, in the pleasure of nearing our journey's end, that we were surrounded by the marks of the havoc of last winter, and when we passed one large building after another (for these houses are built like granaries or fortifications, very high and solid, and quite different from those of the southern plains) with no sign of life, and all more or less dilapidated, it seemed at first as if we had fallen upon some recently excavated city of the past, and then, in a moment of course, the real state of the case rushed into the mind. Of the one hundred houses belonging to this village, the Consular Report gives eighty as having been burned! As we were leaving it, a poor Christian woman suddenly appeared from behind a building where, no doubt, she had hidden on our approach, and seeing a lady among the party, rushed up to me and took my extended hand with gesticulations more eloquent than words. It was sad to leave her with only the small expression of sympathy I was able to give by a warm hand-clasp, but delay was not possible at the time. I wonder what her tale would have been could we have stayed to listen!' Noteworthy is the fact that in the subsequent letter (p. 130), the name of the village is changed to be 'Khayad', however, the indicated village Qatrabel is found as 'Kitabel' (p. 130). The authors quoted above describe it as a city, a large proportion of the inhabitants of which were murdered.

Apart from this, one must not forget the other districts: Bsheriyye,[29] Lije,[30] Garzan,[31] Kartbart,[32] Adiyaman,[33] Ḥisn Mansur[34] and others. In Mardin, in turn, even if persecution did take place, there was no massacre. However, the exterminations caused great desolation in villages belonging to Mardin, such as Qsur,[35] Bnabil,[36] Ḥesnō d-Attō,[37] Mansuriyye[38]

[29] Turkish maps show for this village the name of Bişeriyye, but some textbooks give the form Besiri. It is situated in a region of fertile land on the northwestern side of Ṭūr ʿAbdīn, stretching from the city of Siʿirt in the west to Batman in the east, with an area of over 150 square kilometres. For historical precision, the following story needs to be recollected: the leader of the province, Sabit-Bey es-Sueydi, together with Nesimi Bey, the head of the province of Lice, were, in 1915, recalled from their offices by the governor of Diyarbakır and subsequently beheaded for refusing to take part in the massacres. The same fate was shared by the head of the town of Midyat.

[30] Lije is also known as Lice, northeast of Diyarbakır.

[31] A locality on the northwestern borders of Bsheriyye. Dāwūd Gharzānī, librarian and social activist from this city is well known in the Syrian city of Qamishli; together with his brother, he runs an art bookbinder's shop. Also known as Hazzo (Gharzan).

[32] Kartbart is probably Kharput.

[33] Adiyaman is located to the north of ancient Samosata, west of the Euphrates river, 200 kilometres to the northeast of Aleppo. 'Under the pretence of road works, all men from Adiyaman and the neighbouring villages were led out and aligned along the road, and then slain with knives. Of the 935 deported, 455 survived and made it to Aleppo' (Ternon, Y., *Ormianie*, pp. 239, 241). A few years ago it was possible to obtain the consent of the local government to use once again a building belonging to one of the ancient churches close to the city, where a monk (now bishop) by the name of Malke was delegated from the Zaʿfarān monastery. This once large Christian community was reduced to just several Assyrian families. Their members have begun learning their national language anew.

[34] Hisn Mansur is an older name for a locality near Adiyaman.

[35] Qsur is probably a locality ten kilometres south of Mardin (nowadays Göllü). Before 1895 the village numbered about 1,000 Assyrians (120 Uniate, 800 Orthodox Christians and 80 Protestants), referred to in Arabic as *qsoraniyye*. Three churches and a school were in operation.

[36] Bnabil (Bnēbīl, Bnāy-Īl, Turkish Bülbül) is a village twelve kilometres to the east of Mardin. In the 16th century it was inhabited by 600 Assyrian families. When, in August 2003, the village was visited by a group of employees and students of the universities of Poznań, the sparse Assyrian populace of the village was busy installing quite a large bell on the church tower. The elderly priest serving the village (who died in 2007) said that it was a joyous day for the little parish.

[37] This town is known in Turkish as Eskikale.

[38] This is a locality, known in Turkish as Yalim, to the north of Mardin. In the 16th century, 357 Assyrian families were recorded as living in the village (about 2,400 people), but 1895 saw a decline to about 1,000 people in total (500 Orthodox, 80 Uniate, 100 Protestants and

and others. Those who fled found shelter in the Zaʿfarān monastery [41].

[On the massacres of the Christian people in some other localities in 1895 see Annex 1].

320 Muslims). It is worth mentioning that many former inhabitants of this village currently residing in Syria bear the name Mansurati.

5

THE YEAR 1914 – THE BEGINNING OF WORLD WAR I

World War I broke out in August 1914. Sentiments of rebellion and unrest felt in many countries, as well as unhealthy competition, contributed to this event; the powerful kingdoms in particular eyed one another with enmity. One threatened another and wanted to dominate in terms of military prowess and diplomatic prestige. The rulers were full of mutual disgust and ambitions of expansion, not only regionally but also spanning broader geographic areas; they were also driven by the will to dominate the world.

The signs of the atmosphere of rivalry included large expenditures of financial resources and gold to strengthen military arsenals and firepower. Investments began in the military industry and in the manufacture of warships, which raised fear in some and reinforced the conviction in those making the investments that any fight or battle shall bring decisive victories, crushing their opponents and bringing in rich spoils of war.

In order to make the assumed goals come true and to be able to cover all the wartime expenses, each country tried on its own to incite enmity towards others in the hearts of their countrymen, to increase their profits and turn on the machine collecting taxes on persons and property, on the harvest and on goods, in order to be able to stand up to anyone that in the way of this insatiable appetite. God only knows what promises and what obligations [42] and what disclosed or undisclosed plans, threats and ultimatums grew in the minds of the kings and presidents, and what kind of turmoil and confusion they brought forth at local level, due to the leaders' sly tricks and the sowing of hostilities by various religious and tribal leaders. As a result, this caused the weakening of ties between the people of the same countries, endangering internal security.

Back then the Ottoman Empire wanted to be party in the conflict but it did not have enough arms. The officers that received the order to collect resources at all costs resorted to the most inhumane of methods. Under threat of death, they forced the people living on the territory of the empire to pay abysmally high taxes for the state. In executing such a policy, they resorted to plunder and takeovers of property, threatening the citizens and terrorising the poorest. Even the humblest, not having enough bread to support themselves, were at times arrested, jailed, tortured to death or banished. [These officers] were devoid of conscience and human feelings. Nothing could stop them from using the drastic and extreme acts of lawlessness that they implemented, indeed exactly the opposite occurred – they received awards, promotions and higher state positions for their acts. None of them was taken to court for these violations of human dignity, and they will most likely receive punishment in the world to come [43].

The First Spark

Among the first sparks that caused the outbreak of the war were the circumstances of the murder of the archduke of the kingdom of Austria and his wife. It so happened that a soldier from Serbia perpetrated this on 28 June 1914.[1] Hearing this news, the Austrians filled with anger and lusted for revenge, and decided that the blood of their archduke could not go to waste. They demanded from the Serbs an inquiry and the punishment of the killer.

[1] The author speaks here of Franz Ferdinand, heir to the throne of Austria-Hungary, who was murdered in Sarajevo on 28 June. The shameful servitude of Franz Ferdinand towards Turkey is proven by the following report: 'Yesterday [27 March 1896] however, was extra grand, because Prince Ferdinand was to be received by the Sultan [of Turkey in Istanbul], and all the world attended; and a gentleman told me afterwards the Sultan was treated as if he were a god!'. Harris, R. and Harris, H., *Letters from the Scenes*, pp. 3–4.

However the Serbs took it lightly. Due to such negligent treatment Austria felt ignored and on 28 July 1914 declared war on Serbia. Seeing the situation worsening, Pope Leo X sent a party of emissaries to the Austrian emperor with a letter of warning for the latter to forgo the war and not to tarnish his old age with blood.[2]

When news about the situation reached Russia, this country mobilised its armies and sent them to the borders of Austria and Germany. This move was met by the Germans with outrage [44]. Germany, not friendly towards Russia, Great Britain or France, awaited an opportunity of confrontation, for which they had been preparing themselves for a while. They were almost certain that any possible war would result in their victory, providing them with control over other countries and permitting them to retake the territories of Alsace and Lorraine, the population of which was German but falling under French control.[3] However, Russia signed a treaty with France and, overtaking Germany, was the first to declare war, on 4 August [of 1914].[4] Following this, a coalition was joined by England [Great Britain], as well as Japan, encouraged by the latter, together with Serbia and Montenegro. Turkey and Bulgaria sided with Germany; Italy as well, in the beginning keeping to itself, engaged on the German side, hoping to solve many of its internal problems.

In this way, these two blocs stood one against another, the fiery rockets thundered, sharpened swords shone, deadly guns roared, people fell as if they were leaves from trees, the earth turned red from the spilt blood, one could hear demolished buildings moaning, and hospitals filled with wounded in

[2] This is somewhat imprecise: Leo X was the Pope of Rome between 1513–21. However, during the time of World War I, the popes were Pius X (1903–14) and Benedict XV (1914–22) – the former called the nations of Europe to instigate and to pray for peace. 'I would gladly give my life if I could redeem peace in Europe through such an act'; the latter sent, in January 1917, a handwritten letter to Kaiser Wilhelm II, on which the emperor remarked: 'The Pope and President Wilson of the United States, are two people equally separated from reality'. Fischer-Wollpert R., *Leksykon papieży*, pp. 143 and 186–8. Pope Benedict XV also wrote a letter dated 10 September 1915 to the Ottoman Sultan Mehmed V on the genocide. In the letter the pope condemns the Armenian Genocide and urges the Sultan to put an end to suffering of the Armenians. For the content of the letter see: <http://www.imprescriptible.fr/citations/institutions#Benedictus%20XV> (last accessed 21 September 2018).

[3] Error of the author. Alsace and Lorraine became parts of Germany following the Franco-Prussian war of 1870.

[4] On this day, German forces invaded neutral Belgium.

unimaginable numbers [45]. The world was appalled by the scale of the tragedy, helplessness and fear; flourishing cities sank into chaos. Were it not for divine providence that saved a minute portion of humanity, destruction would emerge along the proportions of Sodom and Gomorrah.

Turkey and World War I

It is known that Turkey stood by Germany, responded to its orders and made its will a reality. It is no mystery that the Emperor of Germany, Wilhelm [II], on many occasions announced very clearly: 'May the three hundred million Muslims of the world know that the Emperor of Germany always was, and shall ever remain, their loyal friend'.[5] His message was an attempt at gaining friendship and support of Muslims and the awakening of anti-British sentiment, particularly among those who were subjects of [Great] Britain.[6] He also wanted for these countries to rise against the English, an action that would cause turmoil and disquiet, and for them to liberate themselves from the English regime. Turkey supported this policy, as it sided with the Germans both now and previously. Hence, Turkey began to organise its forces, prepare military equipment to aid the Germans [46] and to prevent enemy armies from infiltrating its territory. Germany, in turn, began to supply Turkey with all sorts of weapons, to support it financially and to send military leaders to train Turkish soldiers and to lead the Turkish army. Germany also sent its naval forces to ensure the effectiveness of warships. It furthermore provided financial help: the largest loan amounted to thirty million dinars in gold. In order to show off his friendship towards and loyalty to Turks, Emperor

[5] These words were uttered by the Emperor of Germany, Wilhelm II, in 1898, during an official visit to Damascus, see Kucharczyk, G., *Pierwszy holocaust*, p. 57. Damascus was at that time within the boundaries of the Ottoman Empire. Philip Hitti also mentions it, adding that the emperor, together with his wife, laid a wreath on the grave of Saladin. *Tārīkh Sūriyyā wa Lubnān wa Filasṭīn*, p. 348. Certain Muslim commentators were appalled by the fact that during his pilgrimage to Syria (4–9 May 2001), Pope John Paul II did not lay flowers on the grave of Saladin. The Grave of Saladin is located by the Umayyad Mosque (once the site of a cathedral dedicated to St John the Baptist), where the pope met with the Muslim leaders of Syria.

[6] Egypt was under control of Great Britain in the years 1880–1923 and after World War I Britain administered and occupied Iraq (1920–32), Jordan (1920–45) and Palestine (1918–47).

Wilhelm constructed in Berlin a grand mosque with a beautiful minaret, twenty-three metres tall, laying the cornerstone of the building himself in a colourful and broadly publicised ceremony.[7]

A month before the outbreak of the war, Germany and Austria clearly indicated that they felt sympathy towards Turks and that they would develop trade and cultural exchanges with this country, as well as strengthen industrial relations to make the country a wealthy land.

Turkey let itself be misled by these promises, withdrew from all privileges it hitherto had extended in relations with [Great] Britain and France and, in line with the will of its allies, toughened its policy and began to distribute propaganda against these latter countries [47]. Muslim clerics also joined in. Their preaching in mosques spoke almost exclusively of war. Preachers also emerged, in city squares and army barracks, where they prepared people for the inevitable war. The Turks already saw themselves victorious within one or two days over [Great] Britain and France, side by side with Germany and Austria. Turkey did not consider that many people in their prime would fall in this war and that its great expanses, stolen from other nations, would be divided up to be lost forever.

Enver Pasha[8] – the Cause of the Demise

It is known that all the misfortune of Turkey was the result of the attitude of Enver Pasha, who treated his country as if it were a toy. He was son-in-law to the sultan and a puppet in the hands of Germany, acting as their servant, having made their wishes come true and having executed their plans. He was a tool in the hands of the German ambassador, who played with

[7] One of the aspects of the multifaceted and broad cooperation of Germans with Turkey was the publication in Berlin of an Arabic-language weekly (until 1923 the Turks used Arabic script) under the title *Al-Jihad*. Its title page was adorned by quotations from the Qur'ān, including the so-called surah of the sword. A copy of the first issue, dated 5 March 1915, received by the editor and translators thanks to German historian Gabriela Yonan from Berlin, is included as Annex 3. Gabriele Yonan is the author of many articles and books about contemporary Assyrians, including *Ein vergessener Holocaust: Die Vernichtung der christlichen Assyrer in der Türkei*. Some of her work has been translated into English, Turkish and Swedish.

[8] Other forms of this name are: Ismail Enver Pasha and İsmail Enver Paşa. He was the minister of war.

him just as children play with a ball [48]. One could say that he bears the blame for Turkey's failure. He was richly rewarded by both sides, Turkey and Germany.[9] His fortune in 1916 amounted to the interesting sum of forty million dinars in gold! An unbelievable amount.[10] And that is why he could promote anyone he wanted and recall anyone he wanted!

Enver Pasha was aware that he would lose the war. His army was badly trained and could not cope with handling the new equipment received from Germany. He also knew that his military arsenal was old and of little effectiveness and that the wealth of the country was but a semblance, based on the loans provided by Germans. Enver did lose and fled the country in shame.[11]

Let us remember that Emperor Wilhelm announced earlier that as long as he is alive, he was a guardian and supporter to Muslims, wherever they might be living. He expressed this through the loans that he provided to Turkey. Muslims of the entire world, not just Turkey but also India, Persia and other countries, believed that this knight was a defender of their interests and an advocate of their faith.[12] They all let themselves be cheated. Wilhelm's

[9] The author may mean to say, rewarded both by Germans as well as by Turks.

[10] De Courtois, S., *The Forgotten Genocide*, p. 104 indicates that one gold Ottoman dinar was, back then, valued at twenty-two gold French francs.

[11] Pursued by Bolshevik forces, he died on the border with Afghanistan on 4 August 1922.

[12] The complete faith of Muslims with regards to the attitude of Germans is proven by reports, such as one written down in the diaries of Palestinian intellectual Khalil as-Sakakini (1878––1953). He writes: 'As a result of the jihad announced by Ottomans and by Germans, Palestinian Muslims began to look upon their Christian neighbours with an evil eye. A German medical doctor residing in Jaffa declared that he will kill 50 Christians with his own hand, and he walked from door to door inciting Muslim citizens to do the same. I have seen Germans invigliating the Muslim cleric circles, encouraging them to mobilise the entire society for the jihad. The Ottomans managed to spread the rumour that Germans have converted to Islam and that together with them they shall conquer many lands, which they shall divide between themselves. The most curious of all, however, was that Muslims were filled with the conviction that emperor Wilhelm took on the name Mohammed and that he will soon depart for a pilgrimage to Mecca.' Furthermore, the author quotes the contents of a song verse sang by choirs of Muslim peasants coming to Jerusalem to join the army: 'Wilhelm, o uncle of ours, we shall avenge ourselves with your sword!' Other rumours concerned alleged mass rapes perpetrated by Christians against Muslim women in the Balkans, together with cutting away their breasts and puncturing stomachs with sharp objects or throwing children up to puncture their bodies with spears or swords while they are in the air. Ottoman and German agents also thought up the so-called 'standard of the prophet', which was walked across city streets not only in Palestine but also across

engagement on the side of Turkey was tactical, and he did not stand with them, thinking only of the Turks.

However, puzzling and unbelievable is the fact that the kingdom of Austria is in fact entirely [sic] Christian, and so, how could it – as Christian – [49] agree to the extermination and destruction of Christians in the territory of Turkey? They were fully aware of what was going on and knew that innocent Christians were being mass murdered. This applies to Germany as well. How could they have slept soundly in light of the destruction of defenceless people? Not only did they not do anything to stop the genocide of Christians but with their attitude they inspired Turks to spill the blood of nations adhering to the same religion as they did. We have the right to ask, how Sandros,[13] the German ambassador in Constantinople, could have not protested against the plans of the genocide of Christians? It's unimaginable! It was well known that the Turks consulted on all of their efforts of extermination, both big and small, with the Germans, and that they only executed them following consent from the Germans. So, how could the Germans and

all Ottoman territory so as to incite the Muslim determination towards the jihad. On 20 November 1914, the standard reached Jerusalem. Even before sunrise, all Muslims of the city came out to greet it. A cleric from Mecca walked in front of the standard, followed by Ottoman and German cavalry in military formation. The people touched the standard with awe, kissed it and shouted 'Allahu Akbar!' – 'God is great!' When the great mass of people made its way to the Al-Aqsa mosque, the Jews gathered on both sides of the road also greeted the standard. The standard remained at the mosque until Saturday, 9 January 1915, when officers led it out and continued with it to the south. al-'Īsa, U., How the Emperor of Germany Became Muslims' Uncle?, elaph.com (2007), <www.elaph.com/ElaphWeb/ElaphLiterature/2007/1/207741.htm>.

13 All available sources, of which the majority pertain in fact to the mass murder of Armenians, provide a different name of the German ambassador in Istanbul: Hans Freiherr von Wangenheim. He died in Constantinople in the night between 23 and 24 November 1915, most probably of a heart attack. A description of the circumstances of his death and his state funeral in the capital of the Ottoman Empire was provided by the contemporary ambassador of the United States in Istanbul, Henry Morgenthau, who served between 1913 and 1916 (*The Murder of a Nation*).The duties of the German ambassador were temporarily taken over by Konstantin von Neurath, and beginning on 1 December 1916 Paul Graf Wolff Metternich zur Gracht became the new ambassador. David Marshall Lang writes: 'The execution of the Armenian genocide plan commenced with the silent consent of Liman von Sanders, the German inspector general of the Ottoman armed forces and baron Hans von Wangenheim, the German ambassador in Istanbul.' *Armenia. Kolebka cywilizacji*, p. 261.

the Austrians allow themselves to take responsibility for the fate of a nation brutally murdered across all of Turkish territory?

[Examples of] Turkish Brutality

It is known that even war has its ethics and that certain laws and regulations of universal character apply, which no country may ever transgress. A state that does not heed to such rules is subject to punishment. One such rule states [50] that wars are played out between regular armies and that no harm may be done to the elderly, women and children.

The first act of law describing the rules of war was passed in the United States of America in 1863.[14] It reflects the care for sites of worship and shelter as well as the humanitarian treatment of works of culture. In 1899 in turn The Hague saw a broad forum take place, in which representatives of twenty-two countries, among them Turkey, participated.[15] This meeting agreed on a set of laws in force in time of war. We read there that, for instance, only the regular armed forces are in enemy relations with each other and that it is forbidden to treat civilians as enemies or to limit their freedom. It is also forbidden to destroy territory that an army takes over. These laws were signed by all countries participating in the conference.

When, on 13 July 1915, great masses of Christians, civilians only, were led to their deaths, the Germans celebrated a festival organised on the very same day. This happened in Berlin, during a banquet given on occasion of refurbishment of the great mosque constructed by Germans for Muslims. One of the guests was Mukhtar Pasha, the ambassador [51] of Turkey [in Germany]. In speeches on this occasion, the speakers praised the Germans and wished prosperity for the country. One of the great Germans said: 'We shall take over rebellious Belgium. In our hands, it shall serve as a hammer

[14] The legal act entitled *The Geneva Convention for the Amelioration of the Condition of the Wounded and Sick in Armed Forces in the Field* was passed in Geneva, Switzerland in 1864. The Russians exhibited the greatest activity during editing and passing of this legal act, see Kocot, K. W. and Wolfke, K., *Wybór dokumentów do nauki prawa międzynarodowego*, p. 325.

[15] Sources indicate that twenty-six states participated in this conference, with the final act being composed of three conventions and three declarations. The title of the second convention is *Convention with Respect to the Laws and Customs of War on Land.* Ibid., p. 281.

with which we shall smash the head of [Great] Britain.' Another said: 'We can leave to our enemies' eyes solely to cry with.' And still another said: 'We cannot let small countries live differently than their power would allow them to.'[16]

Sorrow to the world and to humanity – German victory shall bring doom to nations!

Here is an example of the falsehood and arrogance of Germans. In order to justify the use of aggression, they used devilish tactics. They sent to the Armenians living in the Dört-Yol[17] valley four spies presenting themselves as English. In secret, these four met with the leaders of the Armenians and convinced them that they arrived to aid them. The Armenians believed them and started lamenting bad treatment by the Turks and blaming them for the hardships and suffering they have experienced. As suggested, the Armenians wrote down their requests and pleas for the English, asking them for aid in solving their problems and pleading for them to come at once in order to liberate them from the Turks. Following this, these spies went to Constantinople and gave these letters to the Turkish authorities. This happened in December 1915. From this moment on, a dramatic turn of events took place: Christians, particularly Armenians, began to be called 'traitors'. In order to shame and punish them, the public opinion was carefully prepared, and the army was mobilised.

Soon after the massacre of Christians in Mesopotamia, the Germans arrived [52]. The Turks accommodated them in empty homes belonging to Christians who were murdered earlier. It is almost certain that the tenants [from Europe] saw on the walls of many of the homes crosses and images that could indicate prior habitation by Christians. However, did the Germans ask themselves to whom did these homes belong, and what happened to their owners? It is doubtful that they would concern themselves with these matters!

[16] The author does not quote the names of the speakers; one may surmise, however, that if they participated in such an important event at all they must have certainly belonged to the German political or intellectual elite.

[17] Dört-Yol, a small city located on the shores of the Mediterranean Sea on the bay of Alexandretta (now called the Gulf of İskenderun, southwestern Turkey), inhabited almost exclusively by Armenians. On the tragic fate of the inhabitants of this locality see Ternon, Y., *Ormianie*, p. 209.

In fact, many of them saw with their own eyes the bodies of the elderly slain and left in skips, and tufts of hair of girls and married [women]. They never asked who these people where, why were they befallen with such misfortune and why did the Muslims treat these girls so mercilessly and brutally? It is truly a thing unheard of!

The Germans have no arguments that would justify their participation in the massacres of Christians. Had the Germans wanted for these people to stay alive, one sign, one word would have sufficed. Sadly, they had only one goal: to win the war at any cost. And let Christianity die and disappear! Christianity can cry from the bottom of its soul, with its strongest voice, without any regret: 'God, break the force of evil and raise the power of good'. May God, whose judgements are unknown to us, let truth always win and triumph, and may the evil of tyranny be buried forever [53]!

Turkey would have not instigated these persecutions without reason; it is just, and justice is one of the foundations of a state. The first cause of the war was the suspicion that Christians have weapons and that in the future they shall use them against the state by providing support to the enemy, meaning the English and the French and their allies. Task forces set up for this purpose called in city streets and squares for every Christian to quickly return their weapons that they had to the state and, under this pretence, Turkish gangs entered houses and took from them anything they wanted. Even if a small kitchen knife was found it was sufficient for the entire adult members of the family to be considered collaborators and the enemy. These forces of habitual criminals and robbers were instructed by authorities to hunt down every man that was aged between twenty and forty-five. The caught were arranged into groups and driven on foot, without any food, to war. The elderly in turn were placed under arrest and in jails. Their wildness with respect to women is difficult to describe; no force and no begging could stop their animal-like drives and actions; young, beautiful girls in particular had no chance. When their relatives attempted to defend them, it equalled execution. Death also awaited those that refused to follow this or another bandit. Nobody is able to estimate how many sisters, wives and mothers were shamed, kidnapped for harems or forced to convert to Islam, and how many of them took their own lives so as not to fall into the hands of these wild beasts [54]!

The Situation in the Cities of Turkey at the Beginning of the War

The moment Turkey was bound to prepare its soldiers for war, the officers and local government representatives were overcome with joy, with an atmosphere of triumph permeating their ranks. Immediately, and without any warning, they commenced their work and started taking people almost directly from the street. They were governed by no rules at all, even those saying that a 'soldier' should usually possess the physical and psychological predispositions required and be of good health. Out of the men captured so haphazardly they wanted to form strong army units. People were overwhelmed by fear; they escaped to churches and monasteries or hid away in their own homes. Officers searched for them, however, found them, punished them and forcibly transferred them to the units being created. Without any training, money or equipment, those unfortunate men were driven on foot to Amida, Bitlis, Van, Kartbart, Erzurum.[18] Many of them died en route because of cold, thirst, lack of food and exhaustion. Some of them escaped, risking their lives, fleeing to the mountains and woods. Those that managed to make it back home, hid away and did not leave their households for months on end. They lived in constant fear and under the threat of yet another 'drafting action'. The nightmare of army service, which equalled death, forced them to bear such risks. Sadness was everywhere and hearts were filled with grief [55]. Many inhabitants of beautiful and well-maintained villages and cities fled where they could, many reaching the Sinjar mountains[19] where they hid, fearing derision, humiliation, shaming by officers and impending death. Woe to anyone who tried to flee the army. Desertion meant death for the entire family, loss of property and take over or burning down of houses.

Probably some voices of protest against the inhuman treatment of soldiers reached the authorities. Under the pretence of improvement of the conditions of army service, the government obliged the followers of all religions,

[18] Erzurum is a city approximately 200 kilometres to the southeast of Trabzon on the Black Sea. The original Arab name was directly translated into Turkish: *arḍ/arz* ('Earth') and *rum* (Byzantine people).

[19] The Sinjar mountains are found in northern Iraq. The hospitality of the inhabitants, the Yezidis, of this area, and their heroic defence of the defectors shall be described in the following pages.

in particular Christians, to support the army institutions through charity and gifts. For some, the amounts were even designated so that it would make the service of a relative easier. On the other hand these amounts often surpassed the financial abilities of the family, even if they sold all the valuable items that they possessed. Sadly, the unjustly taken money only went to the pockets of officers and was used for entirely unrelated purposes. There were instances when those from whom money was demanded and who were not able to provide the entire amount were treated as if they were slaves. They were the object of market trade or thrown into jail, until redeemed by the family or a kind-hearted rich person. The Turkish government's begging drive did not omit even churches and monasteries. Against the will of their keepers, everything that could be sold was taken – liturgical items (some of them with embedded precious gems), crosses of gold and silver and other religious items of value. Only God knows what the fate of these items was, many of great historic value, and whose vaults they enriched? The soldiers still died of hunger in the war, and the exhausted were left in the field for the enemy to take them.

Provisions for the army were transported using donkeys [56] and oxen. Due to bad weather and rains, it often happened that [food] turned bad on the way and was not only unsuitable for consumption but at times even poisonous. However, a hungry soldier will eat anything. One army doctor indicated firmly that, due to food poisoning, more than 6,000 soldiers died every day.[20]

[20] This figure is almost certainly exaggerated, however no reliable data could be found that would be helpful in correcting it.

6

MY DIARY

At the Za'farān Monastery (Mardin)

Since the beginning of the outbreak of the war, I have endeavoured to write down the events important from my point of view, those that I have seen with my own eyes or those that I have heard about from trusted people that have experienced them. Initially, I mused, probably like most of my generation, that the war was going to last only a few months. It turned out, however, that we were naive; our forecasts did not come true, and we were disillusioned enormously. The war lasted for four years. Its course, in all of its tragedy, was accompanied by murders of civilians executed without any limit, the plunder of churches, the pillage of property, hunger, the expropriation of children, plagues and orphanhood. It was as grave in its result as if it had lasted a century. Does the history of mankind know a similar example? I don't believe it does yet.

On Monday evening of 3 August 1914 the rumour was disseminated that Austria and Germany had waged war against Russia, England and France [57]. On the same day, the order of full mobilisation of the army was issued in Turkey. The streets and homes filled with disbelief and hopelessness, while the cries and sighs could be heard of women and sisters worried about the future of their sons, brothers and relatives.

Figure 5 The remains of cells, monasteries and churches on a high mountain to the east of the monastery of Zaʿfarān

On Thursday [6 August], 150 boys were called to arms.[1] They were taken to war. This was already the fifth column; the first was dispatched on 3 August. They were sent to Amida, without food reserves, on foot; some of them walked barefoot. And August days in our region are the hottest of the entire year.

On Saturday, 8 August, news arrived that the countries at war made peace and signed a treaty. It is hard to describe with what manner of joy and relief the people took such news in. Some began dancing in the streets and squares, others fired shots into the air.

Hearing gunshots, the mayor of Mardin thought that Muslims had begun killing Christians. His fear was probably justified, as apparently the Muslim elite of the city gathered each night in secret to discuss a plan of extermination of the Christians at the first opportunity that might emerge; news of this had been delivered to the mayor in confidence. Christians did

[1] Most probably from Mardin itself.

not know anything about this treachery and were not able to do anything about it, as the government had confiscated all of their weapons, each and every piece that they had in their possession. In order to calm the atmosphere down, the mayor sent out his people to notify the inhabitants that these rumours were not true, that the war continued and that there were no accords between the opposing countries. To confirm this fact, almost 200 men and boys were drafted within a single night, to be sent to Amida. Joy quickly turned to sadness.

On Sunday, 9 August, a delegation representing the Muslims from the city of Shauro [Sauro] came to the head officer of the army, bearing a large sum of money in gold, which they offered in exchange [58] for an order releasing their boys from the obligation to serve in the army. The officer explained to them that presently only Christians can pay to be exempt from joining the army and the set amount per person is fifty gold dinars per year. However, within a short while, the Muslims could also hope for deferment for the same amount. This was the first day that some representatives and elite members of the Christians (Assyrians, including Syrian Catholics and Chaldeans, as well as Armenians and Protestants) found out that there existed the possibility of deferment of military service. Their civilian leaders (mayors and village headmen) as well as the clerics of all rites of the Armenians and Assyrians commenced drawing up lists of people of draft age (twenty to forty-five years) and collecting money, fifty gold dinars each, which they gave to the government along with the lists of names. Even though many Christians paid so that their sons could stay home, at least for a time, they were still burdened by other fees such as the land tax and poll tax.[2]

On Wednesday, 12 August 1914, orders arrived to send the hastily formed army to Baghdad, as Diyarbakır could not host everyone. The mayor [of Mardin] also ordered for everyone to be loaded with as much arms as possible. And as the government had no means of transport, donkeys and mules found in households and in the streets were confiscated [59]. Those protesting against such treatment of their property by the authorities were

2 Non-Muslims were obliged to pay such taxes to Muslim governments ever since Muslims took over those lands in the seventh century. The amounts varied depending on the needs and whims of the rulers.

calmed down by the mayor, who said that in ten days the animals would be returned to their owners. But God only knows when they woud return or be given back. On this same day, the Yezidis, inhabitants of the village of Bajinne[3] chose to stand up to the authorities by not releasing their boys to go to war. The mayor of Mardin sent a penal military expedition to them. The inhabitants defended themselves bravely and the army was not successful in breaking their resistance. The soldiers returned to their bases in shame.

On Thursday, 13 August, news arrived that Germany had defeated France. On this very day, the Assyrian inhabitants of Ṭūr ʿAbdīn sent a letter to the mayor of Mardin, expressing their readiness to defend their lands against any enemy that might arrive with their own force, provided that they are equipped with appropriate arms after they join the army and provided that they form special units, with the state not needing to worry about their maintenance. On the same day, Turkish soldiers arrived in Mardin with swords at their sides and began writing down the goods that were found at stores and wholesalers, promising their owners that the state would not take more than twenty per cent of the goods [60].

On Friday, 14 August, the officers continued their unfortunate inspection of the town, going from store to store. This time they did not write down the goods but took what they liked. The rumour began circulating that the war spans the entire world, with Turkey proclaiming war on Russia.

On Saturday, 15 August, when the Assumption of Mary was supposed to be celebrated, from sunrise onwards military patrols circulated the city, announcing: 'every young man that is sick or married to an orphan, or who is the sole provider for their elderly father, is exempt from military service.' The announcement was met with relief by all inhabitants. On this day, Turkish newspapers announced that England and France had defeated Germany and Austria at sea and in the air and that German infantry experienced a crushing defeat from the Russian forces on land.

On Sunday, 16 August, the streets of the Turkish cities filled with soldiers. The officers and soldiers were quick and precise in scouring the markets, stores and warehouses to take particular clothing, textiles, sheep, *meshḥō*[4] and wheat

[3] The author explains the meaning of this name in quotes as Bet Ganne ('Castles in between').

[4] *Meshḥō* is pure milk fat derived from butter obtained as a result of shaking yoghurt in water-

as well as other durable products, and to move them to the barracks to provide for the fighting units. The city inhabitants cursed these robbers; the Muslims did this more loudly and decisively than the fearful Christians. The helpless locals, including those from the villages, did not know how to act in such a situation. They could not do anything about it. On this day, Bishop Ivannis Elias Halluli departed from the monastery of Zaʿfarān and travelled to the seat of the patriarch in Mardin, in order to take over the duties of the elderly and sick Bishop Kirill Givargis. In the evening, in turn, travelling representatives of the authorities circulated all the city districts, shouting loudly [61]: 'There need to be prepared full lists with names of all men aged 30–45 to draft them into the army.' Announcements of such wording were attached to church doors by the soldiers accompanying them. They also gave everyone the chance to pay the sum of fifty gold dinars in exchange for exemption from service. On the same night, many had already reported at the office to provide payment, however the mayor did not accept their money but told them to come at dawn. When they came in the morning they were surprised, because all the lists of people drafted into the army only contained names of Christians, without any breakdown by church: Assyrians, Armenians and Papists.[5]

On Thursday, 21 August, we had heard that in Amida 1,578 stores, warehouses and wholesalers were set alight, with the fire consuming all of their contents. All of these belonged exclusively to Christians. It later turned out that the governor himself, an uncommonly evil man, was behind this idea. The action plan was agreed upon three days prior with certain Muslim citizens: first the stores were looted of goods and then set on fire. The fires raged for three days and three nights. The Christian owners lost their livelihoods, turning from rich to the poorest in an instant. When they complained to the governor they saw that the one who was supposed to be their protector,was the thief, saboteur and arsonist all in one.

skins, which is then melted after salt is added. It is a valuable and in demand product in the Near East, popular with Bedouins in particular, known in Arabic as *samn*. It is commonly used for frying foods.

[5] The author means the lists did not contain subdivisions by confession into Gregorian and Unitarian Armenians, Orthodox and Unitarian (including Chaldean) Assyrians and Protestants. Likewise, the extermination process to follow spanned all Christians, irrespective of nationality and adherence to an Armenian or any other church.

Today [on Thursday, 20 August], the sun set before the end of the day [at an unusual hour]. And on Saturday, 19 August [rather 22 August], between midday and the evening [62], the skies went dark over our region, and one could see the stars [in the sky]. The darkness lasted an hour and ten minutes. After this period, the sky went bright again.

On Monday, 24 August, the soldiers plundered stores and warehouses [in Mardin] and took from them textiles, cotton, wool, socks and shoes for the army. On the following day, all of the looted goods were loaded on to 100 camels and sent to Amida. In the evening, when the sun was setting, a group of 350 soldiers equipped with arms went through the town. Some of them said, however, that they are on their way to Ṭūr 'Abdīn to arrest the local chieftain Alike Batte, who had made himself known to the authorities. Together with his men, numbering about a thousand, he revolted against the state.[6]

On 14 September, the Feast of the Cross, the army suddenly attacked churches [in Mardin], as clergy and lay Christian activists were brutally arrested and led to the city authorities. Only those that surreptitiously were able to pass appropriate 'bribes' to the officers were able to flee. This scenario was repeated by the army every Sunday, and in this way they held many deacons, men and teenagers [63]. A large proportion of the faithful stopped attending church for fear of arrest.

Saturday, 19 September, was a particularly sad day, as close to 200 Christian youths were detained as a result of a round-up and kidnapped under officer escort to Amida. They were allowed to take some food for the road. On the city outskirts, close to the water source named 'Ayn Sinje, their families gathered; mothers hugged their sons and cried, as did their younger siblings. The detained also cried. The same happened on the following day, on Sunday, 20 September. On this day, the number of boys taken was close to 300. A similar round-up took place on Monday, 21 September. A further group of about 250 youths was held and forced to march out. The three

[6] Alike Batte was a Kurdish chieftain, friend to legendary Assyrian revolutionary Shamune Hanne from the village of Sare (Ṭūr 'Abdīn). The gravesite of the latter is found in the neighbouring village of Bsorino. The adventures of both these heroes, as well as the bright and dark sides of their friendship, live on in the stories recorded on magnetic tapes in Syriac and in sung poetry in the Kurdish dialect of Kurmanji.

days of repeated round-ups took the spirits of the citizens of Mardin away. Fear roamed. There were no youths to be seen in the city streets and squares, once full of them. Cries and lamentations could be heard from almost every household.

On 22 September the army brought about 400 men and boys from such Christian villages as Qsur, Tella and Ḥesnō d-Atṯō to draft them into the army. They were followed by their families: mothers, siblings and grandparents. All cried. They knew that the men were being led to their deaths [64].

[Turkish Preparations for War]: Collection of Wheat, Sheep and Other Food Products as well as Equipment for the Armed Forces

On Tuesday, 6 October, the Turkish government, following much pressure, was able to convince the representatives of the national administration to commence the operation of gathering wheat from Christian citizens to provide for the army. All Christians responded positively to the plea by the government and agreed to deliver the wheat voluntarily after cooking it.[7] Half was sent to Amida, while the second half {most likely made its way to an unknown tyrant}.

On Thursday, 8 October, the mayor of Mardin sent troops to rural areas to collect sheep from Arabs. As a result of this operation, 300,000 sheep were collected. Some of them were sent to Amida, the rest was slaughtered, the meat cooked and baked, whereafter it was loaded on to crates to be sent to the army. However, as we found out, all of the meat spoilt and was thrown away, while the part that was edible was taken by the officers for themselves and their families, with the bounty being shared with the highest representatives of the local administration.

On Monday, 12 October, the army attacked homes by surprise, taking from them all the food reserves that the inhabitants had. On the following day, the authorities turned to the citizens, asking them to prepare all kinds of food packets for the army. On Wednesday, [14 October], great amounts

[7] Before cooking, the seeds required careful cleaning by hand, and after cooking they needed to be sun-dried. Assyrians perform this centuries-old procedure using fresh wheat seeds in order to obtain a quickly boiling semi-finished cereal product in the form of groats named *bulgur*, which can be stored for a long time. It is broadly used in culinary art and is very popular in all of the Near East.

of wheat grain were taken, loaded on to 100 camels and sent to Amida [65]. On Thursday, 12 November, in turn, announcements were posted on walls and at well frequented spots in the city, with the following wording: 'In the name of the Sultan, our country has waged war against France, England and Russia. It is a holy war.' Other announcements said: 'The king of England is threatening Muslims and seeks to destroy them entirely', with the following sentence placed underneath this slogan: 'the king of England says: "The world cannot be safe, and the people of earth cannot live in peace, until the Qur'ān will disappear and cease to exist"'.[8]

This deception was spread by Germans to encourage the Muslims to accept the war and to incite in them the highest enmity towards Christians living in Turkey.

On Thursday, 19 November, Muslims gathered in mosques in great numbers. Holy war was the topic of the fiery preaches of the imams, as a duty of every Muslim against the enemies [of Islam]. They said:

> The Balkan states have started a war against Turkey. The English have taken the city of Busra[9] to the south of Baghdad, and Russians are bombing Trabzon.[10] In light of such challenges, every Muslim, irrespective of their age, has the holy duty to fight our enemies. Slay them! Burn them! Spill their blood! Destroy them all until the nation of Mohammed is free of those that hate our faith.

On Sunday, 27 December, the Turkish army had taken four Russian cities in the Sari Kamesh region [66]. However, three days later, the Russians attacked the Turks, reclaimed their cities and took 90,000 Turkish soldiers captive; only the injured, handicapped and the suppliers and medical personnel prevailed. Both Enver Pasha as well as the German general fled the battleground in secret. In the cover of night they reached the city of Erzurum on foot.

8 It is not hard to foresee the fatal effects of such announcements for Christians. It is not known whether they were also posted in other cities in which Christians resided. It is also doubtful for them to have been hung in cities where the people were all Muslim, if there were any like this back then in Turkey.

9 Basra – presently the second largest city of Iraq. The locality of Busra is located in Syria.

10 Trabzon (ancient Trapezund) – a city on the Black Sea.

{The Beginnings of the Extermination of Christians}

On Thursday, 18 February [1915], twelve young Assyrians from the village of Qarabash were sentenced to death by firing squad for, as stated by Turkish officials, fleeing from the army. Here is the true story behind this incident.

The boys were caught following a round-up and drafted into the army by force. Before leaving Amida, they fled together, travelling to the vicinity of the locality named Tachte Kala. When they spoke this name before the military court, the court reporters purposefully deformed the name and recorded it as Chanak Kala, which in Turkish means 'battlefield'.[11] This hideous ruse was enough to sentence them to death. The boys were separated from each other. Their public execution was to serve as a warning and to scare others. Two were executed in Mardin, two in Al-Madine, two in Kartbart, two in Edessa and four in Amida. Those shot in Mardin, in the southern part of the town, were Neman and Abednuhro [67]. The treacherous execution of these boys was considered by the Christians to be a bad omen for the coming times. Father David Antun took their bodies, celebrated the funeral mass and buried them in the crypt of the St Michael Church in the southern part of Mardin. The funeral was attended by the current Armenian bishop, who came from Amida and took this tragedy and lawlessness with great dismay, even more so as he offered the authorities a large sum of money to spare their lives: 50,000 gold dinars. However, the offer was refused. His attempts at providing legal defence for the unlucky boys ended up empty. It seemed that the calculations of the authorities showed that this was not profitable. Despite the fact that the boys were good Assyrians, the Syrian Orthodox Church rejected them. The [Armenian] bishop declared mourning in the Armenian Church in his parish and declared them martyrs of the faith, He even created a liturgy in their honour, celebrated to remember them every year.

Here are the names of the boys: Ṣalībā Bār Eramia, Kadarsha Bār Garbo, 'Abd an-Nūr Bār 'Īsā, Asyā Bār Saydē, Kadarsha Bār Yaqin, Pheṭrus Bār

[11] Remarks of the translator: This is not correct. The words Chanak Kala refer to a war that took place in Turkey in 1915. It is also the name of a city not far from ancient Troy. The literal meaning of the words is 'pot fortress', as *chanak* means pot and *kala* means fortress. The Turkish word for battlefield is *savaş meydanı* or *harp meydanı*.

Hannush, Ḥannā Shaghule, Karim Ḥannā, Ne'man 'Abd al-Aḥad, Gara/h/bet Ya'qūb, Ḥannush Gir and Phaulos Ḥannā [68].[12]

The Christians were convinced that as of that moment they were the object of revenge and hate by the authorities, and that no legal arguments or calls to conscience and tolerance shall move their tormentors, following the murder of the twelve youths from Qarabash and their fruitless defence by the Armenian bishop of Amida, whose intense efforts included expressing a readiness to redeem them with a generous hand. The Christians felt that there was nobody to help them, that the world had turned away from them and had destined them to become cannon fodder, in light of the fact that Germans and Austrians, seemingly Christians, were witnesses to many lawless operations aimed against them; they saw with what premeditation and fanaticism the Turks and Kurds spilt their venom, destroyed and murdered – without any reaction [by their allies]. It was clear that Christianity never found a home in the hearts and minds of these people. They only called themselves Christians. In their actions, they were barbarians. They chose not only to be spectators of the tragedy of Christians, but also mocked them; more than this, they enticed Turks and Kurds to spill the blood of the 'infidels'. Not me, and not any one of my countrymen had ever set eyes on an Englishman, a Frenchman or a Russian; none of us knew their languages, and despite this we were guilty of the defeat of the Germans, Austrians and Turks during the war.

The Turks, seeing that our alleged brothers did not react to our pain and that they did not protest against these inhumane actions, felt even more sure of themselves and became convinced that what they did to us was the right thing. In order for their operations to be more effective and more destructive they asked the Kurds for support, formed a devilish pact with them, and convinced their leaders that Christians are of no use and that they needed to be swept away from the face of the earth [69]. The actions of both of these groups were devoid of mercy; the stronger kills the weaker, against

[12] The list includes two men executed in Mardin: Ne'man and Abed Nurho, whereby the second name is included in the list not in the Syriac version the author had used earlier, but in its Arabic translation as Abd an-Nur. Following this paragraph, the manuscript includes the same subheading – 'The beginnings of the extermination of Christians' – hence it was omitted from the translation.

whom they can make up hundreds of reasons; the most important of these being that since Christians are not Muslims they cannot be loyal to the state. Hence, Christians are traitors and collaborators – this was the way they spoke of us, convincing themselves and others. The world probably does not know such barbarism – such imagined and unfounded joint responsibility, which in the Turkish and Kurdish sense meant condemning an entire nation and every one of its representatives individually to total, unprecedented annihilation: our villages and cities were burned, their inhabitants were murdered or banished, ancient monasteries and churches were razed to the ground. The scale of destruction was unimaginable, and the number of rapes carried out without any restraint on young women and the number of immature girls and children taken from their parents is difficult to describe. I do not know whether this could have happened anywhere else. Any language can give up when describing the scale of this catastrophe. The news reaching us minute after minute of the death marches stunned a person, caused nausea and a feeling as if one would want to vomit. That is why I have decided to move on from describing incidents of general scope to specific examples. I am fully convinced that the children and grandchildren of those that survived will have doubts as to such immense cruelty of man and their degeneration, and they might accuse me of bloating the facts. I also confess that any kind of barbarism should not only be condemned, but one needs to know what it is, what threats does it bring with itself and, using our specific example, one needs to know how it played itself out and what were its repercussions for the life of the nation and its future. Knowledge about this is necessary and important, so that a similar tragedy does not repeat itself, be it here or elsewhere.

But is it possible for people like the local Turks and Kurds, whom one can only call people but who are not really human, to also live elsewhere? Their actions are almost identical to how wild beasts of the jungle act. I have become witness to probably the most tragic of times in my nation's history. I declare hereby, for history and for memory, that what I was able to record is but a drop in the ocean of events. We expected the twentieth century to bring us and humanity hope, peace, freedom and light. The opposite occurred: we are witnesses to greater wildness and barbarism than we experienced in centuries past. We are dealing with animal mutations of the human character, straight out of the jungle [70].

[Slavelike Labour and Death Transports][13]

On the first day of March 1915, in the province of Amida, the Ottoman state ordinance requiring Christians to give up their weapons was published and implemented. It concerned particularly those who had relatives in the army. A further operation of searching for alleged weapons, however, now had a different goal. The country desperately needed hands to work for free in road construction. All work related to this was carried out manually and stones were transported by people on their backs. The workers only received food and water sporadically. Many of our countrymen died of exhaustion, hunger or thirst. For this work people of very good build were selected, in the homes of whom no weapons were found but who were accused by the authorities of having hidden weapons before the operation initiated.

Hundreds of selected young men were drawn out of their homes and treated almost like slaves. On the long road towards their place of work each of them was burdened with a load of forty kilograms. This load comprised food rations of officers as well as arms and ammunition. In addition, each worker was permitted to have a bag of personal belongings and bread, weighing not more than fifteen kilograms. If the officer's 'package' would weigh more than forty kilograms, then the carrier needed to have a lighter personal bag. The upper load limit was fifty-five kilograms. These unlucky men carried this load on foot, irrespective of the road or weather conditions, in rain and snow. Each group was escorted by twenty to thirty armed officers and soldiers [71], wielding bats, leather straps and other torture equipment. If the tired column slowed down, the guards would attempt to hurry them with whips, hit the exhausted with bats, most often on the heads, and curse them in a manner below human dignity. {In most cases these unlucky men helped themselves out; when any one of them could not walk any more, another would take his load to carry, and if he fell, another would have tried to help him stand up again.} As the column moved away from their families, the hope of these 'slaves' of survival and of returning home would wane and fade away. Many died during these marches because of exhaustion, dehydration

[13] This subheading stems from the translator and editor of the Syriac text into Polish and covers the description on pages 71–3 of the manuscript. It was lifted from chapter VII.

and beatings. It was not permitted to bury the dying or the killed, and others needed to carry their loads. Of any group numbering in the beginning a hundred men, only [about] thirty would reach their destination.

On Friday, 9 April [1915], the governor[14] of Amida issued an order to his deputy (the *javer*), meaning the one that accompanied him [and carried out his orders] (his name was Shakir Bey and he was Cherkess by birth) to mobilise army units in preparation of an operation to detain the more important Christian elite across the province. Over the course of three days, 1,200 men were arrested. All of them were led to Amida and placed in a building called the Msafir Khane, or the House of the Traveller.

The detained were subjected to torture and pain: fingernails were pulled with pliers, ears were cut off, finger bones were broken and various parts of the body were punctured with a hot rod. Simple tools were used to deliver the pain and torture, because – as they said – it would be a pity to use valuable bullets for this. The tortured were not informed what they were accused of or why were they treated this way – they had no option of defence and nobody, not even their closest family members, could be allowed to visit them.

On 25 April, meaning after seventeen days, the arms of each man were tied with a rope and, following this, the entire group, one man after another, was bound with a cord. Formed into a long chain they were led out through the gate of Mardin[15] towards the River Tigris. The march took about half an hour. On the river, fifteen rafts were waiting, prepared to transport these people to Mosul. This was the official version of the authorities. About 500 soldiers were to supervise a swift transport.

The official version of the authorities was not true. The governor of Amida notified a locally known Kurdish bandit and thief by the name of Amarke[16] to murder the entire group in concert with the soldiers [72] when it entered the territory he controlled: more precisely, close to the village of Shkafto.[17] Amarke could only dream of such an occasion. He led 100 well-armed men to the indicated spot and took position on the riverbank. When the officers

[14] Reshid Bey, Cherkess by birth, was appointed to become the governor of Diyarbakır on 25 March 1915.

[15] This is one of the gates of Amida.

[16] This may be the diminutive Kurdish form of the Arab name of Omar.

[17] The Kurdish name means cave or grotto.

escorting the rafts reached this spot after two days and noticed the people of Amarke, they stopped and released the hostages on to land. There, these men were stripped naked, led to a nearby ravine and shot, with the bodies being burned afterwards. At the place of execution, the smoke rose from the glowing and burning bodies for three days. One of the soldiers taking part in the hostage escort, originally from the Bar-Ave region, said: 'Three days after the execution, somebody notified us that they had seen a priest accompanied by three men, who most probably did not die, at the place of execution, walking around with candles in hand around the burned remains, praying.' Hearing this, the soldiers travelled there, but saw nobody.

After the soldiers returned to Amida, the governor started a new round-up. This time, more than 500 men were caught. They were escorted out of the city, but not too far away, and shot; afterwards some of the bodies were burned and some were thrown into a well. Valleys, ditches and meadows filled with human bodies. For a long time, people avoided this place. The decomposing bodies gave out a very unpleasant stench.

{Following this horrendous operation, the Muslims became even more aggressive. Particularly ruthless were those who perhaps recalled that some Christian once insulted them, or demanded the repayment of a loan, or simply seemed better off in life. To avenge themselves, armed gangs entered homes or workplaces, took Christians and murdered them, leaving their bodies in the streets or roads. The bodies lying in the streets interested nobody but the victims' families.}[18]

[18] This paragraph was moved from page 75.

7

EYEWITNESS REPORTS – THE STORY OF A ROAD WORKER NAMED ABED MSHIHO, WHO SAW THE MOST

On 5 March [1915] they took me to work at the construction site of a road running to Aleppo. {The task assigned to me spanned levelling out the ground, moving stones and grinding them down, carrying soil, digging ditches, and so on.} The base was located close to a village named Gozli, a three-hour walk from Amida. Our group numbered about 300 [73] people. Having reached the chosen spot, the leader told me to be the works foreman (the Turks call such a post *bayluk amini*[1]). Every day, about thirty new workers arrived. When we numbered 1,100, no new persons were brought in anymore. The work was extremely arduous and slavelike, we were treated very rudely and were given insufficient amounts of food and drink. We were hungry all the time.

At the camp, there were many higher level Turkish foremen. Each of them had a thick bat with them, with which he would walk from morning until nightfall and frighten us. Those that could not stand the required pace were beaten on their heads with all force available. However, they had to continue working, with dried blood on their head, face and clothes. Every day, each foreman would break two or three bats on our heads, but the stores

[1] Or *chawish*, meaning group elder.

were filled with this torture device. This is not everything, though. An injured worker had an additional penalty for reluctancy; over the course of a single day he had to perform work planned for three days. Very few were able to become such heroes. If at the end of the day they came to the conclusion that one did not fulfil an order, he was taken to the commander, who would impose the penalty foreseen in such cases. He would, for instance, order to put the unlucky man on the ground and bind him: one soldier would sit on his head and another would sit on his legs, tied together with a rope. When the man was in such a position, executioners of strong build would take positions on either side of the man and beat him with bats, a hundred hits each, with all the force they had. One could see blood squeezing out from the clothes of the punished. It happened often that the beaten would die during such a torture.

One day [continues Abed Mshiho] the commander ordered me to gather fifty workers and together with them to fetch large stones from the other side of the village of Gozli. The spot was a 45-minute walk away from our camp. This was very difficult and tiring work. When we were carrying the stones, at about 5pm, two vehicles stopped by our camp. The governor himself came from Amida to – as they announced – inspect the progress of the work [74] and to make sure that it was progressing as planned. The governor stopped close to us. First he took a look at the workers and afterwards he turned to me, not knowing that I was Christian: 'What is your function here?' 'My lord, I am your servant who supervises the work of this group' I replied. 'This is in order, but why do you let them carry such small stones? Are you here to play and relax? Open your eyes, these cut stones are to be dyed with your blood!' he commented on our hard work, whereafter he made his way to the commander and told him to immediately execute the order.

I would have thought that the governor would praise us for our devoted work, but from this moment on he turned our lives into hell. We gave absolutely everything we had. Once again, their criminal nature only saw slaves in us.

One day, when we were nourishing ourselves with dry bread an officer by the name of Hasane Sado, accompanied by two others, suddenly approached us. He pointed his finger at a worker and said: 'This is Manug from the village of Ka'biyye. The authorities in Amida have business with him.' Hearing this, our commander ordered Manug to be caught. By his order, the soldiers bound his arms and moved him away, pretending to be taking him to the offices. However, after about thirty minutes, a dull shot could be heard. They had murdered Manug up on a hill named Talla-Tape. Manug was an Armenian of uncommon strength and courage. In a fair fight he would probably be able to prevail over thirty men [75]. And most probably this is the reason why he was murdered so treacherously and tragically.

O treacherous time, how many disasters you bring us!

Four days after this crime, the same Hasane Sado came up to us again, together with Mhammade Khave-Rashsh[2] and two soldiers. From our group they took two good, honest, valiant workers who had respect among Armenians: Beshar and Nishan. They took them to a valley to the south of the village of Sirme and shot them dead. The same angel of death also appeared on the following day, in the morning, this time accompanied by officer Ibrahim the Tall[3] and five soldiers. Their prey was five Armenians of uncommon physical strength: Khoren, Hag, Ya'qūb, Mato and Khuro. They had bound them with handcuffs and chains, took them to the vicinity of the village of Alme and murdered them there.

The recurring round-ups, which – and this is the most painful thing – always ended with tragic deaths and the bodies being buried in shallow ditches, without a proper funeral mass and without the participation of relatives, brought about an atmosphere of rebellion, sadness and sorrow. The workers began to pray constantly; nobody knew what the next day would bring. It made no difference to them, how many days of life they had left. The life of a slave under such torture, without any hope, is worse than death. Some of them felt as if they were dead; they related themselves to victims of brutality, falsehood, lies and impunity. Their working conditions became rather a nuisance, and they were treated less and less humanely. On long and hot days of June, they laboured from nine in the morning until nightfall, even on Sundays, with one break of a few minutes to eat some stone-dry bread and to drink some warm water. This was their daily lunch. Only Fridays were free.

[2] In Kurmanji: 'black-eyed'.

[3] The author used the Syriac word *arikho* (in this case 'tall'). He was Kurdish and went by the nickname of *Drezh* ('tall').

Their clothes, not washed for [76] months, were stiff from the sweat, and the white stains caused by the salt the body lost became black as tar. Under such conditions, can one wonder that they preferred death over life? However, the heavens probably neither see nor hear.

One day in the evening in the village of Sirme[4] I was supposed to hand out dinner to the workers. The dinner consisted of a piece of bread, dry and black as coal. I think not even a hungry fox would eat it. It was already midnight when the first line group reported for dinner, but those from the second, third and fourth lines did not report in; each line numbered 160 workers. When I asked the commander about the cause of the workers not coming in at the right time he said that right now they are making up the backlog from the day and that they will report in for their bread only at two o'clock in the morning. Not being able to handle such outrage and inhumanity I boldly went to the head manager. Having kissed his hands and feet, I pleaded and begged for mercy for these suffering and orphaned people, for whom nobody had any compassion. And as he respected me somewhat, he accepted my plea. Willing to spare these poor men the hardships of having to reach me, I went to them, departing quickly. I knew they were in a pitiful condition. I took along my friend, John, who always prevailed in such instances. As a few years earlier he had been on a pilgrimage to the Holy Land we called him *Maqdeshyo*.[5] We ran so fast that our heads overtook our feet. We had already heard cries and moans from a great distance. When we reached the spot we informed the guards about the will of the head manager [77] to release the workers. In the guards' hands we saw no bats, but only pieces of them scattered about. Instead of bats, they held stones in their hands. It turned out that having broken all hard and thick bats on the workers' heads, they started throwing rocks at them, aiming for heads. On the way to the camp, the poor men were barely able to walk; blood was dripping from the heads of many of them, others had broken fingers and many bruises on their bodies. They were in terrible condition. But who knows about it, and who has the opportunity to see it and describe it? Only a handful took their bread into their hands, the

4 This is the same village, close to which the mentioned two Armenians, Beshar and Nishan, were killed.

5 From Ar'ō Qadishtō ('Holy Land').

rest preferred to lie down without dinner so that on the following morning they could begin a new day of struggling beyond human perseverance.

The work, planned for ten days, was carried out in five – an extension of a road section to the village of Habashi.

A certain Kurd by the name of Nado lived in the village of Habashi. Noticing that the workers walked around hungry, he came up with the idea of selling bread brought from the town, offering a loaf, usually worth ten [78] copper coins, for the sum of five or six silver coins. Those who had a few coins spent them within a few weeks. And when their money ran out, just as luck would have it, the foremen began torturing them even more crassly, limiting not only the bread but also the water rations. Were they in league with this Kurd? Is this not clear proof of harassing one's victims? Some could not even speak a word; tongues and lips went dry from thirst. They cried like little children and begged the heavens for a quick death.

This is just a drop in a sea of despair.

After a short while, we were transferred from the village of Habashi to the village of Sarsang, and from there onwards to the village of Shaytan Dare, meaning Valley of Satan. The distance was quite long. And as there were no villages on the way, in the night we needed to sleep at the roadside and under the stars. This country is close to the mountain range named Mosho, which is often covered with snow. We were shivering. We had nothing to cover ourselves with and protect ourselves from heavy rains, which sometimes continued all night. Our torn clothes barely covered our bodies. In a climate harsh for us, close to twenty per cent of the workers got ill. But despite fever and other complaints, they had to work. They were forced to wake up.

It so happened that the commander took me along for the wake-up call. A man sleeping or shivering of cold and disease was first hit by an officer with a strong bat. When the man woke up, the officer would order him to stand up immediately, shouting: '*Kōfūrō* [*giaur* – infidel]![6] Wake up!' Out of fear, everyone tried to stand up as quickly as they could. Afterwards the officer would order the man to stick his tongue out, so that he could hit it with a metal bar he held in his hand, surprisingly and swiftly

[6] From an Arabic word from the Qur'ān: *kāfir* (infidel).

[79]. In this way, without any reason at all and without any resistance, he treated every single person, shouting, cursing and beating. As a result, he forced everyone, without respect to health, to murderous daily work. The saddest thing was that many of the sick were just hours away from dying. However the commander would accuse them of pretending and lack of will to work. In this way, every day, there were a few workers less. They fell down, not to get up again, exhausted by illnesses, hunger or the beatings of merciless barbarians using any available torture tool.

On 8 June, in the evening, the commander called me over and told me to select 200 workers who at dawn were to move on to work in Amida. When I finished my task the commander appointed a party of officers to escort them. And as the group included my relatives and people from my village, I begged the commander to let me go along with them, irrespective of whether he is sending them to death or not. He advised me to abandon this idea, as the group might be a great and troublesome burden for me. As the commander had relative respect for me, though, in light of my forceful persistence, he gave me his permission. We made the trip to Amida, which usually takes fourteen hours, in ten hours. We were stopped at a citadel on the northern outskirts of the city. To our surprise we were imprisoned here [80] for three days. As it turned out, the citadel held a great number of other workers. All were Christians.

After three days passed, the head construction engineer appeared, accompanied by the commander of 1,000 soldiers.[7] In the speeches they gave, they appealed to us for more effective work during the construction of the road to the city of Bitlis, indicating a group of foremen who will be reckless in ensuring this. They also stated that we were to sleep in the village of Ka'biyye that night. When we entered the village, we saw no men aged between twenty and fifty. The children that we met ran up to us and started crying, kissing our hands and shouting: 'Is my father with you? The Muslims have decimated us!' In light of this incredible situation our entire group was

7 This does not mean that this commander arrived with 1,000 soldiers – but it could mean he was a *binbashi*. The author merely indicates the commander's renown, without indicating his military rank. He mentions more often commanders of units numbering 50 soldiers. Perhaps that was the contemporary commander classification, or perhaps the young author did not know how to pronounce military ranks.

in tears, and everyone started hugging the crying and broken children. We wept over our fates and over that which awaits us and our children, from whom we were separated, and they wept for their parents and brothers who were taken away. Seeing what was happening, the escorting soldiers started beating us with bats over our bodies, with a rage typical of the wildest beasts. They shouted: '*Kōfūrē* (*giaurs*), you shall not see the day of your return to your children!'

With that, they crushed in us the most valiant of feelings. We could not speak a word. In the morning, they drove us to work on the road towards Bitlis.

However, let us return to this almost 200-strong group that was left in the Valley of Satan. On 16 June they were attacked by an army summoned from Amida, numbering 150 soldiers, led by three fanatical officers known among Christians as Sidqi, Yihia and Tharwat. Each had fifty soldiers with him. The army was supported by 300 Kurds armed to the teeth. Having surrounded the camp on all sides, the workers remaining there, who – as we already know – were at their physical and mental limits, were bound with rope and taken on to the road. Their target was to be the locality of Sibaberk. When they came close to the night camp of Karabahche (black garden), fire was opened on them. Of the entire group, numbering about 190 people, only two prevailed who were able to flee and travel to Amida. These two related the course of this mass murder on their colleagues [81].

The operations of leading Christians to death were called *gōlūṯō*.[8]

On 19 June, during the construction work on the road to Bitlis, we were transferred from Ka'biyye to the village of Sa'diyye. When, late in the evening, we were preparing to have dinner we were surrounded by the army. We heard the loud voice of the commander, Sidqi: 'The workers are to come out to work.' It wasn't difficult to read the clear signs of deep fear on our faces, our knees were trembling, we made the sign of the cross, exchanged the sign of peace, hugged and said our goodbyes. They led us out to the square like one would lead out wild dogs. At the camp gates guards were posted. In light of such an uncertain moment, one of us, who previously served in the church as a deacon, suddenly got up and said: 'Brothers! Have no fear! Remember the

[8] This word means 'expulsion'.

words of the Gospel: "And fear not them which kill the body but are not able to kill the soul"'.[9]

After two hours of standing in the square, the commander called me personally and asked: 'Do you know what awaits you?' 'Of course,' I replied, 'the end of our journey on earth is coming to an end. Soon we will all die.' To this he responded: 'You will not be harmed. We want to separate the Armenians from the other Christians. Such are the orders we have received from the sultan.' Following this statement, the commander took the list of workers in his hand and started reading out Armenian names, one by one. This lasted until five in the morning. And we were still without dinner.

We were 212 people in all. The number of Armenians was 102. They made up less than half. After they separated them, they bound their arms with us watching [82], whereafter they tied all of them together and pushed them into a nearby shed. The remaining 110 workers were told to go to work, however only after we sang out loudly a hymn of praise to the sultan. The grandly merciful sultan had granted us our lives and had forgiven us our Christian affiliation. On the next day they led our poor Armenian colleagues from the shed and took them to the place of execution – between the villages of Qarabash and Matraniyye –where they were told to strip and thereafter they were all shot dead.

On the following day we found out that commander Sidqi travelled with a group of sixty soldiers to the village of Akpınar, where the camp was located housing those who worked on constructing the road to Mardin. And there again he separated the Armenians from the remaining Christians. Among the Armenians was a young man from Qarabash, who had the Armenian name Megerdetch but who was not Armenian but Assyrian. In the face of death, he told the commander that he is not Armenian, which can be testified on by the village leader of Qarabash, priest Salim Bar Bshara. By order of the commander, the soldiers went and brought the village leader. Even when he confirmed that the young man was not Armenian the commander refused to believe that a non-Armenian could bear a typical Armenian name. Following this exchange, the commander treated the respected [village] leader

[9] Matthew 10: 28.

as a Muslim treats a dog. He signalled the soldiers to move the priest to the Armenians and to kill him as well. They were lined up between trees, by a water spring, and shot.

From that moment on the uncertainty of tomorrow became our nightmare. We were treated very badly, beaten with bats for any reason until we passed out and until all our clothes were coloured with blood. Those that were late for work, even by ten minutes, were immediately ordered to be shot without mercy.

After ten days of such treatment, the principal engineer visited us [83] and ordered all of us to travel to Amida on the following day. There we were placed in a night shelter called Rola, where we stayed for two days, without food or drink. The guard that watched us did not let anyone move, for instance to beg a piece of bread in the city. Some bought water from him, paying a silver coin for a glass.

On the third day the manager for agriculture came to us, stating that he will employ us for the wheat harvest and that he shall send five to ten workers to each village. I, together with thirteen other prisoners [from the village of Qarabash] were assigned to Mr Fayiz Beg,[10] who sent us to the village of Chanaqchi belonging to the community of Havarchay. Kurds lived there. They threatened us every day: some said that we had five days to live, others said that we had ten. And as it was quite realistic that they would kill us we were afraid to sleep at night.

Harvest work was very tough. From dawn until dusk, squatting, we cut the wheat with sickles. Our legs and arms were stiff. The days were scalding hot. Some had blood flowing out of their noses. We received very little water, and the food we were given would be enough for two to three people, not fourteen; apart from that, it was unpalatable and bitter as bile. Our guard would not listen to our complaints, just the opposite – all complaints were punished with lashing. We were confronted with death. However death would not come naturally; it would be inflicted at will by barbarians that do not fear God and that do not know what it means to be human.

10 Fayiz Beg was a member of the Turkish parliament from the Amida (Diyarbakır) region from the Committee of Union and Progress.

Will these people ever know that their actions are worse than how wild beasts behave?[11] [84, top sixteen lines].

One day, while we were busy with the harvest close to the village of Pre-Hage, we saw a military unit leading a column of Armenians, made up of women and children, representatives of a brave nation. They were wonderfully dressed, groomed and pretty. All wept. When they reached the river bridge, the soldiers told them to sit down and take a drink of water. After a moment, the soldiers moved about 200 metres away and the column was attacked by the Cherkess waiting close by. The Cherkess took all their valuable property – jewellery and money [85, bottom seven lines] – whereafter they told them to march in front. Soldiers flanked the column and more and more armed Kurds joined them. The elderly and sick women who could not keep up the pace were murdered on the spot. The column reached the top of the mountain called Havarchay, close to the village of Gulli, and from there it went downhill again to where a water spring is located.

I do not wish to describe the blood-curdling scenes that occurred that night; women were mass raped, the heads of children and babies were smashed, yet at the same time I believe that the day will come, even if it is Judgement Day, when these bandits and their commanders shall answer for their deeds.

In the morning they stripped all women and children that remained alive and, as usual, they shot each of them one by one.

Three days after this incident I was passing by a mill belonging to [the inhabitants of the village of] Chankchi. There I saw a boy swimming in the river, aged about ten. When he saw me, he came out of the water on to the shore and told me that only he of the entire column was able to escape. I had two loaves of bread with me. I gave them to the boy and I told him to surreptitiously travel to Amida. When the boy was close to the city, a shepherd met him and killed him on the spot.

Two days later, on Friday, we were out in the village as this is a day off work. Around midnight, we heard mortar and machine gun shots fired,

[11] Nineteen lines from this spot on (five on page 84 and fourteen on page 85 of the manuscript), speaking of different affairs than the remaining story, were moved along with the title recorded by the author and included in curly brackets at the beginning of the subsequent eighth chapter.

as in a real war [86]. When the Kurds heard the shooting, they gathered, armed themselves, agreed on something and moved away quickly. We were aware of the reasons for this mobilisation and were overcome by fear. In the morning the Kurds returned with an uncommon 'bounty'. They brought over 100 women and just as many girls of unmatched beauty. We found out later that the Turks showed great mercy, because they let these women live and let Kurds take them for themselves. As it turned out, this group was but a part of the women that the Kurds had chosen as their mistresses and slaves. Similar groups were assigned to other villages taken by Kurds. Anyone was permitted to 'take' as many women and girls as they wanted. And the entire column, from which they were forcibly taken, was supposed to number 40,000 people. This transport did not originate from Amida, but Fiji, Pal, Sebastia,[12] Rishkalo (Bakale), Erzincan and other localities. The ones that arranged the column told the Kurds that originally they planned to kill 2,000 people a day, but that it would take too long, 20 days in all. Hence, he asked the Kurdish chieftains to help out and to take as many people as they were able to kill. However they only killed the men; they chose to keep the women for themselves as mistresses and slaves.

Two days later, on Sunday, when my compatriots were busy reaping the wheat, I, having filled several bags with wheatears and transported them, sat down by the tent to rest a bit [87]. Suddenly, a girl slipped into the tent. She was aged about ten, she was completely naked, had bruises on her neck and cut wounds and signs of having been beaten all over her body. She asked, in an innocent and quiet voice, speaking perfect Turkish, for water. I gave

[12] Sebastia (now Sivas) – in times of Emperor Diocletian (third century) the city was the capital of the province of Armenia Minor, and Emperor Justinian I (6th century) turned it into a metropolis. Towards the end of the eleventh century, it was conquered by Turks, and the name Sivas stems from this time; in 1400 Tamerlane conquered and ravaged it (most of the inhabitants were murdered); in the 16th century the city was rebuilt by the Turkish Sultan Mehmet II (note from the translator into English: Mehmet II lived in the 15th century). In 1838 Horatio Southgate (1843: p. 301) wrote: 'The city is a dirty one, and it is inhabited by twenty-two thousand Muslims and eight thousand Armenians'. It is currently a provincial capital and numbers about 300,000 people. The church commemorates the person of Eustathius of Sebaste (d. 380), who is considered one of the fathers of monasticism in Asia Minor; the memory of the Forty Martyrs of Sebaste is also vivid and celebrated by Christian churches, including those of the Near East.

her an empty sack to cover herself and, after she was done drinking, I asked whether she was hungry.

'Yes', she replied.

I gave her a piece of bread, some cheese and butter and a cucumber. After she was done eating, I asked with tears in my eyes:

'Daughter, I know that the bandits hurt you. Where are you from, and did they leave anybody from your family alive?'

'I come from the city of Erzincan. I was with my mother, elder sister and my two brothers . . .'

The girl could not finish the sentence. She broke down crying, and after a moment, she indicated to the hill, saying:

'Yesterday the army and Kurds massacred and killed us. My mother held me tight. When they killed her, I ran to my brothers. They killed them as well. Then I fled to my sister, but they killed her as well. They caught me, stripped me and toyed with me until I passed out. I think they thought I was dead and they left me alone. When I awoke around me were just dead bodies, one by another or one on another. I fled. They could have killed me as well, but they did not. Now I am alone. I have nobody.'

While the girl was relaying all this, my compatriots returned to the tent. Nobody from the group could hold back tears.

After some deep sighs, the little girl looked at me beggingly, a look I will never forget: 'Father, let me also be sacrificed for you, take me to any Christian village. I am afraid!'

'Daughter, if I could be certain that they would kill only me, leaving you alive, I would fulfill your plea [88]. However, it is quite probable that they will find us and kill only you. Then our pain would be even stronger,' I replied caringly.

The girl did not protest and did not repeat her request.

We all concluded that the best solution would be to seek out a hiding place for this girl nearby. Our choice was the closest bushes by the river. Nobody goes there and nobody will see her. As our discussion continued, we saw two shepherds coming towards the tent in which we were sitting. One of us quickly hid the girl so that they would not see her. It was only after they left and walked away that we mustered up the courage to execute our idea. We left some bread and water for this girl. Sadly, she only survived two days. When I went to bring her food on the third day, she was lying stiff.

O justice, do you exist at all? Human life has no value here.

It is Friday today, a day off work, for us as well, so we spent it in a mud hut that we had available in the village. Around midday we decided to venture into the village to test the reaction of the Kurdish inhabitants. In the centre of the village a large tree stood. We sat in its shadow. After a while we were joined by three local Kurds. Before we started talking, however, we saw five boys approaching the village. They were completely naked. Seeing them, the Kurds started whispering 'these are lost children of infidels' and started a chase immediately. The boys must have felt their evil intentions and began running as fast as they could. However, the adults got to them on the rice plantation, pushed them to the ground and then pressed their heads against the mud, and held them by their legs until all five passed on. They were five or six years of age.

The souls of these innocent beings, which lost everything and all relatives on a single day, shall remember these criminals, and shall be their accusers before the divine tribunal.

There is no other tribunal!

The overpowering sadness and despair forced us to return home. When we entered we all started crying. When, after an hour, we emerged again we saw and heard how these murderers, proud and satisfied, described their heroic deeds to the gathered and onlooking peasants [89]. However, this was not an end to the sorrow of the day. In the afternoon we heard gunshots from the direction of a hill about two kilometres away. Immediately the Kurds ran to their houses, took their weapons and loudly encouraged others to do the same and to join them. They all ran out towards the shots. They returned in the evening, carrying large bags of clothes taken from people who lost their lives close to the village. They also brought girls. The imam (whom they called Sofi Hasan) had the largest take of the bounty: he took three girls. Most probably they were the only ones to survive from a further death march, the size of which was hard to estimate.[13]

[13] Each of the available sources on the genocide stresses that for their participation in the extermination of Christians, Kurds had the right to take not only the clothes of the unlucky but

I could not restrain myself from trying to get to know from these young women what happened to them and how they ended up there. I boldly approached the imam and asked whether or not he was planning to go to town tomorrow. My goal, however, was initiating some sort of contact, even eye contact, with these women. Their looks betrayed their intelligence and uncommon education.

On the second day, in the morning, when I was walking down the stairs to go to work, I noticed that the girls were following me with some uncertainty. I eagerly wanted to indicate to them that I am Christian, but in a manner that the Kurds would not notice. I managed to slow my gait and whisper several words in Armenian. They heard this and were greatly surprised. The oldest of them asked me in disbelief whether I was Muslim.

'No, sister,' I replied. 'I am Christian [90]!'

When they heard this their faces lit up, but I also noticed some uneasiness. They approached me and asked with more trust:

'Is it not curious that they keep you alive while they killed every one of ours?'

'We are of the Old Assyrians.[14] We were also hit by massacres. The Turks and their Kurdish allies left but a few alive, but in the end the sultan pardoned us. {He did this for reasons unknown to us.} We do not know who got lost where, and we live like slaves, away from our families and homes, if they even still exist.'

This news saddened the women. Having sighed, with sad voices, they concluded: 'Meaning we will not find Christian husbands for us. If this

also selected women for harems. The condition was always the same: 'If you accept Islam, we will spare your lives!' Rhétoré, J. (*Al-Masīḥiyyūn*, p. 206) adds that 'children, particularly aged five to seven, were also bounty for the Kurds; they are particularly susceptible to fast Islamisation. Infants were killed without hesitation; it was assumed that their upbringing may cause problems.'

[14] 'Old Assyrians' or *Süryani Kadim*, was how Assyrians on the territory of Ottoman Turkey were officially called, probably to distinguish them from those that entered into a union with the Roman Catholic Church (17th–18th century), called in Turkish (and Arabic) *Suryani Katulik*. Both names emerged later, accordingly, and for a time they were included in identity cards and other documents in Syria as well, maybe even in other Arab countries formed after the dissolution of the Ottoman Empire.

would prove to be impossible, we would prefer to die the next day. Our death would be sweet then!'

'Where are you from?' I asked.

'One of us is from Sebastia, another from Erzincan, and the third comes from a village near Erzincan.'

While we were talking, I noticed that we were being watched by a woman standing on the roof of a nearby house. Not particularly worried by this I parted ways with the women and went to work. The girls were most probably punished for talking to me; in the evening, when I returned from work, I saw them on the roof of that house in the company of that same woman. Noticing me, they turned their backs. They probably had no choice.

After three days we managed to meet again in a desolated spot. One of them, the oldest, took sixty silver coins from her pocket and gave them to me, saying: 'Take this money for food for yourself and your colleagues!'

When I tried to convince them that they needed money more than we did, she replied: 'We will die soon. When we were caught, Sofi Hasan took sixty gold dinars from me [91]. Had I known that I would meet Christians, I would let myself be killed so the money ends up in your hands!' And she added with tears in her eyes: 'Please, do not abandon us. We are joyous when we see you. Please, continue to try to meet us. Pray for us!'

Trying to console them, I said:

'And you should also not forget to pray! It is likely that neither our, nor your deaths will be natural. We have to drink from the bitter chalice that is prepared for us, as our Saviour did. Remember the millions of Christians who have died for the faith. We are happy that you are educated; you know history, and you know what Christianity is and what its mission is, from the crucifixion of our Lord at Golgotha!'

And when the young women found out that I could write, they said to me:

> If our Lord keeps you alive, write about us this: When we were driven out of our land, there were 50,000 of us. For fifty-three days we were driven across desolate country into the unknown. It is written in the Gospel: 'And woe

> unto them that are with child, and to them that give suck in those days!'[15] All women that could not keep up with the pace, the pregnant, the sick and those that carried their infants, were murdered. Some of the mothers committed their children who died of hunger and thirst during the march to the desert [92]. My older sister had two children. She carried one, and me the other. She got ill on the way and could not walk. They murdered her before my eyes. Then I carried both children. When we reached this place, about 40,000 of us were left. About 10,000 corpses lie along the march path. Why was it only here that the rest were murdered? I do not know! We shall be murdered soon as well. Please, write . . . !

Our secret meetings, some of them very short, lasted twenty days more. The discussions got sadder and sadder with time, and they concerned killings and the death of a nation. The oldest of the women suddenly fell ill. It was only after three days that Sofi Hasan announced far and wide that he would take her to a medic in the city. She believed him and got up. After a ten-minute march, when they were in the middle of the road between the villages of Chanaqchi and Maqsi-Oghli, Sofi Hasan ruthlessly killed her, left the body in the road and returned home. The two other girls, seeing that Sofi Hasan is returning alone, concluded that he killed their older colleague and caretaker to some extent. They fell ill after a short while.

We were working on the harvest. At noon shots could be heard from the direction of the river. We thought that these are hunters shooting at wild game. After we returned home, we went to the spot. There the bodies of both women lay on the shore. As it turned out, this time it was the wife of Sofi, Aishe, who invited the girls to go to the river to take a bath together in the warm water that she had prepared. After they left, Sofi Hasan followed them. He was armed and he killed both girls [93].

We saw Sofi Hasan sitting calmly on the roof of his house. When I asked him: 'Where are your Christian women?' he replied 'I took them to a hospital in the city', whereupon he laughed his face off, just like a wild wolf. He was very proud of himself. He most likely thought that what he did deserved praise.

[15] Matthew 24:19 (author's note).

On the next day, in the evening, I went to the river to bring back a horse belonging to our keeper who was grazing there. Suddenly, a woman jumped out from the bushes, with long hair and naked. Her sight confused me; I even got scared a bit. I tried to pretend I had not seen anything and I hastened my pace. She screamed, however: 'Please, please, give me a piece of bread, and then kill me!' I stopped and told her to wait. I walked quickly to get a loaf of bread. When I returned, the woman was not to be seen. I called out: 'I have bread for you!' She remained silent. I repeated my statement that I have returned with a loaf of bread for her. She still did not wish to reveal herself. She was probably afraid that I would kill her. But when I said: 'Sister, do not fear me [94]. I am Christian, just like you are', she emerged from the bushes. Not believing this, she asked me repeatedly whether this was true and requested that I swear to Christ that I am not lying. I did this, whereupon I threw her a piece of cloth that I had on, so she could cover herself. She took the bread and began eating hastily. For a long time she wished to talk with me but, fearing the Kurds for her and my own life, I excused myself and left.

In the village I met one of its inhabitants, bearing the name Zolfo. He had a shotgun with him and was walking towards these bushes. He probably felt or found out that a lost person was hiding there. Could it be possible that he decided to kill her just like one kills a dog? After a few minutes, I heard two shots fired. Sadly, he killed her and returned, so satisfied as if he had done a great deed.

Three days later, I interrupted my work harvesting a field named Arde-Danga (Pottery Field) for a moment and went with one of the colleagues to fetch some water. By the river, between the grass and the reeds, we noticed a woman. She was sleeping. By her side was a little girl aged about three. We did not know what to do [95]: If we wake her, she might get scared, and if we leave her, one of the Kurds is bound to find and murder her. We waited for a moment. The woman opened her eyes, and when she noticed us, she took her daughter into her arms and wanted to jump into the water with her. We tried to calm her down.

'Sister do not fear. We are Christians too!'

Hearing this, she froze. She looked at us. Her nose was bleeding.

'Where are you from, and how did you get here?' I asked.

'I am from the column of forty thousand!' she replied.

'Are you hungry?'

'I have not had anything in my mouth for three days!'

I hurried to the tent and brought her four loaves of bread and yoghurt. As she ate, her daughter asked her:

'Mother, is this man going to kill us?'

'No, daughter! He's an uncle!'

Having heard this, the little girl ran to me. Seeing this, both myself and the mother broke into tears. After she composed herself, the woman lifted her eyes and asked in sorrow: 'God, why did you do this?'

I replied: 'Perhaps because of the vastness of our sins.'[16]

After which she asked [96]: 'And you, who are you, why did they not kill you?'

'They killed our people too. There are but a few of us left. We do not know, how many. We also do not know when they will kill us,' I replied and asked her to understand as we needed to leave. I advised her not to move from that spot and to be cautious so that nobody noticed her. I promised that as long as we are alive, I will bring her bread every morning. Then I said goodbye to her.

As I promised, the following morning I brought her four loaves of bread and some onions. On the third day, in turn, I found an opportunity to stay with her for an hour and talk. One cannot wonder that she was shaken and fearful. And her daughter, as soon as she noticed me, ran up to me, crying: 'Uncle, uncle!'

When I approached, I heard her saying: 'Brother, I am ill!'

I soothed her: 'God is gracious and merciful!'

The innocent eyes of her daughter and her angel-like voice gave me hope. I knew, however, that this would soon end with great bitterness for me. Her calling me 'uncle' will accompany me for the rest of my life.

Sadly, when I went to her on the fourth day, I was stunned: there she was lying dead and even her daughter was not aware that her mother was dead.

[16] This was the most frequent way that old people commented on the causes of the genocide. It is hard to wonder, as they could not understand that education based on xenophobia, subordinate to a specific ideology, can cause sadistic behaviour in one.

She must have thought that she slept. The woman's body showed no signs of wounds, such as from bullets [97].

I asked the little girl: 'Will you eat the bread that your uncle brought you?'

'Yes,' she replied, 'but please, moisten it in water so it is soft.'

I did not know what to do. When the girl ate the bread, I was crying. I left her by her mother and departed.

The following day, I turned up there in the morning. The little girl was sitting by her mother, holding her head on her breast, in tears. Seeing me, she started crying louder and shouting stronger: 'Mother, mother, mother, get up, uncle's here.'

The girl's mother was already swollen. I left the bread and went away.

On the following day I preferred visiting the little girl together with one of my colleagues. I feared that if something happened to her this could be the biggest sadness of my life and that I might not survive this. The bread that we took for her was not necessary; the girl lay dead beside her mother. We made the sign of the cross over them and recited the Lord's Prayer, in the end raising our eyes to the sky as if wanting to ask: How many innocent victims will this earth swallow? God, is this why you created us, so we could perish like animals?

One day when I was working on thresh [98], we heard an exchange of fire. Initially the village inhabitants, ready to collect bounty, moved on to where the sounds were coming from. They returned around noon, accompanied by two soldiers. The soldiers went straight to our keeper's home. And as he was not home, his wife asked me, as it is customary, to stop working, take the guests and accompany them. I did so. The soldiers had a girl with them of uncommon beauty. When they sat down and rested a while, one of them looked at the girl and suggested: 'Take on Islam!'

She responded, however: 'My parents and all relatives warned me before submitting to the will of Muslims, even if I was to die for it.'

Hearing such a statement, the second soldier, somewhat older than the first, reminded her: 'Did you not see how your parents and relatives died?'

'I saw it all,' she responded with a strong voice, and added: 'They continued to say that you could murder me, because you are Muslim. And they died. I want to be with my parents, relatives and the thousands of others whom you killed, but not with you!'

When the soldiers convinced themselves that the girl is steadfast, they turned to me to speak with her in Armenian. This was an opportunity for me to find out how she ended up here and where she had travelled from.

'Are you from Amida?'

'Yes, I am,' she replied [99].

It was she, however, who asked the second question. She wanted to know how I learned Armenian and whether I was Christian. And if so, then why was she kept alive.

My response was terse: 'You saw how they killed your parents, but I was not able to see how and where they killed my parents.'

I left.

Our keeper turned back after this conversation. Following a few days of absence I greeted him and asked where he was in this time.

'I was a guard escorting a column of Christians from Sebastia to Mardin,[17] and after we stopped on the city outskirts I was supposed to guard them for five hours. We thought that everyone in the column would be destined to die. They were not killed, though, but taken inside the city. There, in the city, awkward things happened.'

When I asked him what he had in mind, when he spoke of 'awkward things', he explained:

> The column numbered about 40,000 people. Everyone was led out through the gate of Mardin[18] to walk towards the river. When they were at the bridge, a group of about fifty women, some of them with small children, separated from the rest and paused on the bridge, which has a height of almost fifty metres. We were thinking that they might try to escape. To our surprise, though, they shouted as one [100]: 'In the name of Christ', and on that command they jumped, together with the children, into the deep river. The soldiers did not manage to shoot anybody; instantaneously, they were in the water. The women must have preferred this kind of death. They must

[17] In this quote, the author had used this version of the city name.

[18] This concerns most probably the city of Amida, one of the gates of which is called the Gate of Mardin. Amida, not Mardin, lies on the shores of the Tigris.

have been very brave and strong, decisive in keeping their dignity. Before they jumped into the water, one comforted another. It was incredible. None of us expected anything like this.[19]

When I was close to the village of Zunme on my way home, I saw a group of Christians numbering about fifty people. The soldiers guarding them took their clothes and then shot them. There was a pretty woman in the column. The commander did not want to kill her. Instead, he suggested she converted to Islam, promising very comfortable living conditions. The woman mocked the commander and assured him that she would never do that and that she would not change her religion for any other. He restated his proposal many times. Without effect. Finally, he got angry and he put the gun to her chest, saying [101]:

'Are you foolish? Don't you know what you are saying and what awaits you!'

She responded: 'Look up. Up there, Christ the Saviour is opening his arms for me and calling to me. Kill me quickly now!'

The officer pulled the trigger.

The woman fell to the ground and passed on.

Anyone who would see her would have thought she was dead for a month already [102].

[19] Many similar stories concerning the bravery of women, who proceeded the same way so as not to give their hunters any satisfaction, prevail among Assyrian Christians. Most probably the oldest such story speaks of 2,000 young women. It took place in Persian times and is recorded in various historical sources. See Mōr Mīkhōyel Rābō, *Tārīkh*, p. 203.

8

{THE CHRISTIANS OF THE CITY OF AMIDA AND ITS SUBORDINATE VILLAGES – EXECUTIONS AND THE EXODUS OF 1915}[1]

{The order concerning the Christians of Amida was clear: 'All Armenian families are to leave the city'.

Every day, forty to fifty families were led out by force. The families were notified the day before. Some were told that they were being relocated to Mardin, others that they will be transferred to Tella. The women in turn heard again and again that they will be taken to their husbands residing in Mosul.

The deportation activities initially covered the wealthiest and most influential families. Usually around three in the morning, vehicles were driven to their homes; they were told to come out of their houses and get on the provided trucks. Everything they had at home was supposed to stay. After the families reached the locality of Dara, located between Nisibis and Mardin, the escorting soldiers would execute them. The bodies were thrown into large pits and wells.

[1] In order to maintain order and flow of the text, the contents in curly brackets (including the title) were moved to this spot from pages 84 (five final lines) and 85 (nineteen first lines) of the manuscript. This measure was facilitated by the fact that the text on page 103 discusses villages subordinate to the city of Amida. This fragment also covers selected paragraphs found in pages 103–29 of the manuscript.

In many instances the soldiers received orders for the Kurds to be the executioners instead of them. Hence, when they reached the designated spots they engaged bloodthirsty Kurdish bandits and made them carry out the executions. The executions themselves were carried out perfectly: some people were chopped up with axes, others beheaded with swords, still others had a *khanjar*[2] impaled in their chests or they were sawn in half, had their skulls crushed with mallets, or lost their fingers to men with pliers. Nobody would listen to the begging of children and mothers. Some preferred to throw themselves into the deep wells or beg the soldiers on their knees for a bullet, calling on them: 'Son!', than to die in such an ordeal.

When all wells, valleys, gorges and meadows in and around Dara filled with bodies, they started taking the corpses to valleys in Anbarchay, Duhokgidi, Havarchay and Akabe – which became mass graves for people delivered in twelve caravan transports}.[3]

The Village of Qarabash

Qarabash is a large village and one of but a few in the district of Amida to be inhabited solely by Assyrian Christians.[4] It is home to a church dedicated to St Qawme, where two priests serve: Paul and Behnam. They are first cousins. Father Abd al-Ahad is father to one of them and the other is son to archdeacon Qawme. The latter died in the massacres of 1895.

On 20 April 1915, around 9 o'clock in the evening, two officers showed up in the village: Yihia Yasin Agha and Sidqi Pirinjichi, leading fifty soldiers. They surrounded the village from all sides and entered it at dusk. The first thing they did was to call for the village leader – named Bshara – and when he arrived, he was told: 'Gather immediately all weapons from the inhabitants, or you shall all die!' The leader, accompanied by two of the inhabitants and five soldiers [103] searched house by house. They took everything that could be considered arms: knives, swords, spears, *khanjars*, shields, helmets, rifles

[2] A *khanjar* is a double-edged dagger.

[3] Based on many sources, Sébastien de Courtois (*The Forgotten Genocide*, p. 198) calculates that as a result of the massacres in Diyarbakır the Armenian population was reduced by ninety-five per cent and the Assyrian population by seventy per cent.

[4] David Gaunt cites a prewar population estimate of 600 persons. *Massacres, Resistance, Protectors: Muslim-Christian Relations in Eastern Anatolia During World War I*, pp. 246–7.

and so on; they brought everything and laid it out before the officers. The officers praised the village leader for his effective performance, confiscated the weapons and left. They returned about an hour later, arresting surprisingly and without any reason 200 men, binding them and leading them to Amida. There the men were kept in a building referred to as Msafir Khane, or the House of the Traveller. Five days later, the men were led out, bound with ropes and were told that they would be taken to Chabakchur, to work in road construction. They never reached that locality, however; following a seven-hour-long march, when the group reached the outskirts of the village of Sharabi on the shores of the Tigris, the men were halted, stripped and all were killed.

Following this measure, the Turkish officers surreptitiously notified the Kurds that the village of Qarabash is free of weapons, with not even a knife left, and that they may attack it and treat the inhabitants as they pleased. This was precisely what the inhabitants feared most.

Two days after this event, on 22 April, at midnight, Yihia Yasin and Sidqi Pirinjichi arrived at the village again, accompanied by fifty soldiers. This time they arrested all men and the elderly and led them to Amida. These people were also told that they were to be employed in road construction [104]. They were all shot, however, before they reached Amida. When the Kurds found out that there were no men left in the village, who in the end were even able to defend it without weapons, they stormed it the next night, on 23 April, wanting to exterminate each and every inhabitant. Like hungry and angry wolves, they murdered everybody, plundered house by house. Most of the decimated inhabitants had already fled for Amida before the attack, while others found their way to the village of Darakli, about a half hour's walk away from Qarabash. There they barricaded themselves in houses. However, the Kurds destroyed gates and doors, smashed locks and murdered entire families hiding inside. Others blocked roads to prevent any escapes. Some of the inhabitants that survived the massacre [in Darakli] escaped under the cloak of night to Qarabash, where they hid in the wheat stores, in hay, in tobacco stores, in the pigeon towers and on house roofs. Others attempted to make their way to Amida. When they reached the Tigris in the morning, and tried to cross it, they happened upon a group of Turkish soldiers walking the other way. The soldiers told them that they were assigned the task of protecting the inhabitants of Qarabash from Kurds and encouraged the escaping to return under their escort. However, it turned out that their words were not true. They were far worse than Kurds.

Two days later, a rich Bedouin, owner of large sheep herds, who every year stopped at the village, arrived here. He was called Hajji Mustafa and had friends in the village. He gave water to his sheep and made his way to his friend's home [105], not knowing anything of the tragedy that befell the villagers. The house gate was closed, something that was not usual before. Unsettled, he started calling his friend by name. Getting no response, he called the owner's wife. Her name was Mariam. Mariam hid in hay together with other women. She recognised the voice of the family friend, emerged from her hiding place and got down on her knees before the visitor, begging for help. Seeing this, the Hajji broke down in tears and promised his help, saying: 'By the living God, I am prepared to give my life to save you!' He ordered the shepherds accompanying him to bring yoghurt and buttermilk for the women to drink, as it was very hot, and he asked the scared women to come out of hiding with their children and to tell him what happened.

Hearing about the massacres and the treatment of the remaining inhabitants by the soldiers, Hajji Mustafa notified the governor and asked him to recall this army unit, and to appoint a different one, headed by a more understanding leader. And as Hajji Mustafa was the governor's friend, his plea was heard.

When the new officer arrived – bearing the name Ibrahim – the inhabitants felt that he was a good person. Speaking with him, Hajji Mustafa decried the ordeal that the villagers had to endure, stressing their good characters and peaceful stance towards others, irrespective of their religion, of which he himself was an example. Those few that survived, he stressed, are exhausted in the extreme, had lost most of their families and almost everything they had, and it was hard to count them among the living. They will soon die, if not of hunger then of disease. This thriving village shall become a ghost town [106]. Hearing this, the officer swore that he would defend them and that he would not let the Kurds harm anyone else anymore.

The new officer gathered the remaining villagers to speak with them. He said:

> In order to save you from these Kurds I have prepared the following plan: Each day, twenty of you shall set out for Amida with a load of wheat grain. You shall pretend to be travelling to the mill. Ten people from this group shall remain in the town, and the rest will return to the village. On the following day, you shall proceed in a similar manner. And so forth, until everyone leaves the village.

When ten days had passed the only ones left in the village were elderly women, who finally left escorted by the officer.

After all the village inhabitants successfully made their way to Amida, the officer reported to the governor in Amida. He announced to him:

> You sent me to the village of Qarabash, where I was supposed to protect its inhabitants. All I found there were decaying corpses and but a handful of children and elderly women. If you still wish it so, I shall bring this group to the city and shoot them here, or else we can leave them to their fates, until they die of hunger and diseases in the streets and at the walls. I consider this second solution more reasonable than staining our hands with the blood of people who will die soon, even for lack of care.

The governor consented to the second suggestion. And thus, the inhabitants lost their village, in which Muslims settled very quickly.

A few remarks on the fate of father Behnam, the son of archdeacon Qawme: when in the night he left the village of Qarabash, making his way to Darakli, he met on his way a group of bandits who stopped him and killed him on the spot [107]. His paternal uncle, Father Paul, son to priest Abd al-Ahad, met a similarly tragic fate. Khalil Agha, a known and brutal bandit, killed him after inflicting terrible tortures. {He [Khalil Agha] thought up truly devilish torture methods. He would mount his stone-loaded horse and ordered the victim to walk in front of the horse. During the run, he would hit the person with a whip and aim stones at his head. He would make him tip over so that he would be trampled by the horse, then help him up later to continue walking in front of the horse and repeat target him with the whip and stones. This ordeal lasted until the priest passed on close to the village of Matraniyye and, according to other reports, close to the village of Sharabi. The second report may be closer to the truth, as the executioner lived in the latter village. Other details concerning the death of this priest are as follows. After the first wave of persecutions, a handful of inhabitants returned to their village of Qarabash. A particularly brutal Kurd, referred to as Khalaf Agha, found out about the return of these few. Earlier, this Kurd had left a certain amount of grain to be guarded by the village inhabitants, with a helmet hidden in one of the grain sacks. When he reported in to collect his grain, he found only a few sacks. The rest was stolen in the course of one of the Kurdish raids on the village. The Agha was, however, more concerned with the helmet than he was with the grain. When asked about the helmet, one of the women joked that Father Paul had taken it. Hearing this, the Kurd had a fit of rage and decided to avenge himself on the innocent priest.

Where is heavenly justice? God, did this priest not serve You before Your altar, for You to let him die at the hands of such a barbarian in such a horrible manner? God, You are omniscient. Bestow upon him your favours.}[5]

However, during those few days, the Kurds attacked the village several times. The aim of the attacks was to kidnap as many girls as possible. During the first attack one of the Kurdish beasts started chasing a young woman named Miran. The woman grabbed her infant and set off. However, the attacker caught up with her and impaled her with his *khanjar*. The infant by her side continued to suck the breast of its dying mother. Seeing this scene this officer ordered three local women to bury the mother and to care for the infant child. He was a good man.

Two other Kurds kidnapped two young women, the wedding celebrations of which took place two or three months earlier. Their names were Mariam and Sadye. Each attacker took one of the kidnapped women and forced her to sit on his horse, to gallop away with them. Both women were able to escape from the hands of their kidnappers. Shouting 'In the name of Christ' they jumped off the horses. The bandits stopped and cut off the breasts of these two women, after which they trampled them and impaled them with daggers. But these women did not die. The aforementioned officer

[5] The fragment in curly brackets, in line with the author's indication (page reference on the left margin), is an amendment to the report found on the ultimate page of the manuscript, bearing the number 203.

sent them to a hospital in Amida where they were cared for by a doctor from the United States, named Ward.

This is but a drop in the sea of despair that befell the inhabitants of Qarabash [108].

It was only after the military activities subsided, and foremost after Turkey came to the conclusion that it was losing the war on all fronts – a war in course of which it would lose much of the territory it had controlled hitherto – that the Turks began to realise that the extermination of its Christian citizens needed to be halted. A summary report drawn up by someone unknown returned the result that Christian-Muslim Turkey would become a Muslim country; the few Christians to have survived were not able to reinvigorate their minority, even though they obtained permission from the authorities to return to their villages. Sadly, the village of Qarabash was mostly taken over not so much by Kurds as by Muslim Bulgarians resettled there officially by the Turkish authorities. These settlers knew only pillage, which, together with their Kurdish falsity and betrayal, became a new shadow not only for the few original inhabitants of the village but to other Christian villages as well. The basis of unification of the forces of evil of these two clearly differing and, up to that point, distant societies was solely Islam. Organised gangs sowed fear in the entire region: they attacked houses, terrorised citizens, burned crops, devastated fields and vineyards and stole cattle and grain belonging to Christians. Nobody was able to stop them and the authorities looked upon their actions passively. Representatives of the family of Djemal Pasha of Amida enjoyed the worst reputation. Lawlessly they laid claim to the possessions of Assyrian Christians of Qarabash, with the entire village soon becoming their property. In such a situation, the original inhabitants had to finally leave their village, never to return. Such was the fate of many other Assyrian villages as well.

My dear Qarabash! My mother! We shall only return to you in our dreams. Having lost you, scattered, we will probably lose our identity as well![6] [109]

6 The last four Assyrian families left their homes in Qarabash in 1948.

The Village of Ka'biyye

On 1 April 1915 the order of the sultan to confiscate weapons owned by Christian citizens was made public. Accordingly, on 10 April, three officers of the Turkish army set out from Amida to the village of Ka'biyye: Sidqi Pirinjichi, Yihia Yasin [Agha] and Tharwat Osman, with a group of about seventy armed soldiers. They reached the village at 6pm. They surrounded it from all sides to prevent anyone from escaping.

The following day, in the morning, the officers entered the village. They called the village leader, George, and ordered that every man, aged fifteen and above, to be led out of their houses. Additionally, they warned that if they found anyone hiding they would burn down the entire house and have all family members shot.

The village leader had to carry out the order. He took a position in the square, surrounded by the army, and started repeating loudly: 'My dear countrymen, fellow villagers, the authorities demand for every man, aged fifteen and over, to come out from their homes. If they do not submit, they shall die!' Everyone listened, without exception, and exited their homes to move to the village square [110]. The men numbered 152 in total. At this time the officers demanded that the village leader release forty coils of grass to them,[7] in order for the soldiers to bind the gathered men.

With almost the entire male population of the village bound, the officers demanded the collection of all weapons from the homes. Within a few minutes, knives, *khanjars* and scissors formed a pile in front of the officers. However, the authorities were not satisfied with this, accusing the inhabitants of hiding automatic rifles, helmets, cannons and other weaponry. At the same time they warned that if even one item of weaponry was found in any household then they would not shy away from killing all of the inhabitants. Saying this, the officers indicated to the soldiers that they should choose one person from each family to be lashed as a prelude to what might await them. Assurance by the villagers that they

[7] A very compact coil of green grass, one to three metres in length, twisted so that it retains its freshness in a dark room as long as possible. Such coils were used in the winter as 'green' and 'fresh' supplementary animal feed.

did not have anything more that could be considered weapons did not help.

The soldiers turned out to be merciless. They beat the defenseless villagers with uncommon fury. They raised their legs and beat their naked feet with bats, as hard as they could, 200 to 300 times. The squirting blood wet their clothes, covered their faces and flowed on the ground. The pleas and cries of the victims and witnesses to this barbarism brought no help.

Following nine hours of constant beatings, after which almost half of the victims lay on the ground moaning from pain, the officers ordered the soldiers to bring five of the most respected inhabitants forward. These were [111]: *maqdeshyo* Gabriel and Ablahad; the sons of the priest, Ishaiah, Manug and Mahran; sons of Thomas; and Rezqo, son of Ello. They led these condemned men outside of the village and, with everyone watching, took their lives in cold blood.

Afterwards, they caught the provost, who bore the name Moses, and a monk, Father Noah. First, they subjected each of these to the torture of 200 lashes and afterwards they threw them both into a pit filled with thrash and refuse. After their clothes were soaked in the sewage and stench, they were dragged out for further beatings, this time using metal rods. During these tortures all the time they mocked these members of the clergy, saying: 'O you servants of Christ! Day and night you teach of the miracles that your Christ caused, but where is he now? We do not see him being able to help you! Beg him even more loudly. Maybe he will finally listen to you!' The priests' throats were completely dry, so that they could not utter a single word. Blood could be pressed out of their clothes. They looked as if they had emerged from their graves. Didn't Christ also remain silent, when Herod accused him groundlessly?

Around 11pm the officers ordered the women to prepare a tasty and rich dinner for them and the soldiers, whereby each was supposed to get a lamb or a baby goat. That night the villagers slaughtered eighty lambs [112]. While the women were busy preparing dinner for these bloodthirsty creatures, the soldiers played with the virgins, noble daughters of noble families; each would be raped several times with her relatives watching. Wild and angry animals would have not behaved in such a way, and even the devil would be shamed to act like this.

Following the dinner and further appeasement of animal instincts using the terrorised girls, the soldiers, without any remorse and limitations, bound all the males and took them to Amida, placing them in the building called Msafir Khane, meaning House of the Traveller. It was already morning.

Their stay lasted five days, until 15 April, and during this entire time they were subjected to terrible tortures. On that day, the Turks announced that they would lead them out of there to engage them in road construction, where they would crush rocks and stones in quarries. The plan, however, was entirely different; they were driven along a mountain road towards Igil, to a hill overlooking the Euphrates.[8] There they were stripped and shot, with the bodies thrown into the river.

I believe that their souls entered heaven, and on Judgement Day they shall testify on the genocide conducted against them before the [heavenly] tribunal of justice.

On 20 April, at 5pm, the orphaned village of Ka'biyye was attacked in turn by Kurdish gangs from various tribes, murdering the encountered inhabitants and plundering their homes. While the Kurds were engaged with robbing, most villagers managed to escape in the direction of the city of Malo. During the escape, close to fifty people died; the rest made it to the city. The most painful thing is that when the refugees tried to find shelter in the courtyard of the Church of the Holy Mother, Father Bshara did not accept them. He notified the mayor [113] of Amida, whose name was Rashid Pasha. He in turn immediately issued an order to the police to quickly drive the escapees out of the city. The mayor would not hear the arguments of the injured, that they cannot return to their village as the Kurds rampaging it would kill them. The governor assigned to them four soldiers who were supposed to guard them on the way to the village.

The 'protectors', however, did not execute the ordered task. Before the party reached the village, already en route they killed four people.[9] {This tragedy recalls the earlier execution, perpetrated in the same location to which they were making their way.} The villagers started speculating about the ultimate aim of their forced return to the village and the continued presence

8 Rather, the Tigris.

9 This tragedy recalls the earlier execution, perpetrated in the same location to which they were making their way.

of these soldiers. They did not exclude the possibility of being forced soon into a column that was supposed to share the fate of the many previous caravans. The decimated families elected not to live in their own homes but chose to stay together, as close as possible. Everyone fit into five neighbouring households. They feared being separated – Kurds waited for them outside and they had also lost their trust in the soldiers. If they were to perish, they preferred to die together. Concerned by this situation, the deacon Quriaqos, teacher of children at the village school, wandered the narrow streets of the village, humming religious songs interspersed with words to soothe, and stories of martyrs of the faith, in order to accept the impending fate with dignity. A sad atmosphere persisted: fathers hugged their sons, mothers kissed their daughters, as if they were to soon part ways forever.

Before the outbreak of the storm of persecution, the village counted 165 flourishing households and had fertile soil.

On 30 May the governor of Amida sent his deputy to the village, Shakir Bey, leaving it up to him to treat the inhabitants in any way he wanted. The latter, Cherkess by birth, organised fifty of the greatest Kurdish bandits from the tribe of 'Amarke, who were called Ramma. They were ruthless [114]. At 8pm they surrounded the village and then entered it. First, they rounded up all the men, bound them and punctured their bodies with hot iron rods, telling them to collect all the money they had. Within five hours, the terrorists took in a total of 1,500 gold dinars. Following this, they started abusing the women and children, dealing with them worse than hungry jungle beasts. This lasted until morning.

At eight in the morning they led all the men along the road towards the village of Dērīk.[10] Having passed the bridge on the Tigris and having reached the hill called Kurd Kaya (Wolf Cave), they stopped close to a water source named Kaniyya Bazergane (Trader or Caravan Pond), where they murdered everybody. When night fell they burned the bodies. Among the victims of this fanaticism were the mentioned deacon Quriaqos, who was uninterrupted in strengthening the villagers' spirits, as he knew that they would all soon turn into lanterns of the faith. The glowing bodies continued to light the night until morning.

[10] Dērīk is about twenty-five kilometres to the west of Mardin.

Of the living, only widows and half-orphaned children remained in the village. Despite this, the village was attacked by Kurds every now and then, in order to take this or that chosen woman to a harem. The women could not stand this situation any longer and attempted to leave their households at any cost. This was difficult, however, as the Kurds had seized the neighbouring Assyrian villages through which they needed to pass. The only effective method was to bribe the Muslim women, not with money, which the villagers did not have any more, but with home equipment and jewellery. As a result, the sole people to remain in the village [115] were the oldest women very close to death. The remainder died or fled to Amida.

The person responsible for the party of reapers who collected wheat from the fields belonging to the village of Kaʿbiyye, located to the east of the village, found out somehow that there were still live survivors from this village in Amida. He travelled to the city, summoned these people and encouraged them to return to their homes and fields, promising that if they were Assyrian the governor would consent to give them guarantees that nobody shall harm them anymore. He indicated as well that a precise list of all people would need to be drawn up so that the governor would know what help would they need upon their return. At the same time he warned that persons who did not register would lose their right to return and that nobody would help them. It is not difficult to wonder why these poor people fell for such a ruse again; will the drowning not try to grab on to anything to save themselves?! The prospect of return to their own village was the most logical solution for these beggars.

On 12 September some of those surviving, 550 people in total, returned to the village of Kaʿbiyye. As night fell a group of military police approached the village, composed of about a hundred Cherkess and about fifty Turkish soldiers under the leadership of Khalil Chalabi. This Chalabi and his ancestors had been, for a long time, a nuisance to the village inhabitants. He often threatened that this wonderful land would at some point belong to his family. In the morning they ordered the inhabitants to gather and they told them they needed to return to the city as the governor had overturned his decision. Apparently, he wanted to settle Muslims expelled from Bulgaria in this village.

The scared inhabitants were rounded up in a fenced area. Each of them was given a loaf of bread, after which they were made to run to the city. When the party crossed the river [Tigris] they were stopped and told [116] that they are to choose the road to Mardin. Hearing the name of Mardin, the inhabitants realised that they are being led to death. Suddenly one brave villager ran forward and stood still in an instant. His name was Daniel, and he had six sons, the oldest being fifteen. Before the massacres began, his family numbered thirty people. He and his sons were the only ones remaining. The rest had perished. He called to his fellow villagers in a strong voice: 'Brothers and sisters, today is a day of great joy for us. Eternal life stands before us. Let us all sing *hallelujah* to the Lord!' Suddenly, a choir of voices broke out, mixed with cries.

The column made its way towards the village of Dērīk. When it reached the already mentioned hill of Kurd Kaya, from its eastern side, close to the water source named Kaniyye Malo, a pause to rest was announced. The women were permitted to breastfeed their infant children and everyone was told to drink the water, as they would not find any more water on the way.

After the people drank, the escort told the men and boys to separate from the rest, whereafter they opened fire on them with machine guns. They fell to the ground like lambs, one upon another. Following this massacre, the soldiers signalled the Kurds waiting around to commence their deeds. Wielding any available tools of death they had – knives, swords, bats, sickles, *khanjars*, pickaxes and hoes – the Kurds commenced like beasts [117] first to finish the dying, crush skulls, cut off hands and legs, gouge out eyes and hack the bodies as one usually proceeds in a slaughterhouse with slaughtered animals. These barbaric scenes played out before the eyes of mothers, wives and daughters of the victims. In the same way the women and girls were then killed, only after being raped.

No pen may describe our pain and the bestiality of the enemies of humanity living among us. The milk of mothers mixes in the mouths of infants with blood. Infant children are torn away from their mothers' breasts and killed. Women are raped before everyone's eyes and nobody defends them, nobody feels for them. O earth, take these victims in, bury them! And you, o sun, set, eclipse so that darkness covers what we call intimacy . . .

The desecrated bodies of several hundred people, scattered across a small area, were seen by an accidental traveller – a trader by the name of Abdalla[11] of Mosul. Three days after the massacre, he travelled through this area to have a drink and to quench his horses' thirst. In disbelief, he looked upon the pile of human bodies and the corpses lying here and there. He heard the voice of a woman, calling for help and asking for water to drink. This good man showed mercy and gave the woman some water. When he noticed that she was naked and wounded, he covered her, dragged her to the water source and cleaned her wounds. Afterwards, he asked her, why so many people were massacred, among them so many children, women and the elderly, and whether any more people were alive here. The woman told him everything, and said that over two days Kurds came here to kill the dying, burning some of them. They never found her, though; she was buried under two corpses. And until the day before, she heard the cries and moans of a few children and infants, but she could not get up to help them. Today they cannot be heard any more. When this good man started searching, he encountered two other women who were still alive, and they were naked, as well as three boys aged between five and eight. He helped them climb onto horses and took them to the monastery of Za'farān. He knew the monastery well; he had stayed and slept there on many occasions.

The two mentioned women died two days later.

From the Assyrian village of Ka'biyye, which numbered 1,650 people, only three boys survived [118].

O reader, do not blame time for these tragedies; life is full of contradictions. And do not judge the criminals and savages harshly; they are used to spilling the blood of innocents belonging to a different nation and a different religion. They received hate for others with their mother's milk, it is a piece of their blood and their minds. Let us turn our sorrow and our complaints to the tribunal of justice, because this mass of refugees from Ka'biyye was not able to enter the church. Perhaps maybe then these people would have survived? And because the governor had condemned them to death, carefully preparing their demise, the effects of which they could not foresee. They thought the governor, as a human being, was driven by good intentions.

[11] The author of the diary does not indicate whether this Abdalla was Christian or Muslim. Christians also bear this name; however, it is more often encountered among Muslims.

O God, we resort to your judgement, and await your providence [119].

The Village of Qatrabel

On the first day of April [1915], the mentioned officer [Tharwat] Osman made his way to the village of Qatrabel, leading fifty armed soldiers. Upon arrival at the village, the leader, named Khashsho Baran, was called and told that the unit was sent by the governor to collect the weapons at the disposal of the villagers. The village leader replied then: ‘Everybody knows that nobody from our village ever had any weapons, and that they have none. If you do not believe this, you may search house after house.’ The officer indicated to the soldiers that they are to begin their search. The inhabitants were unlucky in that a hunting rifle was found in one of the houses, of which the village leader knew nothing. The officer became furious. He arrested the village leader and the four most respected men of the village and sent them to the military tribunal in the city of Kartbart.

On 10 April,a different officer, Yihia Yasin [Agha] arrived at the village, leading fifty soldiers. They arrested twenty-three further men, took them, bound, to Amida and placed them at the Msafir Khane [120] in order to release them in the night and make them run the road towards the village of Charurki, following four days of torture. There they were taken to a hill named Bdale-Sor, meaning ‘red hill’, stripped and shot them.

The women and children remaining in the village, having heard of what happened to their relatives, crossed the River Tigris and fled for Amida. In this way, they saved themselves [121].

The Village of Charukhiyye

The village of Charukhiyye was densely populated by Assyrians, some of whom belonged to Chaldeans [Uniate]. It lies on the shores of the River Tigris, about eight kilometres to the south of Amida.

On 2 June, at 8pm, the mentioned officer Yihia Yasin [Agha] appeared here, leading fifty soldiers. He surrounded the village from all sides so that nobody would be able to leave. At dawn, the soldiers entered the village and arrested all men, thirty-five persons in total. There were no male youths in the village; they were drafted into the army earlier, to be sent to war. The arrested were told that they would be taken to work in road construction. Priest Thomas was also arrested and treated very badly; a bell was hung from his neck, one like those worn by rams in a herd of sheep, and a loop of rope was hung from his neck, following which he was bent over and his back was sat on, in a manner one sits on an animal.

The arrested were made to run the road towards Havarchay, and when the group reached the village of Gulle they were stripped and ordered to form rows of five people. The soldiers wanted to check, whether the bullets fired from guns would be able to penetrate through five bodies [122]. In this way, the men were killed, with the soldiers watching them suffer and die for an hour. After the effectiveness of shots was tested, the fallen were picked up from the ground; suddenly one of those lying on the ground rose to his feet. His name was Peter Mushe and he was a priest. As it turned out, he was not hit. He called: 'I am still alive. Please, kill me as you have killed my colleagues.' However, the soldiers were of the opinion that since he did not die, it meant that it wasn't his time yet. They said to him: 'Accept Islam, and you shall be spared.'[12] He declined sharply: 'My Lord God, protect me from betraying the Christian faith. I wish to join my colleagues. They are waiting for me to celebrate a funeral mass for them. Take my life so I can join them.' Seeing this undaunted attitude of the priest, the soldiers shot him.

The orphaned women and children remaining in the village fled for Amida to the Chaldean [Unitarian] church. Salomon, the Chaldean bishop, accepted the refugees and gave them shelter. This commendable attitude of the bishop, full of kindness, brought him great respect. People still remember him with gratitude. May God bless him with love so that he eternally enjoys divine light and for a stream of grace to shine on his grave [123].

The Village of Saʿdiyye Bar-Ave

We were told about what happened in this village by one of the soldiers. He reported:

[12] The author uses the verb *hagar*, meaning *join the people of Hagar*, wife to Abraham, the mother of Ishmael, from whom, according to Muslim tradition, stems the tribe of Mohammed, the founder of Islam.

When the persecution of Christians began, I was accompanying my commander in the village of Taffe, subordinate to the village of [Sa'diyye] Bar-Ave. One day, the *qaymaqam* (sub-governor) of the Al-Madine province turned up at the village, accompanied by about seventy Assyrians originating from Bsheriyye. When they reached the village of Taffe, they noticed beside it a tunnel at the riverside. He paused and ordered the soldiers and the Kurds to move the Christians to this tunnel and kill them, not with gun shots but using swords, pickaxes, shovels, axes and other tools. One of those murdered, even after his head was severed, continued to speak for about ten minutes. He prayed and kept repeating the name of Christ.

Following the murder of this group of hostages, the same *qaymaqam* came to my commander, being from the locality of Pal, and chastised him for not having yet killed the Christians living in his territory.

When the Christians heard this statement, they were convinced that their end would arrive soon. They shared their fears with the [Assyrian] priest of the village of Sa'diyye, David. At this time, the village had no Armenian priest; two months earlier he was transferred to a different locality. The priest gathered the village inhabitants, Assyrians and Armenians, in the church [124]. After the mass, he preached to strengthen and embolden the faithful. Everyone accepted the Holy Communion and left.

We entered the village and commenced arresting the inhabitants. However, we were not able to find Father David or any one of the twelve other men we were searching for. Following our orders, we shot all the inhabitants.

As it turned out, the priest and those twelve hid in a tunnel eroded by the water, where the small river running through the town of Shauro would flow into the Tigris. They stayed there for eight days. A good Muslim would deliver them food every day in secret. When, on the ninth day, this Muslim was walking along the road with bread and food, another Muslim, with whom he was acquainted, noticed him; he knew that none of his relatives worked in the vicinity. The latter notified us and ensured us that there must be some Christians there, and indicated to us the way to the hiding place.

We started watching the food supplier and we followed him to that tunnel. We heard him calling on the priest to pick up the food.

After they had eaten their meal and after that Muslim had left, we attacked this shelter, arrested the priest and his compatriots, bound them and led them to the village of Taffe. There we subjected them, in particular the priest, to various tortures. During their ordeal, one of them was close to breaking, even more so as we assured him that if he renounced Christ, we would stop torturing him and we would spare his life. Seeing this, the priest, himself being tortured horrendously, called out:

'Don't do it!'

He died in a moment [125].

The priest had a small box in his pocket. When it fell out, he picked it up and held it tightly. Despite our efforts, using all kinds of tools to recover this box from him, we could not pry his fingers apart. But when we paused, exhausted, he opened the box instantly, took something out of it, and swallowed it,[13] whereafter he tossed us the empty box, saying:

'There. Now you can have it!'

A second man from the dozen died from the torture. We took the remainder, together with the priest, to a spot close to the water, and shot them all there. We used firearms because we were tired of thinking up ever newer ways of torture, as it would have taken too long.

Watching the priest, I would never have supposed that a man can endure so much pain. He was a true hero; he mocked us, he laughed at the methods of inflicting pain that we used, he took them all lightly, and we thought he would cry, moan, beg for mercy. However, not once did he give us any sign of satisfaction that he was feeling any pain. It was extraordinary. [126]

The Extermination of Christians in the Villages of the Havarchay Region, Also Called Chamme Havar, and in the Anbarchay Region

On 3 May [1915] Shakir Bey, advisor to the governor, along with an officer from Ramma, named 'Amarke, moved towards the Christian villages; they were accompanied by 150 armed men; half of them were regular army, with the rest made up of Kurds from the various villages in Ramma. In the Havarchay region, the following Christian villages could be found: Sileme,

[13] Without any doubt, the priest had a consecrated host in the box. Knowing what might happen to him, he wished for it to be his final meal before death.

Qarte, Der-Bashur, Maqsi-Oghli, Zorava, Havar-Dahle and Havarkhase. All men from these villages were led to the village of Chanaqchi.

The men were gathered at one spot and supplemented by all the Christian men from this village [of Chanaqchi]. Following this, the entire column was sent to a valley near the village of Hawardahle. There they were stripped, bound and opened fire on. All perished. They were 164 people in total. One needs to add that the Christians from this neighbourhood were known for their bravery, virtue, prudence and wealth.

Following the massacre, the soldiers made their way to two other Assyrian villages, Sirme and Gozli, and murdered all the men they met there [127]. The women and children, in turn, who did not manage to flee to Amida on time, were taken by the Kurds. Only those were spared that accepted Islam. The rest were shot.

On 7 May Yihia Yasin [Agha], leading fifty soldiers and supported by twenty known Kurdish bandits armed to the teeth, originating from a village owned by Qasim Bey, set off for the Anbarchay region, specifically for the villages of Baghjachik, Pozpenar, Qoshk, Abbase and Chirnak. They gathered all the Christian males and took them to the village of Malla-Chabre. The column was also joined by men stemming from this Kurdish-Assyrian village, despite the fact that hitherto no conflicts arose in it and the Christians worked years and years for this Qasim Bey and considered him a friend. The latter and his gang started first offending the Christians and then they tortured them. In the end, the victims (114 people in total) were led to a valley called Dera-Chiyane on the eastern side of the village, where they were all shot.

Qasim Bey started treating the mothers, wives and children of the murdered as if they were slaves; they worked on the harvest and collected wheat for him from fields that hitherto were their property. Following the harvest, which took three months [128], Qasim Bey suggested to these people that they convert to Islam. Those that broke down and accepted the offer were spared. The remainder was killed. This was the payment for their hard work.

Many villages around Amida, both the larger ones, such as Kadi Chirnak, Ragle, in which the population was Muslim in the majority, as well as the smaller ones, such as Aynshah, Telhas, Qabaskal, where only Christians lived, turned into purely Muslim villages. Some of the Christian inhabitants were exterminated and the surviving males, who were able to bear arms or work, were drafted into the army or employed in national road construction. None of them returned home. Their families, who in time managed to find shelter in Amida, received no news from them, but they live in the hope that at least some of them had survived, and expect their return [129].

9

EXTERMINATION OF CHRISTIANS IN THE VILLAGES OF THE DISTRICT OF MARDIN IN 1914[1]

{The City of Mardin}

{Mardin is a big and densely populated city. It is inhabited by about 20,000 Assyrian and Armenian Christians, who belong to various churches: Orthodox Church, the Unitarian Church and the Protestant Church, with Syrian Orthodox Church members making up the majority of the population. The city lies on the southern slope of a tall mountain and its houses are arranged in a stair-like form. There is a fortress on the top of the mountain, to which a steep and difficult road leads. It used to be called the Mother of Fortresses and the Battle Centre. In this respect, nothing in

[1] Given the events described, the author probably means 1915. (Gaunt, D., *Massacres*, pp. 168–75, 237, 245, 449, 475; Travis, H., 'Native Christians Massacred', pp. 332–6). The city of Mardin and the surrounding villages may have had an Assyro-Chaldean population of about 47,000 (Gaunt, D., *Massacres*, pp. 424, 435; U.K. National Archives, F.O. 839/23, Eastern Conference Lausanne, Autonomy for Assyrian Christians [Claims of Assyro-Chaldeans]; U.K. National Archives, F.O. 839/23 82893, 87993 & Minute No. 639, Eastern Conference Lausanne, Autonomy for Assyrian Christians, Covering Letter from General Agha Petros, Commander-in-Chief, of the Assyro-Chaldean Forces, to Marquis Curzon of Kendleston, Secretary of State for Foreign Affairs [etc.], 21 December 1922).

the entire Gozarto region can match it. This is why every ruler, in every time period, tried to conquer it. Other than most fortresses, even the strongest ones, from which on many an occasions city names were derived, in the case of Mardin, the name of the city itself means 'fortress' in Assyrian. Inside the fortress, subsequent rulers erected strong castles and vast buildings, drilled wells to reach water and planted various trees in the courtyard so that they could survive through long sieges by enemies. Mardin towers over such ancient localities as Dara, Nisibis, Sinjar, Danisor, Kefrtuth, Hobur, Rish 'Ayna and others in the region.

The inhabitants of Mardin took on Christianity through the missionaries Thaddeus and his student, Aggai, halfway through the second century. It is thus one of the first Christian cities. A testimony to this are old churches and monasteries such as the church of St Shmouni and the monastery of St Michael, located to the north of the town, as well as the grand church of the Forty Martyrs, turned by Muslims into a mosque, which they named the Sohdo Mosque,[2] as Michael the Syrian and the Edessian as well as Bar Hebraeus write in their chronicles. However, it is painful that we know nothing about our ancient Christian fathers, particularly from the first three centuries. The reasons for this are repeating wars and disquiet, pogroms and persecution experienced [by the inhabitants]. Their writings, and knowledge about them, are gone}.[3]

What I am writing here is the description of but a drop in the sea of blood spilled in the Christian villages. The bestial acts of barbarians cannot be fathomed or imagined by any mind. If they were to be described in detail one would need to mobilise a group of people and the notes would fill volumes upon volumes. I shall present only a small sample from a great number of animated descriptions.

At the Za'farān Monastery

{The monastery of Za'farān is one of our oldest monasteries – since the twelfth century it has been the seat of the Orthodox patriarch. It houses a beautiful church, built in the form of a cross, with a length of seventeen metres and a

[2] *Sohdo* means 'martyr'.

[3] This text in curly brackets was placed on pages 150 and 151 of the manuscript.

width of twelve metres. In the year 1696 the altar was adorned by inscriptions [using the *estrangelo* script[4]] from chapter sixteen of the Gospel of Matthew, which speaks of Peter as the first of the Apostles. Around the monastery, from the eastern side, there are numerous hermitages and hermit cells, as well as chapels, churches and small monasteries, such as the d-Neṭfo[5] monastery of the Holy Mother, the monasteries of St Yaʿqūb, St ʿAzazel, St Behnam and other saints.[6] The monastery is surrounded by fields, vineyards and gardens of fig trees, almond, nuts, peaches, apples and punic, as well as olive tree forests}.[7]

The monastery of Zaʿfarān[8] is located at a distance of eight kilometres to the east of Mardin. In the years of the genocide it was home to thousands of people: men, women and children who survived the massacres of the Christian inhabitants of the immediate vicinity. Most came from the villages located not far from the monastery. These were Ḥesnō d-Attō, Bnēbīl, Bkhere and others. The monks of the d-Netfo monastery of the Holy Mother and of the monastery of St Yaʿqūb, both located on the mountain's eastern slope, also sheltered in the Zaʿfarān monastery. These people could not fathom the events that transpired so suddenly. They were very sad, they wept over the members of the families that were murdered and the youths forcibly drafted into the army, the fate of whom, and the question whether they were still alive, were unknowns.

4 *Estrangelo* is the oldest script used for writing or printing Syriac, being a transitional stadium between cuneiform script and writing using letters. It is decorative. It was used to write down the first copies of the Bible (the Gospel), and from here – as is believed – stems its name. It was used as a template for the first Kufic script of Arabic (from the city of Kufa in Iraq), with which the first copies of the Qur'ān were written down. After the introduction of a different letter style – that is *serto* (used by Western Assyrians) – *estrangelo* almost fell out of use, but it was reborn during the late Middle Ages. It is currently available in the newer versions of Microsoft Word.

5 The name comes from the verb *nṭāf* ('to drip, to condense'); water kept condensing and dripping from the rock ceiling of the monastery, filling a container cut out in the rock bottom of the room with cold and uncommonly pure water.

6 On this mountain, there were located seven small monasteries cut in rock. All are presently in a state of ruin. The remaining ones were dedicated to St Theodor, St Stephen and St Joseph.

7 The fragment in curly brackets was moved from pages 133 (final five lines) and 134 (first nine lines) of the manuscript.

8 The monastery is also dedicated to St Ananias.

Both the hosts of the monastery, as well as those residing in it, lived in fear and uncertainty and asked themselves the question: 'When are the Kurds planning to attack the monastery and start killing?' Such a bleak scenario came about on 4 July [1914], on Monday morning; the barbarians among Muslims surrounded the monastery [130] from the southeast, where the Gurna water source is located, as well as from the northern side, where the chapel of the Holy Mother is found. Following this, [army] units arrived, taking the fields from the northern side, all the way to the chapel of the Holy Mother. Some of them forcibly entered the orchard named Ferdayso,[9] just a step away from the monastery.

The situation of those residing in the monastery became difficult. When they saw the armed gangs around the monastery, some climbed onto the roof and started shooting, others exited through the gate to reinforce the defending guards, however the majority gathered in the church and chapels and prayed beggingly to the one and only God that he should not let the barbarians conquer what was one of the last fortresses. The kneeling children cried and repeated loudly: 'Our Lord, have mercy and grace us'.

Those who stood guard in the nearby village of Ḥesnō d-Attō, when they saw the masses of attacking Kurds, started blowing their horns to give a sign to the leaders in Mardin. This is because it was agreed that in the case the monastery is attacked the military stationed in Mardin would come to its aid.

At midday a unit of fifty soldiers arrived at the monastery. From the very beginning it was clear that they had bad intentions; their behaviour towards Christians living in the villages en route to the monastery, through which the soldiers would pass, was bad. As it turned out, the Kurds had earlier agreed upon their attack on the monastery with the head of this [army] unit, who bore the name Farhan. The deal between them stated that the Kurds would pay him 200 dinars in gold in exchange for the fact that, in the case of an alert, his unit would be the first to arrive and would not interfere with the Kurds in conquering the monastery, plundering its property and killing the people inside [131]. When the soldiers attempted to enter the monastery, the guards did not let them do so. Similarly, a part of those inside the monastery were against letting them enter. They feared that they might live the same fate as

[9] This is probably a word of Persian origin, meaning 'garden of paradise'.

the inhabitants of the village of Kasre. However, Bishop Elias Halluli, residing at the monastery, as well as others, agreed to open the gate. Before the soldiers were able to do anything evil, a different military unit arrived from Mardin, numbering 100 men, who were better armed. This unit was sent by the mayor of Mardin following a plea by Kirill Givargis, the Assyrian bishop residing in the town. Having entered the monastery they drove the traitors and plotters headed by Farhan out, which was greeted by the inhabitants with relief. When the soldiers from the new unit climbed onto the roof and saw the masses of barbarians surrounding the site the commander became very upset and ordered his soldiers to open machine gun fire on them. The Kurds left in haste, and their plot, God be thanked, could not be executed.

In gratitude for the soldiers' attitude the prior ordered ten lambs to be slain in order to prepare food. The soldiers remained at the monastery for two days. Considering the fact that their uniforms might have not been washed for a long while the nuns washed them and handed out fresh clothes to some. The commander, in turn, was rewarded with twenty gold liras, which he divided among his soldiers. Before departing, the commander left behind ten soldiers to guard the monastery [132]. They remained there for twenty days, cared for by the inhabitants.

It is true that everyone who was able to find shelter in the monastery survived. It is also true that, with time, the food reserves of the monastery grew thinner; everything that the refugees took with them, as well as everything that was originally found at the monastery, ran out. The lack of food became a great problem and caused the people trouble. The monastery was under constant watch by the Kurds, who also roamed the roads. Nobody had the courage to venture outside of the monastery to arrange deliveries of food. The barbarians would not shy away from killing anyone they met on the road.

These conditions caused the residents of the monastery to start dying of hunger or falling sick and not being able to move. The people were not able to care for themselves or for their surroundings; there was more and more grime and the foul stench got worse and worse. Continued stay at the monastery would mean death from starvation. Some were able to find shelter in Mardin, others were taken in by Arab Bedouins [133].

At this time, the following resided at the monastery: Patriarch Ighnāṭiyyos Abed Mshiho II, wrongly deposed by the Holy Synod, who, having been pardoned, found his way back to his holy nest and into the arms of his mother,[10] as well as Bishop Ivannis Elias Halluli, the monastery bishop of St Malke, Severius Samuel, eight priest monks, twelve novice monks, forty seminarians as well as survivors from the villages Ḥesnō d-Attō, Bnēbīl and Bkhere and individual people from such villages as Dara, Firan, Bafawa, Ma'esrōtō and others. The defenders of the monastery in turn came from the village of Bnēbīl [134]. They were characterised by bravery, vigilance and devotion; many owe them for sacrificing their lives. They guarded the monastery day and night and, with the arrival of the soldiers, they mixed in with the crowd. They feared arrest and being drafted into the army, so much so that they carried weapons, which was strictly forbidden for Christians to do [135].

The Village of Bna Bil (Bnēbīl)

Bnēbīl[11] is a large village, located about fifteen kilometres from Mardin to the east and approximately ten kilometres to the northeast from the Za'farān monastery, inhabited by about 150 Assyrian families, known for their bravery, boldness and valour. It hosts two churches: one dedicated to St Quriaqos, another to St Shmouni, where two priests, Joseph and Thomas, serve. The latter died last year.[12]

On 9 June the village was attacked by about 5,000 wild Kurds from the surrounding villages, among them women. At that time, the village was guarded by ten soldiers, who did not want to aid the inhabitants and who fled. Another sorrowful thing is that the soldiers were commanded by Khalil Ghazale, whom the villagers considered a friend and who always declared that he would defend them.

When the villagers noticed that the guards let the Kurds through without firing a single shot, and when the latter started plundering houses and food stores, they mobilised to defend their name and dignity. In street combat they were crowned with a crushing victory and they forced the attackers and robbers to flee in fear and to leave the village area, chasing them all the way to its borders.

10 The author means back to the (mother) church.

11 The author makes use of three different versions of the village name.

12 The author means in the year 1913.

However, following this success, the traitor Khalil Ghazale [136] brought with him a large army unit, saying that he will now be able to stand up to the Kurds if they should wish to gather their forces to attack the village again. The inhabitants believed him and handed over their weapons, the possession of which was forbidden to them as Christians. The inhabitants met the commander and the soldiers in the village gardens. After the arms were handed over, the army started treacherously shooting at the gathered villagers. Six people were killed.

I fail to understand how the inhabitants could let themselves be cheated by Khalil Ghazale again, after he had already betrayed them once. They had had their experience with people who do not keep their word, who do not stay loyal and who do not respect their dignity and cannot be trusted. This cost them a lot.[13]

[13] A. N. Andrus wrote: 'I saw the Koords [sic] coming on to attack the village and gave the alarm. It was daylight. The villagers assembled and put themselves under my leadership, as I knew Koordish tactics, having lived so much among them. Putting myself at the head of the villagers, we suddenly charged and scattered the Koords. This gave time for the villagers to gather up what they could and seek safety for their families and themselves by fleeing to Deir Zaofaran and Mardin. (Most of the Protestant families came to Mardin and filled up our chapel and the schoolrooms above it.) I then advised the leading men not to accept the invitation of the soldiers, who nominally were sent to protect the village from just such attacks, to eat breakfast with them, as I distrusted them, since they had not helped us to drive the Koords off. They did not take my advice, which I emphasised, by leaving the village with what of my household goods I could take with me (my wife and children I had previously sent on to Mardin foreseeing trouble). In self-confidence, they prepared food for the soldiers and sat down to partake of it with them. When the soldiers finished eating, they turned on their hosts and shot them down. The Koords, learning what had happened, returned and helped the soldiers in plundering the village. The village was all Christian, some 50 houses.' Barton, J. L., *Turkish Atrocities – Statements of American Missionaries on the Destruction of Christian Communities in Ottoman Turkey, 1915–1917*, p. 100. In the introduction to the book, from which the quote stems, A .N. Andrus writes that the author of the report is a preacher by the name of Garabed Laḥdō, whom he took in as an orphaned child following the massacres of 1895. It is curious that the name of the village is found in this report written as Bendbeel. A few words about Alpheus N. Andrus: he was an educated member of the clergy and a missionary of the American Board of Commissions for Foreign Missions, beginning operations in Mardin in 1868. He knew oriental languages and remained at his work until the end of World War I, when, together with his co-worker and medical doctor named Thom, they were forced by Turkish authorities to move to Sivas. Following Thom's death of typhus, A. N. Andrus moved to Constantinople. At this time his wife, remaining in Mardin, died. He

When the inhabitants were left unarmed and when they were constantly attacked by Kurds they decided to leave their beautiful and rich village and make their way to the monastery of Za'farān. Their stay at the monastery lasted three months and they lived off the modest resources they had taken along with them. After this time, they returned to their village[14] [137].

The Village of Dara

Dara is an ancient locality, located on a plain extending between the cities of Nisibis[15] and Amida.[16] At the beginning of June, before the *jihad* against Christians was proclaimed, the village leader, together with the local Muslim Sheikh and Ahmad Khalil, turned to the Christians and specifically to twenty-five young men, for them to come to a meeting. They were told that by order of the state they were to travel to the city[17] to be drafted into the army. This was a tactical move, as these people had prepared a devious plot and wanted to get rid of the Christians. Together with other Muslims they took these males to a place where a deep well was constructed, not far from the village, about a half hour's walk away; there, they shot all of them and threw the bodies into the well. Together with the men a Christian woman that would not submit was also killed.

Only one person from this group managed to save himself; he escaped, naked, to the village of Bkhere and he told the story about what happened. The widows remaining in the village of Dara as well as their daughters refuse to marry Muslims even today.

Three months after the massacre of these men, a woman named Sayde, together with her eight-year-old son, managed to escape from the village and hid in the monastery of Za'farān. She said that the herd of 53 goats belonging

returned to the United States, encouraged by the U.S. ambassador in Constantinople, following the severance of diplomatic relations between the United States and Turkey in 1917. Ibid., p. 96.

14 The inhabitants of Bnēbīl, traditionally, had the privilege of carrying the patriarch sitting in an armchair to the altar and a selected group of men would protect him during every trip.

15 Nisibis, today Nusaybin, is a city in southeastern Turkey close to the Syrian border.

16 Today it is a city in northeastern Syria, to the west of Qamishli. Kurds are the majority of the population; however, many Assyrians continue to live there and they were able to retain one of their churches.

17 Most probably to Nisibis.

to her was left with the village leader of Amida named Farhan and that she would like to recover them and transfer them to the monastery. Hearing this, the church patriarch Elias III Shakir turned to the authorities for aid in recovering the goats. Soldiers were sent to the village leader and they were able to recover all the animals.

Following a year spent at the monastery Sayde wanted to visit her village. She took her son with her and left. There, she was killed by the same Kurd from whom she had escaped [138].

The Village of Ma'sarte[18]

On 2 June two known avengers and tyrants, Hussein and Shendy, living in this village attacked their Christian neighbours, according to a plan prepared earlier concerning the extermination of these people that had been agreed upon with influential Muslims of Mardin bearing the names Khider Chalabi, Mahmad Ali Chalabi and Shawkat Milliyye. In order to prepare the extermination plan very carefully, the aforementioned tyrants travelled to Mardin.

After they returned they called a meeting in the evening, to which they invited all thirty Christian farmers. They announced that they had received from the leaders of Mardin the task of protecting Christians, as they were under threat, whereafter they guided everybody to the spot where they were supposed to take shelter in case of a sudden attack. There, close to a well, they killed all of them.

On the way to that spot a few men left this group. When they heard what happened to their countrymen they fled the village. Two were successful in making their way to the monastery of Za'farān. Two others tried to escape to the [Assyrian] village of Bafawa, but they were caught on the road and murdered. It needs to be stressed that certain Muslim women, against the will of their husbands, provided shelter to Christian women and their children and afterwards secretly and gradually smuggled three or four women each day to Mardin, to the Church of Forty Martyrs [139]. Kirill Givargis, the patriarch's emissary residing there, granted shelter to the refugees and rewarded the

[18] This village was about twenty kilometres to the southeast of Mardin, on the road to Midyat (Turkish, Omerli).

brave Muslim women for their attitudes and the risk they took on, and asked them to try to save all the women and children remaining there and to bring them to the church [140].

The Village of Bafawa

On 4 June Turkish soldiers arrived at the village of Bafawa and started looting houses and taking what they pleased. After a while they were joined by Kurds, with whom the soldiers shared the bounty, after which they commenced jointly murdering the villagers. The village priest became a symbol of the extermination. He was burned alive.

Seeing the burning priest, Joseph, son to George, the village leader, grabbed an automatic rifle and wanted to shoot the executioners. However, his father, famous in the region as a man of a big and kind heart, did not let his son shoot, saying: 'Do not stain your soul and honour with blood!' The son asked the father again: 'Father, please let me kill these few bandits, as they are certain to kill us anyway!' However the father declined. In light of such an attitude from his father the son released the rifle, took the Gospel in his hand and started reading from it. Seeing this, the Kurds grabbed the village leader and threw him into the fire, whereupon they took the Gospel from the son, threw it into the fire as well, and beheaded him with a sword.

Only eight Assyrians managed to flee from the village of Bafawa. Two fled in the direction of the village of Rasin, but they were murdered by Kurds; four reached the village of Bnēbīl and the remaining two hid in the monastery of Za'farān, which they reached after eight days. The rest of the villagers was led out and taken to the city of Shauro [141].

The Village of Bkhere

The village of Bkhere belongs to the monastery of Za'farān. When the information on the preparation of the extermination of Christians spread the monastery's prior, together with the monastery's property representative, travelled to the Ottoman leader Khalil Ghazale with the plea to spare this village. The leader was a despot with a range of methods to exercise his powers, and also a clear enemy of Christians. The prior even suggested that the church was prepared to make attempts to obtain consent of the state authorities to employ guards to watch the village and its inhabitants. Khalil assured the church, however, that this was not necessary and swore that he was able to take care of this himself.

This despicable and disloyal man proceeded entirely differently. After attacking the village of Bnēbīl, with disastrous effects for its inhabitants, he turned against the village of Bkhere, the inhabitants of which he had promised to protect. This village was, at that time, also home to several people from Bnēbīl. They thought they would be safe there. In order not to raise any suspicions, and in order to win over the sympathy of the inhabitants, he decided to invite all men and women to a dinner he had prepared for them. After the dinner he announced that he was planning to make his way to the monastery of Zaʿfarān together with them, in order to convince the prior that everything is under control and that the inhabitants are satisfied and safe.

The column made its way to the monastery along a road running through the village of Khurmiyye. When it was half way, close to the water source called Bir Mammo, Khalil started shooting down the men. He killed all fifteen. Afterwards he and his men gathered brush and wood and burned the bodies of the murdered. He took their wives for himself. However, before they departed with him, three jumped into the well. They preferred to die this way than live like slaves for the killer of their husbands.

The majority of the women he had enslaved made their way to the monastery later, each of them at a different point in time and using a different route. One of them, of exquisite beauty [142], did not manage to take along her little child. She left it behind and escaped to the monastery in the night.

The Village of Mansuriyye

On Wednesday, 11 June, the Muslims living in the village of Mansuriyye suddenly attacked their Christian neighbours living in a different part of the village. However, before they were able to wipe them out, military men arriving from Mardin showed up and were able to save the inhabitants from the second part of the village. However, the rescued were afraid to leave their households; Muslims were waiting for them. Thus, they were not able to collect the remaining crop from the fields and lack of food supplies became a burden to them.

When it seemed that the situation had calmed down somewhat, about forty women decided to venture to their abandoned houses to collect some minor household furniture and food supplies. On the way they were attacked by Muslims and most were murdered (according to different reports, they were all murdered). A local Muslim woman by the name of Dashiyye, watching the women being slaughtered, was said to voice her greatest surprise at their courage, perseverance, and strong faith, which they did not renounce to stay alive.

A young boy, who had been taken by Muslims to become a slave after his family was murdered but who was able to flee for the monastery, told us about the tragedies that had befallen this village and its Assyrian inhabitants [143].

The Village of Qsur

The village of Qsur was a large locality, inhabited by more than 400 families. All of its inhabitants were Assyrian. On 14 June (1914), a Saturday, Kurds and Arabs from around Mardin and the nearby mountain villages launched an attack on it, the attack having been in preparation for a long time, even though the village was guarded by 120 soldiers. Initially the soldiers fired on the attackers and were able to halt their march, but in the end they came to an agreement with them on the sharing of the bounty and let them inside the village, encouraging the attack in hopes of much loot. The Kurds, as usual, showed no mercy to anyone and in the end they set the houses on fire; pillars of fire and clouds of smoke hovered over the burning village for eight days. Most inhabitants perished in the flames, and the ones that escaped were killed in cold blood.

The few that survived escaped to Mardin under the cloak of night.

It was only after eight days, when only ashes were left of the village, that the governor of Amida came to Mardin. Hearing about what had happened he sent a public officer to the already non-existent village, ordering him to count the charred bodies. As it turned out, 1,700 bodies were there. At the site, he met the son of Sheikh Ramazan,[19] the highest religious authority for the local Muslims, who was considered a miracle worker. He was armed and, along with his gang of several dozen people, was scouring the ashes for

[19] The Turkish variant of the name Ramadan, popular among Muslims, referring to the name of the month in which the fasting period of the same name is celebrated.

remains of precious items, such as gold that melted and resolidified, worn by women as jewellery.[20] The officer arrested him and brought him before the governor. However, the governor released him[21] [144].

The Village of Qille̱t

Qille̱t is a grand village, entirely Assyrian, of which only a handful people entered into union with Rome and others joined the Protestant churches. {There was an old church in the village, dedicated to the Saints Simon the Zealot and John of Daylam. The inhabitants numbered more than 200 families, had five priests and ran calm lives. They had broad fields of arable land, well-maintained vineyards and gardens, as well as numerous herds of farm animals}.[22]

[20] He could only have found himself there by order of his 'God-fearing' father.

[21] Describing the faith of the inhabitants of this village, also referred to as Goliyye, Gōrgīs adds: 'The Kurds represented three tribes: Milliyye, Dakuriyye and Kikiyye. When some were busy with the burning, others would lead the bound villagers to the well. There, they would make them lie side by side on the ground in such a way so that their heads would hang over the well opening. Shouting *In the name of Allah the loving and merciful,* they would behead these people one by one. The heads would fall into the well, and the bodies would be thrown in afterwards. One of the torturers climbed onto the roof of a tall building, which a group of children chose as their shelter, and began throwing child after child from the roof – in one instance, straight onto the sharp end of a spear held by another Kurd, other times onto rocks, repeating each time: 'Go look after the grazing goats!' (*Ǧirāḥ fī tārīkh*, p. 28). Gōrgīs estimates the number of people burned and killed on one day to be 2,000. 'Goele, still another of our outstations, two hours south of Mardin and on the plain. Report of Ibrahim Bahdi Divrha, a Protestant brother. The leading men of this village of 300 houses (all Christian) fearing an attack by the lawless Koords [sic], who had interpreted the deportations of the Armenians as another decree against all Christians, had asked and obtained from the government at Mardin a detachment of soldiers to guard the village. But when the Koords came and demanded of the soldiers the surrender to them of the chief men of the village, who had taken refuge in the houses where the soldiers were quartered, threatening to kill the soldiers if they should refuse to hand them over, the soldiers not only opened the door but helped the Koords to kill the men, carry off women and children, and plunder the village. To cover the slain, they burned the house in which the villagers had taken refuge. Later the government assigned the deserted houses to Koords who had fled before Russians who were advancing around Kara Hissar. From our house we saw the flames and smoke of the burning house, and by the aid of a glass we could see the Koords making off with the spoil.' (Andrus, A. N., *Turkish Atrocities*, p. 101). The population of Goele was mostly Syrians, with about an equal number of Syrian Catholics and Syrian Protestants.

{Earlier on, three priests from this village were arrested: Thomas, Masud and Abraham, as well as the well-known businessman and philanthropist, the kind-hearted Malke Gabro, and other important personalities. They were placed in a prison in the city of Shauro and subjected to various tortures, whereupon they were murdered along with numerous inhabitants of Shauro in a place named Babayn, which means 'two doors' [in Arabic]}.[23]

On 3 June Kurdish gangs gathered and surrounded Qilleṯ from all sides. The military unit stationed in the village, comprised of twenty-five men, not only did not intervene but also helped the attackers gain access to the village. The soldiers, up to that point supported entirely by the inhabitants, became traitors.

At this time, the village leader, Beniamin, and his son, Simon, were under arrest in Amida; they were taken a few days earlier, which can explain the deceitful plans of the authorities. However, the court released them from their accusations and let them free. En route home they were attacked by soldiers and murdered.

Having heard of the death of the leader, the inhabitants gathered at his house to pay their respects to the family. The Kurds made use of this circumstance and attacked the house, murdering most people inside. The blood flowed across the floor and the yard, all the way to the gates.

I am ashamed to mention the brutality of the Kurds and their beast-like acts on women and girls, both inside the house of the village leader as well as outside. Even corpses were a sexual object for them, used in a truly sadistic manner. Each body that showed any signs of life, such as twitching of eyelids, heartbeat or voice, was pierced with a red-hot metal rod. The wildness of these Kurds became so disproportionate that they would pierce bodies already dead with such rods as well. The more beautiful women and girls were taken to the city of Shauro and forced to live in harems. Those declining to be treated this way were murdered or committed suicide[145].

Peter Gabriel reported:

[22] The fragment, placed in curly brackets, was transferred from the end of the text describing this village in the manuscript, from page 148.

[23] The portion in curly brackets was moved here from its original position at the end of page 145 (two lines) and the beginning of page 146 (four lines) of the manuscript.

Myself, *maqdeshyo* Hanna and the orphan[24] Malke made our way to Shauro. A *karbandekyo* [horse trainer], named Rashido, was with us. From there on, we ventured accompanied by a soldier, who was our friend, to Qillet̠, where we stayed at the house of Jibbo Galle Saboo. On the following morning, the mother of Galle came around, named Zero, and announced as follows: 'The Kurds have notified the elite of our village that official authorities, accompanied by soldiers, plan to visit our village, to take our boys and draft them into the army, and to take the girls to serve in military hospitals, hence it would be good for the adult youths to leave the village for this time, to hide away in caves on the mountaintop, taking with them raisins as food. It would also be recommended for a few adults to accompany them'.

We listened to these stories with calmness. With respect to military service, we are not worried. We are not deserters. I have paid the sum required to postpone my service, and my friend is still too young.[25]

An hour later a barrage of machine gun fire exploded, after which we have heard cries, shouting and laments of the older women. When we came out, we saw seven boys killed in the gardens. At 15.00, the military unit from Shauro arrived. As there were only old people in the village then, they detained three women, who were raped and beaten, whereupon they were stripped and each of them crucified; following this, they arrested our three priests, whom they stripped, shamed, beat, to later take them to Shauro, where they were put in prison[26] [146].

[24] An orphan in the literal sense. Assyrians also use the term 'orphan' when referring to a person who is not gifted and fails at anything.

[25] This young friend could have been the orphan Malke. One can surmise that since John had been on a pilgrimage to the Holy Land, as indicated by the byname *maqdeshyo*, he was older than Malke.

[26] This was already mentioned earlier. 'Statements of eyewitnesses respecting the work of Koords [sic] encouraged by the government: Kulleth, one of our out-stations. Report of a young man (I have forgotten his name) who escaped massacre by climbing up the chimney of an open fire-place. "Koords from the surrounding villages of the Rajhdeeya, Makhashneeya, and Devovareeya districts attacked the village in the early morning hour. pastor Hanoosh Ibrahim (Protestant) was killed on the threshold of the parsonage, and his aged mother on top of him. As many of the villagers as had arms and daggers defended their firesides, but most were slain, many women and children were made captives while very few escaped. The Koords did not assist the government in the deportations, but only in the killing, the taking of captives and booty. The entire village of some 250 houses (there were

The City of Shauro[27]

The number of Christians in this city was smaller than the number of Muslims. When the persecutions broke out people wanted to get rid of the leaders of the local Christian community. In executing this plan, the soldiers arrested the following people: Alexander Gabbe, Amsih Lulo, Malko Bahhe Sabbagh, Baho Kajjun, Sehyun, Zayno David and his brother Abel, George Shammas, Murad Haddad, Sado Naelband and his son Alexander, Barro Isa bano, who was murdered, and many others. After torturing them in prison, they were led out, and it was pretended that they were being taken to Mardin. At the same time, they forced some of them to pay the amount of fifty gold liras for the deferment of their military service. After a short march, Amsih Lulo was murdered, before which he was tortured in an indescribable manner. And when the party reached the locality of Tren Tar'e,[28] Father Abraham died before they could torture him to death. Father Thomas, in turn, was killed while he was praying, exactly when his hands were raised towards the sky.[29] The majority suffered before death by a known community leader, Alexander. It is unknown why the executioners wanted so much to convert Barro Isa Bano [147] to hagarism [Islam],[30] tempting him with various treats. Despite the fact that he consented to their demands, he was still murdered. People said the Muslims saw pillars of fiery light joining the bodies of the martyrs with heaven in that place. They thought it was smoke but these bodies were not set alight [148].

no Moslems in it) was wiped out, and the houses and lands were appropriated by Koords. The village was about 2/3 Syrian and 1/3 Syrian-Protestant.' (Barton, J. L. and Sarafian, A., *Turkish Atrocities*, p. 100).

27 Some inhabitants of this village, who found their way to Syria, bear the last name Sorani.

28 Here the author provides the Assyrian name of this locality, which he later quoted in Arabic as Bābān.

29 Described here are two of three priests stemming from Qilleṯ, whom the author mentioned earlier. There is no agreement concerning the circumstances of the death of Father Abraham.

30 The author uses the very rare verb *hagar*, relating to the name of Hagar, mistress to Abraham, mother to Ishmael, whom the Muslims consider their ancestor.

The Monastery of St Āḥō in Arzun[31]

When the extermination of Christians began, the monks serving at the monastery of St Āhō, Ya'qūb Ḥabsnosoyo, Gabriel Bshiroyo as well as the priest and the faithful, looked for shelter at the house of Jamile Chatto, who was considered a friend. Even though he did in fact take them in and promised to protect them, he failed to keep his promise and released them when pressed by the barbarians, who apparently gave him the following choice: 'the heads of Christians or his head with their heads'. First the clergy was taken care of. They were brave, they never lost their faith, they sang songs and quoted psalms from memory. Having taken care of them, the executioners took two persons each from every village[32] to shoot. This lasted an entire day. Everyone perished. The faith of one of the victims waned in the face of death, as he proclaimed readiness to accept Islam, however he was also murdered. In this way, the entire Christian population of the region was exterminated [149].

[31] St Āḥō (420–525 CE) was born in the city of Rish 'Ayno (today it is Ra's al-'Ayn in Syria).
[32] The author does not provide the names of these villages.

10

THE SINJAR MOUNTAINS SUFFER ON BEHALF OF CHRISTIANS

The Sinjar area is a tall and difficult mountain range, rich in fruit trees, particularly fig trees. It is here that Christianity found fertile soil to grow its roots in the first centuries and here that churches and monasteries were built, the prime of them all being the monastery of St Sergius, located at the top of Ṭūrō Ṣahyō [Thirsty Mountain]. In this region, extraordinary fathers and scholars were educated, of whom I shall name David Bar Faulos d-Bēṯ Raban.[1] However, the growing number of Yezidis in the region beginning in the twelfth century caused the reduction of the number of Christians and the destruction of their numerous cult sites.

The Yezidis trace their roots to Yezid, son to Muawiyah, son to Abu

[1] David Bar Faulos d-Bēṯ Raban died around the year 816. He was born in the village of Bēṯ Shahak not far from Mosul, in a family of writers and teachers, hence his byname Raban – 'the wealthy'. He studied at a church school, whereafter he joined the monastery of Khnushnya near Mount Sinjar, where he became a monk; subsequently he moved to the St Sergius monastery on Mount Sinjar and became its prior. He left behind works in theology, philology, exegesis, as well as descriptions of nature and works concerning social issues. Apart from that he authored many letters, songs and church hymns. He knew Greek and Arabic well, however he wrote in Assyrian. See Ighnāṭiyyos Aphrem I Barṣōm, *Maktbōnūṯō*, pp. 327–9.

Sufyan.[2] They accept the one Great God, to which six lesser gods, a step lower, are subject: Yezid, the Sheikh Ade,[3] the Peacock Angel, Sharaf ad-Din, Shams ad-Din and Fakhr ad-Din. The Yezidis believe in reincarnation and in immortality of the soul.

Yezid was born in 659, and in 688 he killed many Arab inhabitants of Kufa and Busra.[4] In 879 Ahmad, the grandfather of Sheikh Ade, took over leadership of the Yezidis, and after him this duty passed on to Msayfer, who was replaced in turn by Ade. Ade preached [152] to the Yezidis the divinity of Yezid,and it is during his reign and from his initiative that the pogrom of the Assyrian monks and hermits in Sinjar took place. This was around the end of the thirteenth century. Ade died in a region known as Tak, [killed] by units of Hulagu Khan,[5] and his son, Sharaf ad-Din, died in Gzirto.[6]

2 Muawiyah was an Umayyad caliph (666–80 CE), and his son, Yezid (680–3) took over the throne from him. Muawiyah was the first to introduce the hereditary rule later used by the main caliph dynasties, and his son was the first habitual drunkard among caliphs (Hitti, P. K., *Dzieje Arabów*, pp. 167 and 192). The view of the author, popular even among the Yezidis themselves, is not confirmed by science. The idea of the Yezidis stemming from this caliph was to some extent a forced plot of security to avoid persecution by Muslims, which sadly proved to have little effect and, with time, turned out to be very harmful to the historic and cultural awareness of the Yezidis. Those knowledgeable in the subject matter derive the name of this community from the ancient Iranian *yazat*, middle Persian *yazad* – 'divine nature'. The religion of the Yezidis is syncretic, it fuses components of ancient Indo-Iranian religions with beliefs from Judaism, Christianity and Islam (Hauziński, J., 'W kwestii początków wspólnoty jezydów w Iraku', in Abdalla, M. (ed), *Niemuzułmańskie mniejszości Iraku. Historia-Kultura-Problemy przetrwania*, pp. 31–41). It is worth noting that following the weakening of the role of the Baath party in the city of Dohuk (northern Iraq) in 1993 the Yezidi Cultural Centre 'Lalish' was established, which can be proud of valuable publications on various Yezidi topics.

3 This chronology is questionable. Yezidi publications write the name as Adi. He was said to be the son of Msafer (the manuscript's author gives the name as Msayfer). ('Izz ad-Dīn Bāqasre, S., *Al-Izīdiyya*, p. 17.)

4 Kufa and Al-Basra are large cities in southern Iraq. The caliph Yezid died in 683 and probably never visited these cities, presently having Shiite majorities. The city bearing the name Al-Busra is located in Syria.

5 The author means that the time between the grandfather Ahmad and his grandson Ade would amount to about 500 years. This would mean that each of the three: the grandfather, the son and the grandson, would live more than 150 years, which is of little probability. The Mongol ruler Hulagu Khan, grandson to Genghis Khan, following the capture of Baghdad in 1258, set out northeast towards Syria, where he captured two large cities: Homs and Hama, whereafter he returned to Persia.

The Yezidis have two leaders. One of them refers to himself as Al-Hajj. Both fast for forty days in the summer and forty days in the winter. They are known for their kindness, philanthropy and mercy. The Yezidis also have other spiritual leaders.

From the customs of the Yezidis: when a son is born, his father remains with him at home for seven days, after which relatives and friends gather and circumcise the boy and, during the following summer, they baptise him in water. The Yezidis may kidnap women and enter marriages throughout the year except for April,[7] whereby any man can have up to seven wives at the same time. During the wedding celebrations, the guests share raisins with the newly weds. No marriage may take place without the consent of the parents. For a Yezidi it makes no difference whether his future wife is a virgin or not. The burial of a Yezidi is divided into several parts: the people prepare a mare, covered in violet, which is led in front of the the coffin, they dance with swords and spears in hand, shoot guns, put ashes on their heads, tear away their clothes and cut hair and throw them into the grave where their relative is supposed to be buried.

There are three holidays in the Yezidi calendar. The first holiday is celebrated as summer [153] begins, to commemorate the murder of Sheikh Ade. It is referred to as the forty-day feast.[8] The second holiday falls on the beginning of November and refers to the murder of Ade by the people of Hulagu Khan.[9] The third holiday falls at the beginning of April and is

[6] This is most probably a reference to the city of Gzirto/Gzorto (Turkish Cizre, Arabic Al-Jazeera) located in southeastern Turkey close to the Syrian-Iraqi border on the Tigris. Its official name today is Cizre, and it is inhabited mainly by Kurds. Qasim Shammo Danani ('Aṣ-Ṣirā' bayna ash-shēkh Ḥasan wa Badr ad-Dīn Lu'lu', *Laliş*, pp. 14–33) provides an incomplete chronological table of the Yezidi Edanite dynasty stemming from Hakkari (southeastern Turkey). Ahmad was father to Msafer and grandfather to Adi. However, Adi never married. One of the grandsons of his brother, Sakher, was Fakhr ad-Din. Sharaf ad-Din in turn was son to Fakhr ad-Din. This same Sharaf ad-Din died in Mosul in 1254.

[7] The situation is similar among Assyrians. April is a unique month in the mythology of Mesopotamia; at this time, nature is reborn and it is the only permissable 'groom', associated with virility and the importance of nature.

[8] Most likely a reference to Easter among Orthodox Christians, celebrated after the forty-day fast known as Lent, even though now it lasts a full seven weeks.

[9] The available sources on Yezidis make it difficult to ascertain the veracity of information concerning the celebration of two holidays with the same intention.

celebrated to commemorate the takeover of the monastery of Nestorius by Ade.[10]

It is forbidden for Yezidis to learn to read and write.[11] This, however, does not apply to the Ade family members. The head emir presides over twenty-five lesser emirs and he has the absolute power to decide on anything, including the killing of this or that person or any attack on this or that person, or the engagement or dismissal of this or that emir.

However, the second emir in the hierarchy does not consume alcoholic drinks and does not see anyone who drinks. The task of the third emir in turn is prayer and teaching. People listen to him, and in his house he keeps bats and handcuffs with which he drives away evil spirits. The fourth emir decides on issues of marriage. The elders are his subjects and they listen to him. The fifth emir in turn keeps servants, who reside in two villages subject to Mosul: Bahzane and Baʿshiqa. They collect for him all fees and gifts. The sixth emir in turn has people who accompany him, called *meskīnē* [the humble]. They dress in black, and mostly belong to the *nukhrōyē* [the alien]. All may wed, save for the head one, referred to as the *shavish*. The seventh emir in turn also has aids, referred to as the *fujkhe* [battalions]. There are many of them [154]. [The emirs] fast for forty days of the year and go on pilgrimages to the grave of Sheikh Ade, and thus they refer to themselves as the 'donkeys of Sheikh Ade'.

The Yezidis would once bow to seven copper idols but two of them were stolen and taken over by Muslims so they are now left with five. They depict birds, and each bird has one eye.

When the Yezidis gather at the house of their leader, they place the idol in a small bowl of water, following which they continue to sing religious songs in Persian until the idol begins to dance. Such an effect can be achieved only once every hour.

10 It is unknown whether this is a reference to Nestorius, the patriarch of Constantinople, or the later patron named Nestorius. Today, the ancient so-called 'Nestorian' Church, from which the Uniate Chaldean Church is derived (16th–17th centuries), is currently referred to as the Holy Apostolic Catholic Assyrian Church of the East. On the holidays and religious observances of the Yezidis in relation to farming traditions and the annual seasonal cycle, see the discussion in Baḥzānī, K. K., 'Az-Zirāʿa: aʿyāduhā, falsafatuhā, asāṭīruhā wa ashyā' ukhra', *Laliş*, pp. 40–73.

11 This has changed, if it was ever true. There are many highly educated people among Yezidis presently.

The Yezidis are fond of Christians but dislike Muslims, as Muslims do not hide their abhorrence of them and their religion. The Yezidis are proud and valiant and like foreigners; these properties have shone through in their treatment of Christians, to whom they have opened their hearts and shown kindness and even defended them when they were persecuted, thus endangering their own lives and property. Thanks to such an attitude, they have gained for themselves great sympathy from all Christians, great respect and gratitude[12] [155].

Christians Flee from Death to Mount Sinjar [156–65][13]

The Christians living in Mardin and its surroundings came to the conclusion that their broad servitude and loyalty went unnoticed by the Turkish authorities and the Muslim community, and any efforts to gain any basic rights, such as the right to live, remained without any response. When such an attitude of the authorities became clear to them they decided, feeling pain and regret, to leave everything they had – land, vineyards, gardens and homes – to look for any spot on earth to survive. The sole location like this in the vicinity was Mount Sinjar, inhabited by good people, the Yezidis, ready to take in the persecuted, the banished and the refugees, and live together with them.

In the spring of 1915 further sad news emerged about the new wave of exterminations of Christians orchestrated by the Turks in the Dusfan and Erzurum regions and the decisive opposing stance among Muslims everywhere against anything that was Christian. Similarly, because of fear of the military, the Christian youth of Mardin and the region began to flee for

[12] The grandfather to the translator and editor of this edition, who died in t 1964 in Qamishli, also maintained gratitude and sympathy for Yezidis until the end of his days. He was one of those who in the time of the genocide found shelter specifically among the Yezidis on Mount Sinjar, and it is there that his wife died. Apart from that, grandfather would always repeat that his only son, meaning the father of the translator and editor, was able to survive thanks to a Yezidi woman who breastfed him. A coincidence allowed the translator and editor to meet this woman at the Yezidi village of Khatuniyye (northeastern Syria) and to speak with her. This happened in the summer of 1967, when, as a youth, wanting to earn some money to buy schoolbooks, he participated in the execution of a scheme of spraying rural households with a solution of DDT. Memory maintains untarnished memories from that stay and other activities in the villages of the southeastern province of Syria.

[13] This part of the text, describing the fate of Christians who hid among the Yezidis, required extensive intervention.

Mount Sinjar. Very few Christians in the army had the chance of returning home: either they would die or their family would die. There, on Mount Sinjar, the Yezidis would take them in happily and with hospitality.

The chieftain of the Yezidis, Hammo Sharro,[14] was most deeply engaged in the rescue of the refugees. This man exhibited love, kindness and philanthropy; he shared with them what he had at his disposal, providing housing, the necessities of life, employment that would ensure survival [156], a grand house that served as a hospital for the ill and the exhausted, and means of collecting alms from other Christians to be used to maintain the hospital. {He would console and commiserate when the refugees would describe the barbaric scenes experienced by their closest family members. He became a popular person, and word of his virtuous attitude in difficult times was spread among Christians through the entire region [the borderlands of what today is Turkey, Syria and Iraq]. And for this they will be ever grateful to him}.

{In July, everybody talked of the death caravans. Their victims were the relatives of those hiding on Mount Sinjar. It is no wonder that there was so much tension among the refugees; everyone asked themselves about the fate of their relatives – did they become fodder for the swords of wild barbarians and under what circumstances did they die? Nobody could provide the answers.}[15]

Disease Decimates the Refugees on Mount Sinjar

{In Autumn 1915 most Christians on Mount Sinjar were afflicted by a deadly fever, a disease hitherto unknown. The cause of this mass illness could be none other but fear, sadness, worry and despair, as if they were living the experiences that were taking place in their homelands.

The reaction of the locals to these circumstances was varied. One of the Yezidi leaders, Ashur, reigning unopposed in the region of Mamidha and fearing the disease could spread, demanded the Christians be driven away or isolated in one location.[16] He feared that they might infect Yezidis.

[14] Hammo Sharro (1850–1933), was also known as Hamu Shiru (Fuccaro, N., *The Other Kurds: Yazidis in Colonial Iraq*, p. 49). He had seven sons: Darvish, Barakat, Khudeda, Sayyido, Ismail, Jundo and Ido.

[15] From the beginning of page 159, together with the second paragraph.

[16] The available Yezidi sources hold no information about a locality bearing a name sound-

Becoming aware of what might await them, the Christians turned to Hammo Sharro, who always supported them. Because of his higher position in the Yezidi hierarchy Hammo Sharro threatened Ashur that he would kill him if he added one more pain to all the pain that these people have suffered. In light of such the leader's attitude Ashur agreed to allocate a portion of the village of Mamidha for the sick until they recovered. However, after the death of twenty people who had no access to medicine, Ashur and the Yezidi inhabitants of Mamidha demanded again for the ill to depart the village. A further intervention by Hammo Sharro resulted this time in moving the ill to a hill that was hitherto uninhabited, lying opposite the village where the leader resided. He believed that they would be safer living closer to his place of residence. He let them build basic shelters and huts of oak wood and live in them through the autumn, hoping that in the winter the situation in their home regions would let them return home.

Winter came. The alarming news coming in from their homelands convinced the refugees to construct mud huts serving as housing and two grand mud houses for public use: at one of these they would meet to celebrate mass, headed by the Chaldean priest Joseph, and the other was planned as a temporary hospital. Within a short while, the priest departed from the area and appointed a deputy by the name of Farjalla, a teacher by trade. As time passed, the numbers of Christians increased. In order to function better, they formed a charity organisation collecting money for the ill}.[17]

{In March 1916 Mount Sinjar was also reached by many Armenian survivors and refugees, mainly from the localities of Shaddada and Deir ez-Zor[18] and the villages nearby. They remained on the mountain's south side. One of the Armenian columns numbered 300 people. Some Muslims, wishing the Christians a bad fate, used to purposefully point them in the wrong direction or keep them in the wastelands near the mountain in order for them to die of hunger and thirst. Having found out about such cases, the Yezidis would venture down to the places where these poor people would be kept, naked, barefoot and exhausted, and having negotiated with the local Muslims, they

ing like this. It is most probably Lalish, which is also the name of the central temple of the Yezidis.

17 From halfway through page 159 of the manuscript until the first line of page 161.

18 Both localities are found in the eastern part of Syria.

would take them in or retake them by force, and then they would lead them to those on the mountain. It happened on occasion that the refugees in the wastelands were guarded by Kurds; in such cases, fighting broke out between them and the Yezidis, who tried to rescue the hostages, particularly children.

Can anyone imagine the condition these people were in? They had barely escaped death and they were kept there until they died, this time from hunger and lack of water. They owed their survival to the Yezidis who, order to retake them also risked their lives. And the Christians were only able to utter the words 'thank you' for such an attitude. The people rescued from one of the round-ups were not only taken in by the local Christians but they also collected help for them in the form of fifty gold lira.

In order to survive the Christians on Mount Sinjar began, in the summer of 1916, to take care of the vineyards and gardens belonging to the Yezidis. Others asked their surviving relatives for sewing needles, chewing gum, sugar and any kind of jewellery, gold and silver, including rings, necklaces and bracelets. They would exchange these for wheat grain, lentils and legumes, which they shared with anyone and everyone. And when hunger, high prices and sicknesses befell the inhabitants of the mountain the Christians ventured to the representatives of the Arab tribe of Tayy with a plea for help. The virtuous Bedouins would welcome these poor people and provide them free wheat, barley, corn, molten butter and other products they needed to survive. The Christians shared these products with their hosts, the Yezidis, as well. Seeing this proof of gratitude, Hammo Sharro was supposed to have said: 'I am proud of you that, compared to us, you are able to arrange your lives and provide for yourselves. Despite the fact that we have so much land, so many vineyards and gardens, we live in poverty, and our children receive many great gifts from you'.}[19]

However, crop shortages, and therefore hunger, caused many Yezidis to attack Christians and take food and other products from them. Hammo Sharro did not hesitate to condemn such deeds. He warned his countrymen: 'If anybody would steal anything from the Christians, they will lose everything and be banished.'

In order to stay true to history, it needs to be said that Hammo Sharro did follow through with his ultimatum and did, in fact, banish some Yezidis.

[19] From the first paragraph of page 157 of the manuscript until the end of page 158.

The Christians will never forget this attitude. It made their defender a true hero. History will record his name in gold.

The Christians stayed with the Yezidis for one-and-a-half years. After this time, persecutions ceased in Mardin and the British forces entered Mosul and started taking over further localities in Iraq. Would peace reign in this country now?

However, the curse of the Turks did not leave the Christians. When the authorities found out that the Christians who survived sheltered on Mount Sinjar they sent an army unit there. The agreed goals were as follows: take over the mountain, scare the inhabitants, and kill the Christians and those who stand in the way.

The Ottoman forces surrounded the Sinjar region [161]. Their leader, at the same time head of the intelligence for this region, Mehyaddin Bey, conveyed to Hammo Sharro a letter with the following contents:

> Release to us all Christians who have fled and who are hiding with you, as well as all weapons in your possession. If you decline, you shall feel much sorrow and you shall be treated so harshly that you cannot imagine; we will destroy your home and the homes of your relatives and tribesmen.

Having received this ultimatum, Hammo Sharro became very upset. He described his position thus:

> My conscience does not let me release to certain death those who shelter with me. I have sworn by my honour, and I have uttered *lauvista*, a word of highest promise among Yezidis. I shall release nobody until my eyes are wet, unless I die, me and my children – only then will the enemies be able to treat them as they please. Despicable must be an officer to state such an ultimatum and to demand our weapons. Do we have to do this to remain defenceless and become an easy target for your forces?

Having read the ultimatum, the chieftain ordered the summoning of all leaders, whereupon he declared that he himself did not plan on surrendering. The present leaders were divided in their opinions. Some of them wanted to accept the ultimatum; others were opposed [162]. The chieftain, however, was able to convince everyone of the need of defence, both of their own community as well as of the guests, which one should not release to enemies like lambs for slaughter. The leaders and commanders grabbed their weapons and barricaded themselves at a location called Shib al-Kasem, circular in shape, considered to be magic and sacred. The chieftain took with himself a unit of 'the humble' and travelled to the locality of Kharse, from which the entire valley can be seen. He noticed three legions of Turkish soldiers, ready to storm the mountain.

On Good Saturday, meaning, the day before Easter, the soldiers moved towards the mountain and started shelling the locality of Shib al-Kasem, where the defending Yezidis were positioned, with rockets. The mountain started to tremble. The local people were overcome with panic. Hammo Sharro and his people watched everything from a secluded spot. When the soldiers came into range of the Yezidi machine guns the latter showered them with bullets. Fifteen Turkish soldiers were killed, with one Yezidi lost. His name was Khalaf Sinjari. He died attempting to collect weapons belonging to the murdered Turks [163].

Observing the numbers of attacking Turks and their arms Hammo Sharro concluded that, with his humble weaponry, he would not be able to stop them. Fearing that the place he chose might become a grave for his people he left it and went to the next village, where the Christians lived. He announced to the Christians with great pain that they are in danger and advised them to take everything they can carry and to move to the south side of the mountain, where it was relatively safe: 'The enemy is at the gates and, using his war machine, he is applying the scorched earth policy.'

The Christians, loaded with food supplies, fled.

Over the course of a single day, the Turks took over the village of Mamidha and other villages, plundering house by house, and by evening they reached the village that the Christians had deserted. They found there only one old man, who was not able to run, and killed him on the spot. With the village of the chieftain himself taken over, the Yezidis surrendered and, to avoid a massacre, declared their loyalty and submission. The Turks put in place a commander of the region with his headquarters in the village of Mamidha, and formed a post in every village, whereupon they retreated [164].[20] The local inhabitants were relieved.

[20] Fuccaro writes that the Ottoman occupation of the mountain occurred in 1918 (*The Other Kurds*, p. 49).

The Turkish soldiers remaining on the mountain could neither accustom themselves to it nor gain the trust of the inhabitants; thus, some of them quit the service. The Yezidis took advantage of the waning numbers; they would attack posts and take the weapons from the soldiers. They proceeded this way until the entire mountain was free of Turks. Some of the Christians fled and found protection among Arab Bedouins from the Tayy tribe where, for a small fee for the leaders, they could hope for their protection; others made their way from one village to another until they reached the city of Nisibis;[21] still others returned to the village originally assigned to them on the mountain and lived there until the situation calmed down entirely. Once again, the Christians scattered due to the fury of the sons of Ottoman.

At this time, British forces entered Mosul and conquered other regions of Iraq [165].

[21] This group also included the grandfather of the translator (M. A.) who died on Mount Sinjar and was buried there.

11

THE FATE OF CHRISTIAN INHABITANTS OF OTHER LOCALITIES

The Demise of the Inhabitants of Bēṯ Zabdāy, Also Called Gzirto

Bēṯ Zabdāy, also called Gzirto d-Bar Umar, is a city with somewhat polluted air. It lies on the shores of the Tigris, about 180 kilometres to the south[east] of Mardin.[1] The city used to be inhabited by a large Assyrian community, including Uniate [Chaldeans and Syrian Catholics],[2] and a small number of Protestants, whereby each community had its own sanctuaries. It was here that bishops resided and where beautiful churches could be found.

In April 1915 the terrible governor of Amida, Reshid Pasha, sent one of his men, named Zolfi,[3] known for his brutality, to the Kurds in order to encourage them to murder Christians. Hearing the arrival of the messenger,

[1] Other versions of the name are Bēṯ Zabdāy, Gzirto, Gazarta and Gozarto (Turkish Cizre). The first of these is also sometimes considered to have been the original name of a different locality, Azakh (İdil in Turkish), inhabited until the end of World War I exclusively by Assyrians. With certainty, the events the author discusses do not apply to Azakh, but to Gzirto, today's Cizre, a small city to the east of Azakh on the Tigris.

[2] The author describes Catholics using the word *papoye* (Papists).

[3] This man may have been a former member of the Turkish parliament from the Amida (Diyarbakır) district, for the ruling Committee of Union and Progress.

the Chaldean bishop, Ya'qūb,[4] paid him – as was customary – a visit. Zolfi, however, treated the guest very rudely and primitively, threatening him: 'There came the time for you to be a carrier, who, just like a mule, shall carry a hundred litres[5] of barley on his back!' The bishop was frightened by the unexpected attitude of the state representative [166].

On 17 August the Kurds took the church of the Assyrian Papists and arrested their bishop Michael and priest Paul, throwing both into jail. Then they made their way to the Chaldean church and arrested Bishop Ya'qūb, along with three priests: John, Elias and Mark. They were also thrown into jail. Bishop Behnam Akrawi made it to Azakh in time to hide away.[6]

On 28 August Bishops Michael and Ya'qūb[7] were led before the court. There they were told to collect the weapons that were alleged to be in the

[4] Bishop Ya'qūb's full name may have been Philippe-Ya'qūb Abraham. He was born in 1848 in the locality of Telkef in northern Iraq. In 1873 he was ordained a priest by the Chaldean Patriarch Yawsēf VI Audo, and in 1875 he was made bishop. He served initially in the Indian Malabar then, beginning in 1882, in Gzirto.

[5] Measuring volume instead of weight was common even in the 1960s in villages inhabited by Assyrians in northeastern Syria. In the stable and dry climate prevalent in the summer in this region, the grain had a low humidity of eight to ten per cent.

[6] So, three bishops resided in this city.

[7] Beṯ-Şawoce, J., *Sayfo b Ṭurcabdin*, pp. 257–8 (narration no. 19) states: 'A good Muslim, who kept repeating that he was the one to have killed the bishop – "When the holocaust was announced, I was stationed in Cizre as a military police officer. I saw bishop Ya'qūb Abraham for the first time when I was made a member of a military unit. We received the order to lead the bishop out, torture him and in the end to hang him. It was only then that I found out why a temporary gallows was being installed in the city centre. We surrounded the house and called the bishop in Arabic to come out. He listened. I have never seen such grace in my life. The soldiers started mercilessly hitting him with bayonets, wherever they could. He was all covered in blood and did not speak. They made him run and kept punching him with bayonets. He must have endured about a hundred hits, and never fell. I did not like such animal-like treatment of a person, without any discernible reason, however I had only one bullet and could not defend him. When we reached the city centre, I saw a crowd of onlookers. They came to see the bishop on the gallows. They shouted *giaur, giaur*! Most probably, there were some Christians among the crowd as well. The military recognised them, because – unlike the others – they stood at the back and wept. The officer gave the order to kill anybody that would cry. Immediately about fifty people were shot. I could not stand this any longer. I decided to take the satisfaction away from these bloodthirsty people, and I decided to use the one bullet that I had. I fired a shot on target from a secluded spot. The bishop died instantly, and until the very end they had no idea that I killed him.' As we can see, the reports on the killing of the bishop are not in agreement.

hands of Christians. When the bishops denied any knowledge of the possession of any weapons they were beaten until their weak bodies became covered in blood. Then three shots were fired at each of them and the bodies were stripped and thrown away on the city outskirts.

{On the following day, meaning 29 August, a mass round-up was organised; all men were caught, placed in barns and sheds, and they remained under such inhuman conditions for four days, without food or drink. Thereafter they were tied with ropes and led outside the city, to a location named Nahro d-Sus [the river Sus], about half an hour's walk away to the south. There all of them were murdered by stoning, by automatic rifle shots or by knives and swords.}[8]

On 1 September the executioners returned to the town and gathered all women, youths and children. They were told that they would be taken to Mosul, to the Christians living there. The victims were arranged into a grand column and taken to the place where the earlier slaughter was committed, where the bodies of their fathers, husbands and brothers lay. En route, girls of outstanding beauty were picked for harems and women were robbed of their jewellery. Other gangs would, during this time, plunder the abandoned homes. The slaughter was carried out just like before. Of all the Christians of Bēṯ Zabdāy – as I heard – only four women survived. A good Muslim woman hid them in her home[9] [167 and the three first lines of page 168].

[8] The paragraph in curly brackets is composed of the six final lines transferred from page 168 of the manuscript.

[9] At this time, close to 700 Christian families (about 6,300 people) lived in this city (see Beṯ-Şawoce, J., *Beth-Zabday Azech. Vad hände 1915?*, p. 237). More details about these four women are provided by Abd al-Karim Bashir, son-in-law to one of them, presently living in Wiesbaden, Germany. Here is a report sent by letter by his son, Fadi Bashir, a graduate of the Poznań University of Technology (1994): 'My mother-in-law, Fahima Gabro Khaddo, would continuously repeat that she was saved by a member of the Muslim elite of the city, named Abd al-Hamid as-Sida. He was a friend of her father's, Gabro Khaddo. He hid her in the dark cellar of his house together with her two sisters, Naze and Mariam. Along with them was also Zakiyya, the wife of her uncle Salim, who was in Mosul at this time. Zakiyya and Salim had only married a month earlier. The cellar, where they resided, allowed them to hear cries of wanderers from the streets: "Anyone hiding a Christian will be punished harshly." They lived in constant fear; however, the kind-hearted house owner would calm them down: "Do not worry. In the name of the friendship between myself and Gabro Efendi, I shall not release you. I am an important person in this town. I shall send you to our uncle Salim in Mosul." One day, two months later, he clad the victims in attire that would

{Some citizens of Mardin told me the names of the leaders who participated in the Christian massacre. These were: Mhammade Rasul, Muhammad Nazo[10] and his brother, Khider Chalabi.}[11]

help them not be recognised, and put each of them into a bag used to carry goods. Each pair of bags with the human load would be put on horseback and smuggled through the city by a servant of Abd al-Hamid. When they reached the spot named Chamme Sus – the river Sus [the informant is using the Kurdish name here], the horses would step on dead bodies or large cut-off pieces of human corpses, which covered the land there. Zakiyya, terrified of this, screamed: "The horse trampled the body of my father, my mother, my brothers. They were all quartered and slaughtered. They lie here!" The servant ordered her to be silent. In a moment, Zakiyya was no longer heard. Her head, hanging from the bag, was powerless. I felt – continued the mother-in-law – that something was wrong. Zakiyya died of grief. Pushing aside the bodies, the servant had dug a temporary shallow grave, in which Zakiyya was put. She remained there, and we, saddened terribly, continued our march to Mosul. In Mosul, my uncle Salim asked: "Where is my wife?" We told him the truth. I have gotten to know [says the informant] this Abd al-Hamid in the 1940s in the city of Dērīk [presently Al-Malikiyye in north eastern Syria, close to the Turkish-Iraqi border]. He used to visit my mother-in-law frequently, and she respected him and was grateful for saving her life. He has a few sons who continue to live in Jazirat Ibn Umar [the informant uses the Arab locality name here]. I know three of them personally: Shaqib, Rifat and Adib. The latter is a solicitor. I wish to add that their mother was Assyrian and had relatives in Dērīk. My mother-in-law would visit them frequently.' It is worth mentioning here that a similar tragedy, in quite similar circumstances, occurred 93 years later. On 9 July 2008, a group of Islamic terrorists in Mosul shot, with bypassers and neighbouring store owners looking on, an Assyrian store-owner, Mazen George Yaqo Abūnā (aged 34). The bandits dragged the body outside and drove away. Hearing the news, the mother of the murdered ran out of the house, stopped by the corpse of her only son lying in a pool of blood, hugged it, and suddenly passed on. Her husband died in the same manner as her son did two years earlier. This tragedy, one of many in Iraq after 2003, had shocked the Assyrian community both in Iraq as well as in the diaspora. Curious is the fact of silence and lack of reaction by other communities, with even the state press not publishing any mention of this tragedy. And, as usual, the perpetrators of this murder go unknown. Once again, voices could be heard proclaiming the necessity of provision of autonomy to the Assyrians on their historic lands in northern Iraq as the sole alternative guaranteeing security and survival. Source: <http://www.ankawa.com/forum/index.php/topic,205055.msg3238190.html#msg3238190> (last accessed 4 November 2016).

10 This name can be found in the work of Beṯ-Şawoce, J., *Sayfo*, p. 237 as Ahmade Nazo. He was supposed to have originated from the region of Mhalmayto and to have used the Arabic dialect of Mardin.

11 The statistics concerning Christians in this diocese, just like in others in southeastern Turkey, allows one to imagine the scale of the genocide: towards the end of the nineteenth century, the Chaldean population counted 18,500, and the Syrian Orthodox counted 20,000 (Gaunt, D., *Massacres*, p. 251; Yonan, G., *Ein vergessener Holocaust*, p. 290). Perhaps as a

The Demise of the Inhabitants of Siʿirt

The city of Siʿirt is the subject of the capital of the region of Bitlis. It is found close to the shores of the River Tigris and it is about a four-day walk away from Mardin to the north. It is surrounded by hills rich in vineyards, fig and punica tree gardens. The city, and the villages belonging to it, were inhabited by more than 12,000 Christians: Armenians and Assyrians, including Chaldean Uniate, with a famous bishop and scholar, Adday Scher. Coeducational schools were in operation, as well as a monastery, libraries and two orphanages run by three nuns. The city was lively and an important regional Christian cultural centre. With the outbreak of World War I in 1914, the members of the Dominican order and the nuns left the city and returned to their home countries [in Europe].

The first attack on the Christians of this city was launched by Kurds halfway through June 1915. Bloodcurdling scenes played out: people were murdered, houses were burned and plundered, without any respect. In order to humiliate the Christians even more, the city's elite was taken prisoner, such as the members of the Assyrian noble family Abbush (more than sixty people), of the family Iwas[12] [169], the family Mousa Gorgis as well as priests and other important dynasties and noble families, 600 men in total. They were thrown into jail and kept without food or drink; they were played with just like [hungry] animals play with a defenceless victim, whereby a true wild man, Ahmad Agha Kachcha, was allowed to enter their cell. He beheaded

result of deaths and displacements during the massacres by Kurdish emirs, principally in 1895, the Chaldean and East Syrian population (plus Protestants, many of whom may have been Armenian) dropped to 2,500–5,000, subdivided into up to 22 parishes, with up to 17 priests and 21 churches. Jean-Baptiste Chabot ('Éttat religieux des diocèses formant le patriarcat chaldéen de Babylone') records 5,000 in 22 parishes with 17 priests and 21 churches, David Wilmshurst (*The Ecclesiastical Organization of the Church of the East, 1318–1913*) records 2,500 Syrians/Chaldeans and Protestants [Assyrians], 27 villages and 7–8 churches in the Siʿirt (Seert) region, and David Gaunt (*Massacres*) records 37 villages, 5,430 Christians, 21 priests, 31 churches, 7 chapels and 9 schools in Siʿirt Chaldean diocese in 1913. By 1928 only 1,600 people were left, without any member of the clergy. Towards the end of the twentieth century all had emigrated. Thus, there are no Assyrians left in this historically Assyrian region.

12 Ighnāṭiyyos Zakkā I ʿIwāṣ, the Syrian Orthodox patriarch, who died in 2014, originated from this family. He was born in Iraq with the given name Sanharib (Sennacherib).

the Assyrian priest, Abraham, with a sword, throwing the head on to a city square. The Muslims present started kicking it around the streets as if it were a ball. A different bloody tyrant named Qasemo and his people then broke into the house of Chaldean priest Gabriel and led him to the court offices. There the priest was stripped, had his body pierced with needles, hit with a spear and a sword, each time being given the choice to renounce Christ and convert to Islam. The priest kept repeating loudly: 'I shall not renounce Christ'. He was most probably still alive when his head was cut off, it being thrown into a sewage duct close to the house of the mentioned Ahmad Agha.

The arrested Christians spent four days in jail. On the fifth day, in the morning, professional murderers arrived. They bound everyone and took them to a valley named Zeriab in the northern part of town, about five kilometres away from the outskirts. Before the executioners commenced their deed, Father Ephrem made a short speech to the gathered crowd, asking for nobody to reject Christ. Hearing the word 'Christ', the barbarians became furious and began to murder people, dividing the clothes of the murdered among themselves[170]. The blood of 600 people did not satiate their thirst. After the slaughter, the murderers hit the town, attacking Christian houses. They assembled the women, elderly, youths and children, who they led out forming three large columns, making them run to their slaughter. During the march the sadists would strip the women and children and commence mass rapes, whereafter they told everyone to strip and take off their shoes, saying that as long as the clothes and shoes are not soiled in blood they can be of use to them. Less than half of the victims reached the murder site; the rest was murdered on the way. The young girls, which they divided among one another, were spared; they were treated as slaves to satisfy the sadistic desires of the murderers.

A handful of boys was also kept alive so that officially everything that the rich families had could be taken over. However, after this goal was reached, the boys were of no further use. When the rumours arrived about the advancing Russian army the Kurds took the boys and murdered all of them in a spot named Sare-Zine.

What was the fate of Bishop Adday Scher?

We know that the mayor, Osman Agha, sent him away to the village of Dirsho, from which the Agha originated. After a week, Ali Naqib al-Ashraf and the *kadi* of the province found out about this and sent off soldiers to bring him back. Before the execution, the bishop asked for five minutes of time. He knelt, hung his cross on his neck and prayed, after which he told the executioners: 'I am ready! Do what you wanted to do.' They murdered him, whereupon they took his vestments off and took them to the aforementioned Ali and *kadi*, as proof of execution of the order.[13]

Following the murder of the world-famous bishop, the Muslims confiscated everything left behind by the Christians (clothing, home appliances and animals) from the orphaned city [171]. In the houses of the Christians, they found jewellery and other very valuable objects, not to speak of tens of thousands of gold lira. From the stores belonging to the Christians, all goods were looted. The attackers divided all of this among themselves. The liturgical items found in churches were melted down or sold as scrap and the books were burned. They turned the Chaldean church into a mosque named Masjid Khalili, from the name of the tyrant Khalil Pasha, the architect of the slaughter of Christians. The schools, in turn, where the Dominicans taught, were turned into a military hospital.

Following the destruction or takeover of all Christian sites in the city of Si'irt, the time came for the surrounding villages. There were attacked one after another, with all inhabitants being killed. In this way, the Muslims soiled their hands with the blood of tens of thousands of innocent

[13] Born in 1867, his name was Sliwa Sher. Adday is the name of the patron saint which he took on following his ordination as bishop in 1902. The execution took place on 15 June 1915 (some sources say it was 17 June), by shooting and beheading. In order to obtain the bishop's ring, the Turkish officer cut off his finger after death. The bishop was invited to lectures and conferences not only by church bodies but also by Orientalists and Syriac studies scholars, particularly to Italy, France and Lebanon. He used every trip to European countries to collect financial aid, which, following his return, he would divide equally between Christians and Muslims. In 1908 he was in Rome and met Pope Pius X. He owned a rich book collection and old manuscripts, the fate of which is unknown. Some said that the bishop felt that the Turks might kill him, hence he wrapped his collection in a material impermeable to water and hid it in a deep well. Others stated that the collection was burned by either Turks or Kurds. The catalogue of the collection, drawn up in true European style in French by the bishop himself, was published by the Dominican Order in Mosul in 1905: *Catalogue des Manusrits Syriaques et Arabes conservés dans la bibliothèque épiscopale de Séert. Avec notes bibliographiques par Mgr. Addai Scher, archevêque chaldéen de Séert* (Mosul: Imprimerie des Pères Dominicains, 1905). The bishop's scientific body of works covers twenty-seven volumes, mainly in history and patrology.

people, who were executed only because they followed the Christian faith [172].

The Slaughter of Kerboran[14]

Kerboran is a large village in the Ṭūr ʿAbdīn region, inhabited primarily by Assyrians. As the extermination of Christians began the district leader called a meeting, to which Muslim fanatics, particularly sons of the Kurdish tyrant Ali Rammo and other tribal Aghas and chieftains,[15] were invited. The meeting was held in secret. The district leader not only gave the assembled a green light but even ordered them to begin murdering Christians and robbing their houses. The order was implemented immediately.

The village was under siege for four days, with selected houses being attacked from time to time, however none of them was taken over. The houses were built akin to a fortress and the inhabitants defended themselves using anything they could. In light of such helplessness, the attackers got the idea to climb on to roofs, drill holes in them, throw in hay and set all of this alight. This devilish tactic, tragic in consequences wherever it was used, turned out to be effective; it caused the death of many victims through smoke asphyxiation. Some inhabitants, who fled the village hastily, totalling about 600 people, were caught and taken prisoner. The massacre was orchestrated by Kurdish leader Mustafa Ali Rammo. He was able to select beautiful women and girls from the crowd and distributed them among those participating in the execution as rewards. Most of these virgins committed suicide before the perpetrators managed to touch them.

The Assyrian bishop Yaʿqūb residing in the village was said to have some

[14] A different name is Kfar Boran. A large group of the inhabitants of this village lives today in the locality of Västerås in Sweden, where they have recently built a church. They normally speak Kurdish, with Syriac being used during liturgy.

[15] Beṯ-Şawoce, J., *Sayfo b Ṭurcabdin*, p. 169 (narration no. 6), names four sons of this Ali Rammo: Darvish, Abd-al-Karim, Khalil and Mustafa. They would burden the inhabitants of Kfar Boran with a further land tax (*haraj*), beside the poll tax taken from the Christians by the state. This important report by Beṯ-Şawoce not only documents the course of the massacres and the attitudes of the executioners but also sheds light on the anti-Christian propaganda, agitation and tactics of education of local military and police forces, and foremost Kurdish leaders, by the state authorities, in order to prepare them for the Christian extermination being planned.

respect with the district leader. Thus the district leader, who – as we can recall – ordered the slaughter of Christians, took the bishop home with him. The Christians who saw this thought that the priest had renounced Christ, which would have been the reason the district leader elected to save him. The truth was different, however: the intentions of the latter were dishonest [173].

Soon the house of the district leader was visited by the architect of this mass slaughter, the aforementioned Mustafa Ali Rammo, accompanied by two people, to fetch the bishop. The governor released the hostage to them. The bishop, tied up with rope, was led out and shot before the house of the district leader. He died as a martyr.[16]

Everything that was found in the Christian homes and churches was appropriated. No baptised person was left alive in Kerboran.[17]

The Monastery of St Gabriel, Called Dayro d-'Umro[18]

This is an ancient monastery, constructed in 397 and expanded halfway through the sixth century. In the autumn of 1917 one of the local bloodthirsty bandits by the name of Shendi set up an army and attacked the monastery. The four people defending it were not able to prevent the monks,

[16] Be̱t-Şawoce, J., *Sayfo b Ṭurcabdin*, pp. 158–66, reports on different circumstances of the death of the bishop. Apparently, it did not take place in front of the governor's house but at the military police post, unless the house of the governor also hosted the military police post, which cannot be excluded. The bishop and the village leader, the name of whom was Abraham Shemun, were hidden there by Tawfiq Chavish, a post commander friendly to Christians. However, he could not proceed contrary to the accords between the Turkish army and the Kurds. 'The Kurds surrounded the post and demanded that the commander released both these men. They, however, wished not to die at the hands of Kurds. They begged the commander for his people to put bayonets on their rifles and to stand in a row, holding them strongly in vertical positions. Both men took to the first floor and threw themselves off the balcony straight onto the blades, which punctured their bodies through in several places.' This version of the tragic death of the bishop is more probable than the version given by Qarabashi.

[17] Gōrgīs, A., *Ğirāḥ fī tārīkh*, pp. 94–8, refers to Kerboran as a city.

[18] *Umro* means monastery. Due to the closeness of this word and the Muslim name Omar, some Muslims say and write that the monastery was allegedly constructed by caliph Umar ibn al-Khattab, which is not true. The founder of the monastery, St Gabriel, came from the village Qartmin, about five kilometres to the southwest of the monastery. Qartmin today is a purely Kurdish village. The correct name of the monastery in Syriac is Umro d-Mor Gabriel. It is still in operation (see Abdalla, M., 'Między świętością a barbarzyństwem. 1600 lat asyryjskiego monasteru w Turcji', *Przegląd Prawosławny*).

altar boys, seminarians and seventy inhabitants of the nearby Assyrian village Kafarbe from being taken from the monastery – they were murdered outside its walls.[19] Only two boys were able to save themselves from this slaughter: one made it to the village of Bsōrīnō, the other to the village of ʿAyn Wardo.[20]

Having taken over the monastery, Shendi and his men desecrated the church and set the rich collection of books on fire. The inhabitants left alive in the village of Kafarbe were able to defend themselves for over half a year until they had to surrender. Only a handful of them survived and these escaped to nearby localities. The village and all its property was commandeered by Kurds.[21] The people continuing to defend themselves for another three months in the church of St Stephen were all killed by the attackers.

The monastery was spared in the years of increased persecution [1915–16] because it was under the protection of certain Kurdish leaders [rest of text stricken in the manuscript] [174].

The Slaughter of the Inhabitants of the Village of Ḥesnō d-Atṯō

Ḥesnō d-Atṯō was a famed village, with a rich history, where Assyrian Christians lived, of whom but a handful joined the ranks of Papists or Protestants. It is located between Mardin and the Zaʿfarān monastery. The church of St George is active in the village. The faithful are provided with the services of two priests, Elias and David.

On Friday, 11 June [1915] certain bold young women of the village made their way to Mardin to notify Bishop Kirill Givargis and the nation's elders of the fact that recently the Kurdish threats of murder of Christians have gained momentum. Hearing this, the bishop advised the villagers to abandon their homes as fast as possible and for them to head to the fortified monastery of Zaʿfarān, whereby they should take with them anything that was of value. The Kurds watching the village for a while found out about

[19] Kfarbo(e), official name: Güngören, about six kilometres to the southeast of the monastery.

[20] Bsōrīnō – other name: Basibrin, official name: Hamerli, about eight kilometres to the southeast of St Gabriel Monastery; ʿAyn Wardo – parallel shortened name: Iwardo, official name: Gülgöze, approximately fourteen kilometres to the northwest of St Gabriel Monastery.

[21] Most of the lost Assyrian villages, including this one, have been repopulated by Kurds, thus shifting the demography.

Figure 6 The bishop of St Gabriel Monastery with three monks from Damascus and the author of the photographs (on the right) showing one of the few surviving manuscripts at the monastery (from the archives of M. Abdalla, 1999)

these plans. Thus, two of their chieftains, Smail Ali Mahmud and Ahmad Mirzo, along with the latter's son, advised the villagers to abandon plans to leave. They would not listen, though. The evacuation was carried out swiftly with the people taking few belongings to the monastery.

On the morning of Sunday, 13 June, fifty-four persons went out of the monastery to make their way to the village in order to collect clothes and minor equipment left behind. They were accompanied by two armed men, Khello and Abde, who, up to that point, guarded the monastery [175]. However the Kurds, who had already taken control of the village the night before, arranged a trap in the village itself. The entire group of Assyrians perished, except two men, George Bār Abe and Simon Bār Malke Ya'qūb, who were able to head towards Mardin with their wounds bleeding. Simon died on the way, but George was able to enter the evangelical hospital where he was accepted and healed by a doctor named Thom from the United States.[22]

[22] It is probably the same medical doctor as the one mentioned earlier (chapter nine).

The villagers residing in the monastery, having heard of the massacre of their neighbours from the village, decided to take the risk of collecting their bodies for the purpose of a proper burial. They made their way to the spot. They put the bodies into bags, and proceeded back to the monastery, carrying them on their backs. However, on the way the Kurds opened fire on them. Divine providence made it so nobody perished this time. Following the funeral mass, the deceased were buried in a mass grave beside the monastery.[23]

On Thursday, 24 June, the military leader Nuri Badlisi, accompanied by fifty armed men, arrived at the monastery. They entered it and selected from among the males found there 450 of the strongest, led them out by force and made them run towards Mardin. When, on the way, the commander found out that there were five Armenians in this group he told them to come forward, whereupon he shot them. These people originated from the village of Payran.

The remainder made it to Mardin. They were supposed to work on the construction of state roads leading to the city. After just a few days the commander was reassigned. This gave the workers a chance to undertake an attempt to escape to the monastery, individually or in groups, by way of a bribe they passed on to their guards. When everyone was already back at the monastery, the same commander surprisingly showed up again. In truth, he never ordered the escapees to return to work but he demanded from each of them forty small coins as a bribe for himself, every month.

As the monastery filled with refugees, in time food became short. Food supplies had run out and the Kurdish siege of the monastery made supplies from the outside impossible. Hunger and lack of hygiene were the cause of death of dozens; many left the monastery in search of help wherever they could find it. Some were taken in by Arab Bedouins, others died lonely in the wastelands or in the mountains, still others found shelter among the Yezidis on the far mountain of Sinjar [176].

[23] In Gōrgīs, A., *Ǧirāḥ fī tārīkh*, pp. 29–30, an identical report is found, to which is added: 'A few days later, sixty men ventured to the village to pick grapes – hunger was prevalent. When they were in the vineyards, they were attacked by Kurds. Six were killed, and Joseph Hanno was burned alive.'

The Slaughter at Nisibis

Nisibis is a city known in ancient Christian times, called the border city as it used to separate two ancient empires: the Roman and the Persian. The famous School of Nisibis, where St Ephrem [fourth century CE] and Narsai taught, existed here.[24] The city has many gardens and it is bisected by a river, called by the Romans Hermas, by the Greeks Gandugnis and by the Arabs Jaqjaq.[25] The city was destroyed and reconstructed on numerous occasions; only the church of St Ya'qūb[26] and what remains of the city walls have survived from ancient times. For years the city was inhabited by Assyrians. At the beginning of the twentieth century several Jewish families also resided in the village and, in the years of the Christian pogroms, spiritual care was provided by a monk, Father Stephen, who suffered martyrdom.[27] In 1916 the

[24] Mar Narsai (399–492 CE) was born in the village of 'Ayn Dalbe close to Dohuk in northern Iraq. His studies at a village school, interrupted due to a Persian invasion and the death of his parents, were continued in the monastery of Kfar Mari not far from Bēṯ Zabdāy, with his paternal uncle Emmanuel, who was prior there; ten years later he moved to the famed school of Edessa. In the year 435 he replaced Theodore, who ran the school of Mopsuestia, to subsequently become the head lecturer of the school of Edessa (a post he kept for twenty years) and the school of Nisibis (for forty years). He spent the final five years of his life at the Kfar Mari monastery. He authored numerous works concerning theology, exegesis and literature, translated into various languages. Abūnā, A., *Adab al-lugha al-ārāmiyya*, pp. 117–25.

[25] The vernacular name is probably Turkish in origin.

[26] St Ya'qūb died in 338 CE and had been a participant of the First Council of Nicaea (325) and founder of the city's famous school where St Ephrem taught. The mud grave of St Ya'qūb is located underground in the ruined and currently non-functioning monastery under his name, the sole surviving testimony to the city's glorious past. In 1999 this historic monument was allegedly maintained by a Muslim family, which had arranged a flat for themselves in the upper level of the structure. Tourists were admitted for a small fee depending on the willingness of the tourists, however, generosity was appealed for. In 2003 a Christian 'guard' watched the site. As of 2020 there are no Assyrians or Christians in the town.

[27] The author stresses the fact that the priest was a monk, as many if not most priests of the Near/Middle East marry. As was previously mentioned, the author had recorded only fragmentary information heard from people residing at the Za'farān monastery. They pertain mainly to the region of Amida and Mardin. During World War I, as estimated by Davis, G., *Genocides Against the Assyrians*, pp. 25–6, 186,000 Assyrians lost their lives in the Amida and Botan/Bohtan provinces, meaning, almost a third of the population, and 186 members of the clergy were killed in a barbaric manner. This number should most probably be

Germans constructed a grand fortress on the left [southeastern] side of the city where they stored food and tools required by the workers employed in the construction of a railway line.[28]

The extermination of Christians commenced on Friday, 4 June [1915]. On this day, Razzo Najma[ddin][29] made his way to the house of Yaʿqūb Aphrahat, bound him and sent him to Mardin, where the latter died along with the local Christians.[30] The brothers of the murdered, Habib and Abd al-Karim, fled to the village of Dadushiyye. They found shelter with Ibrahim, the Arab chieftain of the Tayy tribe, who took them and their families in.

On Sunday [6 June], bad people organised round-ups of Christians in the city [177], and Abdullah Bey Sharkazoyo[31] and Abd el-Aziz Dashi ventured with their gangs into nearby Assyrian villages, bringing into the city large groups of people bound with ropes. At midnight, Riza, the head officer, took a look at the prisoners but said nothing. On Monday, 14 June, an official came and announced to the arrested that the authorities have expressed mercy for the Assyrians and that they may return to their homes. However, they were only released upon the arrival of Mahmud Shawkat, Shakir Hajji Goze, Hajji Assad Chalabi and Qaddur Bey. Not believing that they would be allowed to live in safety from that moment on, some fled to the Yezidis at Mount Sinjar. Abd al-Karim and his brother Basilus were some of these.

On Tuesday, 15 June, the soldiers returned, most certainly following someone's order, and started, without warning, to brutally kidnap Christians

supplemented by a few thousand orphaned children, who had to choose between death or submitting to a form of brainwashing by the killers of their parents and older siblings.

28 This is a reference to the Berlin-Baghdad Railway. One of these workers was the grandfather of the translator of this book (M.A.). 'In the night I smuggled food supplies from this citadel and delivered it to relatives and acquaintances who had nothing to eat,' he would say. He would also smuggle food supplies from the German-built citadel in the village of Qabre Hewore (today it is Al-Kahtaniyya, thirty kilometres to the east of Qamishli), transferring them to his starving countrymen.

29 The author does not indicate the religious affiliation or the post of this man. Perhaps he was a representative of the authorities or one who sided with them. Based on his last name, it cannot be excluded that he was originally Kurdish.

30 We do not know who this martyr was. He most likely belonged to the Christian elite of the city.

31 The Arabic word Ash-Sharkasi may be a last name, as a designation of one's origins as Cherkess.

all over the city. Almost all men and boys were captured this way. They were taken to prison and, at midnight, further to a spot called Kharabe-Kurt (meaning 'abandoned moor'), to execute them. Not one person survived.

Following this massacre, a special military unit was formed, led by Rafiq Nizam ad-Din, the task of which was to kill Christians living in the villages belonging to Nisibis. Wanting to participate in the extermination, the above-mentioned Qaddur Beg, together with Sleman Majda[ddin] organised a trip of the area, encouraging Kurdish chieftains and village leaders to have a hand in the murders of those Christians that were nearby.

Many were keen to participate in the bloodshed. The most surprising thing of all was the attitude of those Kurds who did not think twice before murdering their neighbours and people from the same locality. Such was the way, for instance, of Ibrim, owner of the village of Khezna. He led all Christians living in his village out and shot them all. His example was followed by Ahmade Usuf, owner [178] of the village of Sabha. The latter, however, single-handedly killed not only the Christians of his village but also many others brought in from other localities. Mhammade Bes, owner of the villages of Dukar, and Alike Aysho, owner of the village of Hulva, proceeded similarly. They executed 'their' Christians together with the mentioned military unit commanded by Qaddur Bey. It is obvious that, as usual, everything in possession of the murdered Christians became property of their executioners. The most wealth found its way to the family of Elias Elyudo, and others.

Following these events, the inhabitants of other villages were convinced that their lives rested in the hands of the Kurdish chieftains, aided by Turks. Some of them managed to escape, as was the case with the village of Surujiyye, Kubayba and others. Save for the village of Ger-Sheran, the owner of which, Slemane Abbas, did not harm the Christians, in other villages, such as Mharka, Gerke-Shamo and Khwetla, the Christians were slaughtered, each and every one. The executions were carried out by the people of the mentioned Qaddur, who made a pact with Ahmad Abbas, Ibrahim Khalil and Amar Us, the chieftain of the Kurdish tribe of Dagshuriyye,[32] against the followers of Christ.

[32] The Dagshuriyye was a federation of Kurdish tribes, which cooperated with the Turkish authorities. The second federation, headed by the Hawerkiyye tribe, opposed the authori-

Qaddur Bey took women and girls and gathered them in the church of St Yaʿqūb,[33] whereafter he picked out the most beautiful ones for himself and his people, leading the rest out to shoot them at the spot named Kharabe-Kurt [mentioned earlier]. He exercised particular brutality against minors – he bound all of them with rope, led them out and made horses run over them [179]. The trampling of soft bodies and young bones caused the children to die quickly. How this wildness contrasts with the attitude of the Arab leader of the Tayy tribe, named Mhammad. He imposed on his people the duty to care for Christians and solemnly forbade them to take anything from them. And when he was not able to aid all those in need, he contacted his friend, kind-hearted Yezidi leader Hammo Sharro, asking for cooperation, advice and support.

This Mhammad was said to have once been approached by a Kurdish leader, who offered him the purchase of a signet ring of uncommon artistic value. However, when Mhammad found out that the ring was earlier in the possession of a killed Christian, he declined to speak of the transaction, stating that he would not let himself enjoy owning something that the original owner could not enjoy owning [180].

The Extermination of the Christians of Amida in 1915 [continued]

Despite the fact that the collection of the monastery includes chronicles in our language, I was not able to study them sufficiently thoroughly.[34] I am aware of the fact that mastering the art of writing requires experience that I was not able to gain. However, I believe that even a thorough writer, conscious of the scope of losses, could have had trouble in describing the atmosphere among those remaining after the extermination of Christians in Amida. The darkness that characterises the architecture of this city now gained a second meaning;

ties. Assyrians were members of one as well as the other. A famed Assyrian from the second federation was Malak Barsom Safar of Midyat. He received political asylum from the French mandate forces in Syria, however, under pressure from Turkey he was released to the Turks and hanged in Kharput in 1926. A manuscript in Arabic concerning his life and work was recently found; authored by an unknown person, it counts approximately 150 pages and was supposed to be published as a brochure.

[33] The church of St Yaʿqūb was in Nisibis.

[34] The author appears to mean that the chronicles were in Syriac.

the city was in mourning, and it became, as the predecessors wrote about it, a city of blood.

Evil reached the city when one of the members of the Committee of Union [and Progress], named Reshid [Pasha], was able, as a result of certain connections and manipulations, to convince the central government in the 'city of emperors' that he should become the governor in Amida.[35] He was equipped with unlimited competences, and he was a person who was exceptionally opposed to Christians. The moment he took office he surrounded himself with people who thought just like he did, and under his direct command he organised units, the attitude of which was extremely anti-Christian: their main task was the extermination of Christians.

On 5 April Reshid Pasha came up with a truly despicable idea. He invited from the capital six officers of extremely fanatical attitudes, belonging to the same party as he did [181] and knowing the Armenian language equally well. He used them as spies. [After they arrived] he sent them to the Armenian church, where they pretended to be Armenians who fled from the capital and who arrived there encouraged by those Armenians to incite their countrymen to rise up against Turkey, in which regard they could have hoped for serious support from Russia. Acting in parallel, the people of Reshid Pasha posted in the city the appropriate announcement:

> Six Armenian rebels, themselves high-ranking and influential officers of the Turkish military, deserted from the capital, in order to orchestrate an uprising against the state and to destabilise the country. A dedicated unit is searching for them in Armenian churches and in the houses of the wealthier Armenians.

Two days after the announcement, Reshid Pasha, together with a military commander named Rishdi and other officers and soldiers, organised a parade in the main streets of the city. When they were close to an Armenian church they entered its courtyard and there they 'found and caught' these six alleged 'spies'. The well-arranged measure was supposed to make Reshid Pasha furious. In order to do this justice, he ordered a search of churches and the seat of the Armenian bishop, as he believed weapons to be hidden there. The

[35] Appointed as governor of Diyarbakır on 25 March 1915.

measure was dramatic and lasted five days. The churches were closed down. Under the pretence that the weapons may be hidden in pits under the altar floors and within walls, the churches were ordered to be taken apart, devastated and destroyed. From the morning of Monday, 12 April until Thursday, 15 April, in two city districts, Fatih Pasha and Hasuli, 614 people holding the highest authority and posts among Armenians were arrested. They were placed in a location called the *xenodochion*[36] [182] and subjected to gruesome tortures; fingernails and teeth were pulled away with pliers, while spikes were driven in feet and hands. Some of them, particularly the most resilient, were tortured so severely that they died during the tortures. The bodies of the dead were thrown away in a rubbish site. The location was supplied every day with forty to seventy new people, who were subjected to the same tortures. Similar measures were undertaken in the Christian villages around the city; the murders were merciless, while houses were plundered.

At the same time, soldiers were supposed to bring to Amida 840 Armenian workers who were, up to that point, employed in the construction of roads in Erzurum, Trabzon and Erzincan. The unbound bloodthirst of Reshid Pasha raged so strongly that he could not wait until these unlucky men made it to town, where they were supposed to be executed. He caught them en route and slaughtered each and every one.

On Sunday, 25 April, 807 men were selected from among those remaining at the *xenodochion* who were still alive. They were bound with ropes and led out through the south gate, called the Gate of Mardin. They were led outside the city to the River Tigris. There seventeen rafts were waiting for them. After approximately an hour's journey, on which the unit leader, the aforementioned Rishdi, as well as his officers and a detachment of Cherkess soldiers, embarked, the rafts stopped at a location named the Isthmus of Ramma. There, for no apparent purpose, the victims were told to write letters to their relatives, saying as follows: 'We are on our way to Mosul', whereupon they were all robbed of their possessions, stripped and killed.

Nobody counted how many such actions were conducted. They lasted until all of the arrested were led out and murdered. In each case, an Armenian bishop was witness to the transports. He was forced to stand at the Gate

[36] *Xenodochion* means a lodge or hospital in Greek.

of Mardin to watch all those bound and led to their deaths. After the last transport the Pasha told the soldiers to burn the rafts.

The city of Amida was almost purged of Armenian men. The remaining few, captured in the streets and houses, were led to the Fatih Pasha mosque and tortured. Some were chopped up into bits, others had oil poured on them to be burned alive, while the bishop, together with five priests, was first jailed, where he was subjected to such torture that even the devil could not have thought up worse, whereafter they were led to the court of the provincial office [184]. Here they were told to bend over so that their backs were horizontal and so that they could be sat on, just like one sits on donkeys. And in such positions, carrying on their back's men of heavy build, they were given brooms to sweep the streets. As for the continued unleashing of brutality, the bishop was given a stone-filled pot to put on his head and told to dance in the courtyard while he was being laughed at. They cooked eggs and put them, hot, one each, under the bishop's armpits, while in other instances he was told to hold them in his hands and squeeze them tightly. Burnt skin and meat would fall away from these spots. Finally, they brought a large nail and hammered it into the bishop's head so that it penetrated it; the sharp end pierced the lower jaw. The half-dead bishop was covered with oil and naphtha and set alight. What remained of his body was thrown away with the rubbish.

As to the fate of the five priests: each of them had a long rope tied around his neck and tightened, whereupon their bodies were dragged through the streets so long until they passed away, one after another.

When all men had their lives taken from them the units started arranging the women, youths and children into columns. One such column was led out of the city through the Gate of Rome, another through the Gate of the Mountains and still another through the Gate of Mardin.[37] When the women

[37] De Courtois, S., *The Forgotten Genocide*, p. 63, provides four Arab names of the four gates in the enormous black basalt stone walls surrounding the town. The wall, built by the Byzantines, was eight kilometres in length. The gates are: 'bab el-Mardin' on the west side, 'bab el-Rum' on the north side towards Asia Minor, 'bab el-Jebel' towards the Armenian mountains and 'bab el-Jedeed' on the eastern side towards the River Tigris. The Byzantine citadel in the centre of town was home to two temples, of which one was converted into a mosque and the other currently houses a military museum. From the beginning of the 4th century CE until the year 1933, Assyrian bishops resided in the town; the name of the first

were on their way to their deaths, the Muslims would take their infants from them, keeping them for themselves or killing them with the bound mothers looking on [185].

Jezry Margan of the village of Kasre told me:

> I wandered the wastelands of our suffering earth clothed as a Bedouin, and I saw close to the village of Shirke an Armenian column being led out of Amida. From the column four women were taken each time, stripped, killed, and the bodies were thrown into a deep well. I also saw another column made up of the elderly, women and children. When they approached the village of Taleke, the shootings began, and they were also thrown into a well. I witnessed this massacre. After I ventured away, I heard moans coming from the wells. I had prepared a strong rope, using the pieces left over there, with which the victims had been tied up. I dropped the rope into the well and pulled twelve people out. They included, among others, the son of Wazir and Khatun, daughter of Joseph Torani. I saw a third column in the village of Alye, west of the village of Taleke. The scenario was the same here, shooting people and throwing them into a well. Abd al-Qadir Bey, living not far from there, ventured to the execution site, pulled about fifty people from the well, and took them in. However, despite his efforts, they all died.

The large city of Amida, once an important Christian centre, was left without Christians. By 1917, in the streets of the city, one could only meet older Armenian and Assyrian women, who originated from the surrounding villages, as well as children aged less than twelve. These people suffered the worst that can happen in a person's life: the massacre of one's relatives and the loss of all possessions and banishment from one's village. They had nothing and begged to survive. Some groups occasionally spent nights where the destroyed Christian homes, albeit uninhabitable, remained. After a short while, the city was devastated by a terrible plague caused by lack of hygiene and dirt. Its source lay in Turkish immigrants brought in from the northern countries and from Russia. They did not know what cleanliness of the body, of clothing

one was Simon, and he participated in the First Council of Nicaea (325), while the last one was named Dionosiyyos Abd an-Nur.

and of their environment was. After they arrived, the city filled with a terrible stench. As a result of the plague, the majority of the inhabitants, including all Christians, died [187].

[On the fates of the inhabitants of other Christian localities in 1915 see annex 2].

Christian Property on Sale

Anyone venturing through the cities and villages of Mesopotamia following the extermination of their Christian inhabitants, and following their annihiliation and deportations, would notice a situation hitherto unknown. The murderers, wanting to finish their work, would search here and there for workers and carriers that they needed to carry away from the homes of Christians the entire contents: furniture, clothes rugs, and equipment, and from warehouses and stores the entire stock. When they had difficulties finding anyone willing to cooperate they forced random men from the streets to perform this job. Nobody paid anyone anything for these services. The mentioned equipment was set up for sale for insignificant sums, which strengthened the treasury of the dying [Ottoman] Empire.

I can indicate the city of Mardin as an example. Everything the Christians had in this city became state property. In order to instigate the procedure of takeover of mobile and immobile property, a special committee was set up. It was headed by the son of Hijabi and Najim, who acted following the initiative set up and organised by Hasan Mufti, Mahamad Ali Chalabi and Sadiq Sarri. Using the privileges and rights awarded to them by the authorities, they took a great body of people to aid them and told them to remove from the houses and stores all the belongings of Christians located there. The booty was collected in the largest house in the city and in the Armenian Church, turned into a warehouse, and sold by auction. The carriers never got paid for their efforts, however they gained by taking money found in the homes for themselves, without telling anybody [188].

I saw and heard personally, in various spots throughout the city, specially hired people who would hold in their hands or point to the auctioned goods, loudly encouraging pedestrians to buy. Behind them were mountains of goods that belonged to Christians. To the side, in turn, would sit the above-mentioned committee members, handed money for the sold goods.

Church furniture and liturgical items were sold in the same fashion. Some of the equipment was made of gold, others of silver. On the church floors lay torn old manuscripts and fragments of the Gospel and liturgical books, which these carriers and others would trample with their shoes. To them, these had no value at all [189].

Many Christians were wealthy. As the persecutions broke out, they hid all their jewellery and valuable items in masked pits inside their living quarters or in plastered recesses and small hidden storage units cut out in walls. They proceeded in such a way so that these valuable goods and family memoirs would not fall into the hands of petty robbers. They thought that perhaps some family members would survive and would have something to live off, or that the banished would some day return to their homes. Sadly, this was not so. The enemies were cunning and clever. Using seers and other persons practicing magic, they uncovered the spots where the treasures were hidden, and took everything away [190].

12

POSITIVE AND NEGATIVE ATTITUDES OF SOME PARTICIPANTS IN THE EXTERMINATIONS[1]

Christian Infant Rejects Muslim Breast Milk[2]

A Muslim kidnapped an infant from a lower district of Mardin, called the Gravedigger District. When his wife declined to feed the infant it was taken to a different surrogate mother. However, the infant did not want to drink the milk from her breast. After two days of trying to feed it went without success, the Muslim felt mercy for the child and gave it away to a Christian woman. The infant started sucking from her breast immediately.

The Fate of a Girl Rejecting Conversion to Islam

A soldier during the siege of the Zaʿfarān monastery told us that in the escorted Christian column he eyed for himself a young woman of exquisite looks, whom he wanted for his son's wife. Having found out about the

[1] Original title: *Divine power. Diverse news showing the truth of the faith of Christians.* Altered by the editor.

[2] For clarity, the subheadings of this and the subsequent fourteen paragraphs were edited or reformulated, or otherwise completely changed. The author used shorter titles that would not be understandable to the reader, with some of them not reflecting the contents. The contents of some of the paragraphs were cleared after the 'purging' of repetition.

scheme of the Muslim, the girl refused to submit. Following eight days of persuasion and attempts at convincing her without success, the Muslim led the girl outside the town [191] and killed her with a single shot to the head.

The Care of a Christian Mother for her Child

A Turkish soldier told us this:

> A woman with a child, aged two, in a transport of Christian women, turned to my colleague, the soldier:
>
> 'I know you are taking us to die. Take my child and treat it as if it were your own. Take these three gold coins, all I have, for his support!'
>
> My colleague took the money and put it in his pocket, after which he grabbed the child and mortally hit its head on a nearby rock with the mother watching. After we dropped the transport off in Rish 'Ayna, we returned along the same road. When we were at the spot, where the soldier murdered the child, he stopped at that rock and started boasting of his deed. Before his story was finished, he dropped to the ground, never to get up again [192].

Young Martyrs

An evil Muslim took two little girls, aged eight and twelve, from a transport, and suggested that they converted to Islam. The older one replied: 'I do not want to be with Muslims. I want to be where my parents are!'

The Muslim replied: 'Your parents and relatives are being led to their deaths, and you can survive'.

Hearing this, the girl responded: 'My mother told me that death and life are separated by a little door. And the key to that door is the weapon you are holding!'

The Muslim felt humiliated and killed the girls on the spot.

Her Alternative was Suicide

In a transport of Christian women from Amida, a girl of outstanding beauty was found. One of the soldiers escorting the column wanted to take her as his wife. She looked upon him with contempt, whereupon she took a razor blade from her pocket and cut up her belly, saying: 'This is my answer. Death is better than life with a Muslim.' [193]

The Power of Faith

A young man from Amida, being led to his death, asked his executioners not to hold his hands. He raised his arms towards the sky, whereupon he lay down on the ground and stretched out his neck, saying: 'O Christ, accept my soul!'

The executioners beheaded him with a single blow.

Fear of the Anger of the Saints

Qara Kilise ('Black Church') is a village close to Amida. In it can be found an ancient but badly damaged church, dedicated to St Elias. A large Muslim family that arrived from Van chose it as their living space. Of the Christian inhabitants of the village, only one man was left alive. He worked as a servant for one of the Muslim families. This Christian fled for the Za'farān monastery, and told us this story:

> One day, one of the Muslims living in the church found me and said: 'Up to now, five people from my family have died, and now my brother is ill. Yesterday, a man dressed in black appeared in our dream, and told us to abandon that place before we all die.' That same Muslim reported to me on the following day [194], asking for a shovel, because his brother had died. Two days later, another one of his brothers had died. Following the burial, he asked for his sheep to be separated from the village herd, as he decided to leave the village for good.

An Executioner's Tragic End

A soldier following a column distinguished himself through particular barbarism: he would kill anyone who could not keep up the pace due to weariness, old age or disease, and take their clothes later. On the way back, when he was already close to home, carrying a large sack of clothes, he was attacked by wild dogs. The family that answered his cry for help only found torn pieces of his body. The dogs had quartered him [195].

Divine-Unholy Punishment

Yihia Yasin of Amida was an officer who got wealthy thanks to everything that he had taken from Christian churches and homes. Following the extermination of Christians he began suffering an unknown disease: he lost the ability to recognise even the closest family members and the ability to discern tastes. People said that his brain got damaged. In the night, he would experience terrible nightmares and would shout: 'What are these voices that I hear from churches, demanding that I account for what I caused unto the Christians? Shut your doors and windows!' He died a short while later in the bathroom at his house.

The Intellectual Loser Kills

An eighteen-year-old woman, of exquisite beauty and body, was part of a transport of fourteen thousand people banished from Erzurum. Almost every one of the soldiers escorting the column fell in love with her, including their officer. When the column passed by the village of Harin in the Mardin region, the officer approached the girl [196] and began convincing her to marry him. She responded:

'Can't you see that none of your Muslim women can match my beauty, and the combined intelligence, knowledge and culture of the members of your tribe does not match my intelligence, knowledge and culture? If you say that I am right, then I can talk with you!'

'Yes', he responded, and then asked: 'What are your conditions?'

'Say that you are ready to divorce your wife if you accept my terms!'

When he declined responding to such a difficult question, his colleagues encouraged him to reply affirmatively and then to fulfill his original plan.

'I am ready!' he replied.

'My condition is this: convert to Christianity!'

The officer felt thrown off guard and started cursing her and calling her an infidel. His colleagues, however, calmed him down and advised him to accept her condition this time as well, but still to proceed with his goal in mind.

'Very well!' he responded.

Hearing this, she said:

'See, how for a passing passion you divorced your wife and renounced your religion! You are not a trustworthy man, and certainly not a man that a self-respecting woman would agree to marry. However, what I heard is enough for me, that you accepted Christianity. And do not think I am a traitor like you are, and that I shall renounce my faith like you just did, you, who killed my relatives with his sword. Your treachery is contrary to my noble birth and Christian attitude!' [197]

These words infuriated the suitor and fired up his aggression. He made the decision to kill the girl. However, he did not do this, one of his soldiers did. She took his hits with the words: 'Now I can die in peace. May the name of Christ, whom you accepted a moment ago, triumph!'

The girl passed on close to the locality of Suruj Khan.

The Fate of a Soldier who Believed in Christ

Abo Sheikh Khalaf, a Muslim soldier from Mardin, told me:

> I was one of those who escorted a column of Christians from Mardin to Rish 'aino. Close to a well, in the village of Tumike, we started killing the banished. One of the lower ranking officers left alive a girl he wanted to take as his wife. Despite the persuasion that she will be able to live, she vehemently rejected converting to Islam. The angered officer took out his sword and beheaded her on the spot [198].
>
> All the people who saw this scene witnessed an unexplainable phenomenon: the blood of this girl rose up like a fountain, and not one drop fell to the ground. Seeing this, the officer regretted very much his deed, and shouted: 'I give my life for the Christian faith. It is the one true faith!' His colleagues would chastise him for such a declaration, stating that only Islam is a true religion. When he refused to agree with them, they took out their automatic rifles and killed him on the spot, beside the murdered girl.

Unique, Literary or Proper Understanding of the Message of the Qur'ān?[3]

Joseph Karko lay among hundreds of bodies close to the village of Bnēbīl for two days, from the wounds inflicted upon him. As fate would have it, a Kurd he had known, one Bakir Matto, passed through the area. Joseph asked him:

'Take me to my brothers in the village of Bkhere or the Za'farān monastery!'

The Kurd stated, however: 'Your brothers were killed yesterday, using this automatic rifle, and the monastery is under siege by Kurds and it is waning. It would be better for you if you accepted Islam, because the fate of the Christians is already decided. If you do this, I shall take you in.'

Joseph declined, however: 'If my brothers died, and if the monastery falls, what would be the reason for my life? Please, kill me as well. I wish to join my brothers!'

The Kurd put the rifle nozzle to Joseph's temple, but before pulling the trigger the latter was hastily able to make three signs of the cross on his face, and cry: 'In the name of Christ, I am going to my brothers'.

The same Kurd would often, during feasts, stress the heroism and determination of Christians, repeating: 'How deeply these people adore Christ, for whom they give their lives even! Who is this Christ?'

Another martyr from Bnēbīl, an old man named Simon, would not leave his village during a time when its youths were dying for Christ. His death can serve as an example. A very bitter reflection can be found in it. Namely, when his villager compatriots were being exterminated, he had in his house a Kurdish guest, who was considered a family friend. He was a *sofi* and his name was Asad. Hearing about the extermination of the villagers under way, they exited the house together to find out what was happening. The host questioned, with a dose of doubt: 'Can it be that your fellow worshippers are now killing my relatives, despite everything?'

The guest replied: 'Nothing is going on.'

Whereupon he put an automatic rifle to the body of Simon and shot him on the spot. When Simon fell to the rock, his face turned to the east and a Kurd killed him with a blow to the head.

The last words of Simon were: 'Christ, help me!' [2nd half of page 199, p. 200 and three lines from page 201]

[3] 'O you who believe! Do not take the Jews and the Christians for friends; they are friends of each other; and whoever amongst you takes them for a friend, then surely he is one of them; surely Allah does not guide the unjust people!' (Sura V, 51).

The Faces of Hate

During one of the transports from Amida, 2,500 people were led to their deaths. When the column, into which they were arranged, reached the spot named Shkafto in the Bēṯ Ramma[4] region, they were chased into a valley located there and fire was opened on them. Each soldier had two automatic rifles. When the heated muzzle of one rifle would melt from all the shots, he would put it away and pick another rifle up. The bodies of the victims were burned for three days.

A Kurd passing by notified the soldiers stationed in a nearby village that it might be that not all Christians from the column had died, as he had seen there a priest accompanied by four men.

When the soldiers made their way to that spot, they saw nothing besides dust and glowing human bones[5] [201].

Kind-hearted People: the Yezidis

An Assyrian inhabitant of Mardin, Michael Bar Saliba, told us this:

> I kept my life most probably because until the summer of 1916 I was working on weaving tents for Arab Bedouins in the valley of Mount Sinjar. In this time I have seen many columns made up of Armenian and Assyrian Christians, but Armenians were the majority. Turkish soldiers led them and killed them here without mercy. One day, a great column of Armenians arrived. Its members were placed in many villages, of which I can name Wardiyye, Gzole, Abhara, Hol, 'Ayn Ghazal and Um Diban, to kill them the next day. I, with some Yezidis, decided to undertake an attempt at stealing away and saving as many people as we could. Under the cloak of night, we ventured to the last village. We managed to snatch seventeen men, twenty women and twelve children of the group of several hundred people kept there. We brought the rescued group unharmed before the Yezidi leader, Hammo Sharro, who praised

[4] The region between the city of Amida and the Bsheriyye region was inhabited by a Kurdish tribe of the same name, Ramma.

[5] Repeated story. The author already quoted it under item 4 [Slavelike labour and death transports].

us for our deed and who appealed for us to attempt similar actions in the future.

The same Michael also told us about the attitude of a different man.

One day, I visited a Muslim acquaintance of mine in Mosul. His name was Muhammad Bayyo. When I entered his house, he told me:

'I have good news for you: yesterday I captured three of the most beautiful Armenian women from a column of Armenians – one of them shall be for me, and the two others for my brothers. Never in my life have I seen more beautiful women.'

On that same day I went to my friends, the Yezidis, and I told them about what I heard from Muhammad. We immediately decided to free these women. Twenty-two armed men assembled. We ventured to the house of Muhammad and rescued these Armenians by force. Hammo Sharro received them, and never spared a word of thanks for us. When the rescued found out that the measure was orchestrated by a Christian, with Yezidis taking part, they could not help themselves being moved and crying in thanks for saving their lives. However, their joy quickly turned into sadness; the women got news that all of their relatives from the caravan had died, and that their families have ceased to exist [202].

BIBLIOGRAPHY

Titles originally in Arabic or Assyrian, as well as Arabic or Assyrian author names are transliterated in Latin characters.

Primary Sources

Arabic (and Arabic translations):

Bar Hebraeus. *Tārīkh az-zamān* [Chronicle of the Times]. Translated by Isḥāq Armale. Beirut: Dār al-Mashriq, 1986.

Bar Hebraeus. *Tārīkh mukhtaṣar ad-duwal* [An Abridged History of Countries]. Beirut: Dār ar-Rā'id al-Lubnānī, 1994.

The Hadith of the Prophet Muhammad. Available at <https://sunnah.com> (last accessed 21 September 2018).

'Īwāṣ, Zakkā I Ighnāṭiyyos. '*Qiṣṣat ahl al-kahf fī al-maṣādir as-suriāniyya*' [The Story of the 'People of the Cave' in Assyrian sources]. In *Rā'iḥat al-Masīḥ aḏ-ḏakiyya* [The Sweet Smell of Christ], edited by Zakkā I Ighnāṭiyyos 'Īwāṣ. Damascus: Syrian Orthodox Patriarchate, 1984.

The Qur'ān: Online Translation and Commentary. Available at <http://al-quran.info> (last accessed 21 September 2018).

Rhétoré, Jacques. *Les chrétiens aux bêtes.* Paris: Les Éditions du CERF, 2005. (Arabic version translated from French by 'Amau'īl Ar-Rayyis under title *Al-Masīḥiyyūn bayna anyāb al-wuḥūsh*, 2006).

Scher, Adday. *Tārīkh Kaldo wa Āṯūr* [The History of Chaldea and Assyria], Vol. 2. Beirut: Al-Maṭba'a al-Kaṯūlikiyya li-l-Ābā' al-Yasū'iyyīn, 1912.

Scher, Adday. *Ecole de Nisibe*. Beirut: n.p., 1905.

Ṭabarī (aṭ-). *Tārīkh al-umam wa-l-mulūk* [The History of Nations and Kings], Vol. 2. Beirut: Dār al-Kutub al-'Ilmiyya, 1997.

Greek and Polish translations:

Eusebius of Caesaria, *Eusebius' Ecclesiastical History: Complete and Unabridged.* Translated by C.F. Cruse. Peabody, MA: Hendrickson Publishers, 1998.

Eusebius of Caesaria. *Historia Kościelna. O męczennikach Palestyńskich* [History of the Church. On Palestinian Martyrs]. Edited and translated by Arkadiusz Lisiecki. Poznań, Poland: Fiszer i Majewski, 1924.

Eusebius of Caesarea. *Church History, Life of Constantine the Great, and Oration in Praise of Constantine.* Edited and translated by Arthur McGiffert and Ernest Richardson. New York: The Christian Literature Co., 1890.

Socrates of Constantinople. *Historia Kościoła* [History of the Church]. Translated by Stefan Kazikowski. Warsaw: PAX, 1986.

Sozomen, Hermiasz. *Historia Kościoła* [History of the Church]. Translated from Greek into Polish by Stefan Kazikowski. Warsaw: PAX, 1989.

Syriac translations:

Barṣōm, Aphrem I Ignatius. *The History of Tur Abdin*. Translated by Matti Moosa. Piscataway, NJ: Gorgias Press, 2008.

Barṣōm, Aphrem I Ighnāṭiyyos. *Makṯbonūṯo d-'āl aṯrō d-Ṭūr 'Abdīn* [The History of the Country of Ṭūr 'Abdīn]. Edited and translated by Ġriġorios Faulos Behnam. Lebanon: Diocese of Baghdad and Basra, Ğunie, 1964.

Çiçek, Yulius Yēshū' [Julīos Ješu Cicek] (ed). *Memre de-al sajfe da-sbaln mšīḥaje be-Turkaja men šat 1714–1914 de-sīmīn be-jad ktube surjaje de-Ṭur abdīn* [*Poems of the Sword Years in 1714–1914, Suffered by the Christians in Turkey*]. Glane and Losser, Netherlands: Bar Hebraeus Verlag, 1981.

Ishō, Ṣabrī Y. *Bardaiṣon: Kṯōbō d-nōmūsē d-aṯrāwōṯō* [Bardaisan: The Book of the Laws of the Countries]. Stockholm: Assyrian Teachers Association, 1989.

Mīkhōyel Rābō, Mōr. *Tārīkh* [The Chronicle], Vol. 1. Tranlated by Mōr Ghrighoriyyos Ṣalībā Shem'ūn [from Syriac into Arabic]. Aleppo: Dār Mārdīn, 1996. (Books XV–XXI have been translated into English Amir Harrak under the title *The Chronicle of Michael the Great*, [Piscataway, NJ: Gorgias Press, 2019]. The rest is available in Chabot's French translation at www.archive.org).

Qarabashi, Abed Mshiho Na'man. *Dmo Zliho: Vergoten Bloed: Verhalen over de gruweldaden jegens Christenen in Turkije en over het leed dat hun in 1895 en in 1914–1918 is aangedaan.* Translated by George Toro and Amil Gorgis. Glanerbrug, Netherlands: Bar Hebraeus Verlag, 2002.

Qarabashi, Abed Mshiho Na'man. *Dmo zlīḇo awkīṯ nekesto d-ʿōne da-mšīḥo* [Bloodshed, or the catastrophe of Christ's lambs]. Augsburg, Germany: Assyrian Democratic Organization, 1997.

Secondary Sources

Aktas, Timotheos Samuel. *Report on the Imminent Problems Facing The Syriac Monastery Of St Gabriel in Midyat, Turkey.* http://www.aina.org/reports/rotipftsmomg.pdf, 2008 (last accessed 21 September 2018).

Amnesty International. Extra 07/93: Fear of Torture (21 January 1993), www.amnesty.org.

Amnesty International. Turkey – Escalation in Human Rights Abuses Against Kurdish Villages (30 June 1993), www.amnesty.org.

Anschütz, Helga. *Die Syrischen Christen vom Tur 'Abdin. Eine altchrisliche Bevölkerungsgruppe zwischen Beharrung, Stagnation und Auflösung.* Würzburg, Germany: Augustinus-Verlag, 1985.

Badger, Percy George. *The Nestorians and their Rituals; With the Narratives of a Mission to Mesopotamia and Coordistan in 1842–1844.* London: Darf Publishers Limited, [1852] 1987.

Barryakoub, Afram. 'Academic Conference on Seyfo Held in Sweden'. *Zinda Magazine*, 19 November 2005, http://www.zindamagazine.com/

Barton, James L. and Ara Sarafian. *Turkish Atrocities – Statements of American Missionaries on the Destruction of Christian Communities in Ottoman Turkey, 1915–1917.* Ann Arbor, MI: Gomidas Institute, 1998.

Betts, Brenton Robert. *Christians in the Arab East: A Social Study.* Atlanta, GA: John Knox Press, 1978.

Cutts, Edward Lewes. *The Assyrian Christians. Report of the Journey, Undertaken by Desire of His Grace the Archbishop of Canterbury and His Grace the Archbishop of York.* London: R. Clay, Sons, and Taylor, 1877.

Courtois, Sébastien de. *The Forgotten Genocide of Eastern Christians. The Last Arameans.* Piscataway, NJ: Gorgias Press, 2004.

Davis, George. *Genocides Against the Assyrians.* Chicago, IL: n.p., 1999.

Eilers, Ralf. 'Leichte Beute. Assyrer in der Südosttürkei'. *Pogrom Reihe bedrohte Vólker* 170 (1993): 16–20.

Gaunt, David. *Seyfo: Folkmordet pa°assyrierna: När-var-hur*. Stockholm: Assyriska ungdomsförbundet I Sverige, 2011.

Greenaway, Norma. 'Stock Slaughtered, But Homes Intact: Villagers Return Home After Massive Turkish Fighting Subsides'. *The Vancouver Sun,* 1 May 1995, A10.

Harris, Rendel and Helen Harris. *Letters from the Scenes of the Recent Massacres in Armenia*. London: James Nisbet & Co., Ltd, 1897.

Jastrow, Otto. 'The Turoyo Language Today'. *Journal of the Assyrian Academic Society* 1 (1985–6): 7–12.

Keser-Kayaalp, Elif. 'Church Building in the Ṭūr 'Abdīn in the First Centuries of Islamic Rule'. In *Authority and Control in the Countryside: From Antiquity to Islam in the Mediterranean and Near East (Sixth-Tenth Century)*, edited by Alain Delattre, Marie Legendre and Petra Sijpesteijn, 187–91. Leiden: Brill, 2018.

Makko, Aryo. 'Living Between the Fronts: The Turkish-Kurdish Conflict and the Assyrians'. In *The Slow Disappearance of the Syriacs from Turkey and of the Grounds of the Mor Gabriel Monastery*, edited by Pieter Omtzigt, Markus Tozman and Andrea Tyndall, 63–72. Zurich and Münster: LIT Verlag, 2012.

Masters, Bruce. *Christians and Jews in the Ottoman Arab World: The Roots of Sectarianism*. Cambridge: Cambridge University Press, 2004.

Morghenthau, Henry. *The Murder of a Nation*. American General Benevolent Union of America, New York: Ararat Press, [1918] 1965. Translated into Arabic by Alaksandar Kšīšiyān. *Qatl umma*. Aleppo: Dār Ṭlās, 1990.

Naayem, Jouseph. *Shall this Nation Die?* New York: Chaldean Rescue, 1921.

Rubin, Michael. 'Are Kurds a Pariah Minority?'. *Social Research* 70(1) (2003): 295–332.

Shirinian, George. 'Background to the Late Ottoman Genocides'. In *Genocide in the Ottoman Empire: Armenians, Assyrians, Greeks, edited by* George Shirinian, 19–81. New York: Berghahn Books, 2018.

Southgate, Horatio. *Narrative of a Tour through Armenia, Kurdistan, Persia and Mesopotamia, with an Introduction and Occasional Observations upon the Condition of Mohammedianism and Christianity in those Countries*, Vol. 2. New York: D. Appleton & Co., 1843.

Stafford, Ronald Sempill. *The Tragedy of the Assyrians*. Piscataway, NJ: Gorgias Press, [1933] 2006.

Syriac Institute of Belgium. Press Release: Belgium, Liège: A New Monument Dedicated to the Assyrian (Syriac) Genocide, Atour.com (2013), www.atour.com.

Syriac Strategic Research Center. Impact of Turkish Occupation on Syriac Christians in North East Syria: 30 Day Situation Report (2019), https://www.european-syriac-union.org/news-reader/impact-of-turkish-occupation-on-syriac-christians-in-north-east-syria-30-day-situation-report.html

Talay, Shabo and Soner Onder Barthoma, eds. *Sayfo 1915: An Anthology of Essays on the Genocide of Assyrians/Arameans during the First World War*. Piscataway, NJ: Gorgias Press, 2018.

Travis, Hannibal. 'Native Christians Massacred: The Ottoman Genocide of the Assyrians during World War I'. *Genocide Studies and Prevention* 1(3) (2006): 327–71.

Vööbus, Arthur. 'The Contribution of Ancient Syrian Christianity to the West European Culture'. *Journal of Assyrian Academic Society* 2 (1988): 8–14.

Vööbus, Arthur. *History of the School of Nisibis*. Leuven: Peeters, 1965.

Wigram, William Ainger. *Our Smallest Ally: A Brief Account of the Assyrian Nation in the Great War*. London: Society for Promoting Christian Knowledge/New York: Macmillan, 1920.

Witakowski, Witold. *The Syriac Chronicle of Pseudo-Dionysius of Tel-Maḥrē. A Study in the History of Historiography*. Uppsala, Sweden: Acta Universitatis Upsaliensis, 1987.

Yohannan, Abraham. *The Death of a Nation or the Ever-persecuted Nestorians or Assyrian Christians*. New York: G. P. Putnam's Sons, 1916.

Yonan, Gabriele. *Ein vergessener Holocaust. Die Vernichtung der christlichen Assyrer in der Türkei* [A Forgotten Holocaust: The Extermination of the Christian Assyrians in Turkey]. Göttingen: Gesellschaft für Bedrohte Völker, 1989.

Yonan, Gabriele. *Journalismus bei den Assyrern*. Berlin: Zentralverband der Assyrischen Vereinigungen, 1985.

Young, John. *By Foot to China*. Chicago: Assyrian International News Agency, 1984.

Arabic:

Abūnā, Albert. *Adab al-lugha al-ārāmiyya* [Literature in Aramaic], 2nd edn. Beirut: Dār al-Mashriq, 1996.

Abūnā, Albert. *Tārīkh al-kanīsa as-suriāniyya ash-sharqiyya* [The History of the Assyrian Church of the East], Vol. 1, 3rd edn. Beirut: Dār al-Mashriq, 1992.

Abūnā, Albert. *Shuhadā' al-Mashriq* [Martyrs of the East], Vol. 1. Baghdad: n.p., 1985.

Armala, Ishaq. *Tāriẖ al-kanīsa as-suriāniyya* [History of the Syriac Church]. Beirut: Beth Zabdai, 1996.

Baḥzānī, Khidr Khalāt. 'Az-Zirā'a: a'yāduhā, falsafatuhā, asāṭīruhā wa ashyā' ukhra' [Agriculture and Related Holidays, Philosophy, Legends and other Aspects]. *Laliş* (20) (2003): 40–73.

Bāqasre, Salim 'Izz ad-Dīn. *Al-Izīdiyya* [Yezidism]. Nuhadra: Iraq Laliş Cultural Centre, 2003.

Barṣōm, Augin Mnoufar. *Aḍwā' 'alā adabina as-suriānī al-ḥadīṯ* [On Our Contemporary Assyrian Literature]. Beirut: Dār Qenneshrīn, 1991.

Danani, Qasim Shammo. 'Aṣ-Ṣirā' bayna ash-shēkh Ḥasan wa Badr ad-Dīn Lu'lu' [The Fight between Shēkh Ḥasani and Badr ad-Dīn Lu'lu']. *Laliş* 20 (2003): 14–33.

Gōrgīs, Asmar al-Qass. *Ǧirāḥ fī tārīkh as-Syriān* [Wounds in Assyrian History]. Translated by Ṣubḥī Yonān. Beirut: Union of Assyrians in Beirut, 1986.

Ḥaddād, Benyamen. 'Riḥlat al-abb Vincenzo ilā al-'Irāq' [The Journey of Father Vincenzo to Iraq]. *Magallat Magma' al-Lugha as-Surianiyya*, 1(1) (1975): 179–203.

Hitti, Philip. *Tārīkh Sūriyyā wa Lubnān wa Filasṭīn* [The History of Syria, Lebanon and Palestine], Vol. 2. Translated by K. Al-Yāzǧī. Beirut: Dār Aṯ-Ṯaqāfa, 1972.

Isḥāq, Laḥdō. *Amṯāl ša'biyye min Bāzebde* [Sayings from Bāzebde]. Published independently, 1994.

Isḥāq, Laḥdō and Joseph Asmar. *Sīrat ḥayāt Mār Āhō* [Life of St Āhō]. Damascus: Dar al-'Ilm, 1992.

Morgenthau, Henry. *Qatl umma* [The Murder of a Nation]. Translated by Aleksander Kashishian. Aleppo: Dār Ṭlās, 1990.

Nāmiq, Yūsuf. *Al-Qāfila al-akhīra* [The Last Caravan]. Aleppo: Dār ar-Ruhā, 1991.

Naṣrī, Buṭrus. *Ḏakhīrat al-aḏhān fī tawārīkh al-mashāriqa wa-l-maghāriba as-Syriān* [A Host of Thoughts in the Histories of East and West Assyrians], Vol. 1. Mosul: Dayr al-Ābā' ad-Domnikiyyīn, 1905.

Odisho, William. 'Mawqif almānyā an-nāziyya min al-mas'ala al-āšūriyya' [The Position of Nazi Germany regarding the Assyrian Question]. *Beth-Nahrain Star, Journal of Assyrian Cultural Centre* 1 (1993): 7–16.

Qaṣṣāb (al-), Ya'qūb. 'Al-Iḍṭihād al-arba'īnī wa naṣāra Ḥidyāb: 339–379' [Forty Years of Persecution and the Christians of Adiabene in 339–379]. *Qāla Suryāya* 32–3 (1984): 128–39.

Sākā, Isḥāq. *Kanīsatī As-Suriāniyya* [My Syriac Church], Vol. 1. Damascus, Syria, 1985.

Segal, Judah Benzion. *Ar-Ruhā – al-madīna al-mubāraka* [Edessa – the Blessed City]. Tranlated by Yoseph Ibrahim Jabra. Aleppo: Dār ar-Ruhā, 1988.

Terrazzi, Philip de. *'Aṣr as-Syriān ad-Ḏahabī* [Golden Age of Assyrian Christians]. Aleppo: n.p., 1979.

Ya'qūb, Sewerios T. *Tārīkh al-kanīsa as-suriāniyya al-anṭākiyya* [History of the Syrian Church of Antioch], Vol. 2. Beirut: n.p., 1957.

Modern Assyrian and Syriac:

Beṯ-Şawoce, Jan (ed). *Beth-Zabday Azech. Vad hände 1915?* [Beth-Zabday Azech. What Happened in 1915?]. Norrköping, Sweden: Bokförlaget Azret Azech, 2009.

Beṯ-Şawoce, Jan. *Sayfo b Ṭurcabdin* [The Sword in Ṭūr 'Abdīn]. Södertälje, Sweden: Beṯ-Froso & Bēṯ-Prasa, Nsibin, 2006.

Beth-Kinne, Nahro. 'Yokedilme Yolundaki Bir Hiristiyan Azinlik: Asurlar' [A Christian Minority on its Way to Destruction: Assyrians]. *Nisibin* 54(2) (1994): 14.

Çiçek, Yulius Yēshū' (ed). *Mimrē d-'āl sayfē dasbāl mshīḥōyē d-Turkia mēn shnāṯ 1714–1914* [Poems on the Years of the Sword, 1714–1914, Experienced by Christians in Turkey]. Glane-Losser, Netherlands: Bar Hebraeus Verlag, 1981.

Haddād, Binyamen. 'Rihlat al-abb Vincenzo ilā al-'Irāq'. *Magallat Magma' al-Lugha as-Surianiyya*, 1(1) (1975): 179–203.

Sa'īd, 'Azīz. 'Lecture given on Day 71 in the headquarters of the Assyrian Federation of Ṭūr 'Abdīn in Holland'. *Shemsho* 8(31) (1993): 58–60.

Slēmān, Ḥennō. *Gunḥe d-Suryoye d-Ṭūr 'Abdīn* [Tragedies of the Assyrians in Ṭūr 'Abdīn]. Glane-Losser, Netherlands: Bar Hebraeus Verlag, 1987.

Polish (and translated into Polish):

Abdalla, Michael. 'The Term *Seyfo* in Historical Perspective'. In *The Assyrian Genocide: Cultural and Political Legacies*, edited by Hannibal Travis, 92–105. Abingdon & New York: Routledge, 2018.

Abdalla, Michael. 'Jihad in Practice. The Assyrians of Azakh in Upper Mesopotamia during World War I: Resistance, Agreement, Demilitarization and Exodus'. *Wrocławskie Studia Erazmiańskie* XI (2017): 141–86.

Abdalla, Michael. 'The Fate of Āzakh: An Assyrian Town in Ṭūr 'Abdīn, Turkey'. *Journal of Assyrian Academic Studies* 22(1) (2008): 59–77.

Abdalla, Michael. 'Losy chrześcijan himjaryckich jemeńskiego miasta Nadżran (VI–X w.) w źródłach arabskich i asyryjskich' [The History of Himiarite Christians of the Yemeni City of Najran in Arab and Assyrian sources]. In *Arabowie-*

Islam-Świat, edited by Marek M. Dziekan and Izabela Kończak. Łódź, Poland: Ibidem, 2007, 557–69.

Abdalla, Michael. 'Między świętością a barbarzyństwem. 1600 lat asyryjskiego monasteru w Turcji' [Between Sanctity and Barbarism. 1600 Years of an Assyrian Monastery in Turkey]. *Przegląd Prawosławny* [Orthodox Journal] 1 (1998): 23–4 & 32.

Abdalla, Michael. 'Asyryjska diaspora' [The Assyrian Diaspora]. *Sprawy narodowościowe* [Nationalities Affairs – A New Series] 3/1(4) (1994): 55–75.

Abdalla, Michael. 'Losy Asyryjczyków' [The Fate of the Assyrians]. *Sprawy Narodowościowe – Seria nowa* [Nationalities Affairs – A New Series] 2/1(2) (1993): 67–82.

Abdalla, Michael. 'Śladami asyryjskich misjonarzy' [In the Footsteps of Assyrian Missionaries]. *Przegląd Prawosławny* [Orthodox Journal] 5 & 7 (1993): 23–4 & 26–7.

Abdalla, Michael. 'The Assyrian Community of Qamishli in North-Eastern Syria in the Years 1925–1970'. *Ethnologia Polona* 17 (1992): 74–84.

Abdalla, Michael. 'Z kręgu folkloru chrześcijańskich Asyryjczyków' [From the Folklore of Christian Assyrians]. *Literatura Ludowa* [Folk Literature] 4–6 (1988): 63–76.

Atiya, Aziz Surial. *Historia Kościołów Wschodnich* [A History of Eastern Christianity]. Collective translation into Polish. Warsaw: PAX, 1978.

Daniélou, Jean and Henri Irenée Marrou. *Historia Kościoła* [Nouvelle Histoire de l'Église], Vol. 1. Polish translation by Maria Tarnowska. Warsaw: PAX, 1984.

Fischer-Wollpert, Rudolf. *Leksykon papieży* [Lexikon der Päpste]. Polish translation by Bernard Białecki. Kraków, Poland: Znak, 1990.

Flavius, Josephus. *Wojna żydowska* [The Jewish War]. Edited and translated by Jan Radozycki. Poznań, Poland: Księgarnia św. Wojciecha, 1984.

Hauziński, Jerzy. '*W kwestii początków wspólnoty jezydów w Iraku*' [On the Beginnings of the Yezidi Community in Iraq]. In *Niemuzułmańskie mniejszości Iraku. Historia-Kultura-Problemy przetrwania* [Non-Muslim Minorities of Iraq. History-Culture-Problems of Survival], edited by Michael Abdalla. Poznań, Poland: Wydawnictwo Poznańskie, 2008.

Hitti, Philip. *Dzieje Arabów* [History of the Arabs]. Translated by Wojciech Dembski, Maria Skuratowicz and Edward Szymański. Warsaw: PWN, 1969.

Joannès, Francis. *Historia Mezopotamii w I. tysiącleciu przed Chrystusem* [The Age of Empires: Mesopotamia in the First Millennium BC]. Translated by Stefan Zawadzki. Poznań, Poland: Wydawnictwo Poznańskie, 2007.

Kałużyński, Stanisław. *Tradycje i legendy ludów tureckich* [Traditions and Legends of Turkish Peoples]. Warsaw: Iskry, 1986.

Kocot, Kazimierz Witold and Karol Wolfke. *Wybór dokumentów do nauki prawa międzynarodowego* [Selection of Documents for International Law Studies]. Wrocław-Warsaw: PWN, 1972.

Kucharczyk, Grzegorz. *Pierwszy holocaust XX wieku* [The First Holocaust of the 20th Century]. Warsaw: Biblioteka Frondy, 2004.

Laborde, Józef. 'Wspomnienia z Mezopotamii 1850–1860' [Memories from Mesopotamia 1850–1860]. *Missye katolickie* 9 (7) (1890): 176–80.

Lang, David Marshall. *Armenia. Kolebka cywilizacji* [Armenia. Cradle of Civilization]. Translated into Polish by Tadeusz Szafar. Warsaw: PIW, 1975.

Lang, David Marshall. *Dawna Gruzja* [The Georgians]. Translated by Wojciech Hansel. Warsaw: PIW, 1972.

Layard, Henry Austen. *W poszukiwaniu Niniwy* [In Search of Vineveh]. Translated by Wacław B. Mrugalski. Warsaw: WAiF, 1983.

Paolucci, Giorgio and Camille Eid. *Islam – sto pytań* [Islam – a Hundred Questions]. Translated from Italian into Polish by Karol Klauza. Warsaw: PAX, 2004.

Pigulewska, Nina. *Kultura syryjska we wczesnym średniowieczu* [The Syriac Culture in the Early Middle Ages]. Translated by Czesław Mazur. Warsaw: PAX, 1989.

Popko, Maciej. *Turcja* [Turkey]. Warsaw: Wiedza Powszechna, 1984.

Rufin, Bernard C. *Apostołowie po Kalwarii* [The Twelve. The Lives of the Apostles After Calvary]. Translated by Piotr Kiernicki. Gdańsk, Poland: Exter, 1994.

Santucci, Luigi and Stanisław Klimaszewski. *Legendy chrześcijańskie* [Christian Legends]. Translated by Adam Szymanowski. Warsaw: Wydawnictwo Księży Marianów, 1990.

Simon, Marcel. *Cywilizacja wczesnego chrześcijaństwa* [The Civilisation of Early Christianity]. Translated from French into Polish by Eligia Bąkowska. Warsaw: PIW, 1979.

Starowieyski, Marek. *Dwunastu Pseudo Abdiasza. Historie apostolskie* [The Twelve of Pseudo-Abdias. Apostolic Stories]. Kraków, Poland: WAM, 1996.

Stępień, Tomasz. '*Pseudo-Dionizy Areopagita – u źródeł chrześcijańskiego rozumienia symbolu*' [Pseudo-Dionysius – at the Sources of the Christian Concept of the Symbol]. In *Niemuzułmańskie mniejszości Iraku. Historia – Kultura – Problemy przetrwania* [Non-Muslim Minorities of Iraq. History – Culture – Problems of Survival], edited by Michael Abdalla, 209–16. Poznań, Poland: Wydawnictwo Poznańskie, 2008.

Szymusiak, Jan Maria and Marek Starowieyski. *Słownik wczesnochrześcijańskiego piśmiennictwa* [Lexicon of Early Christian Literature]. Poznań, Poland: Księgarnia św. Wojciecha, 1970.

Ternon, Yves. *Ormianie. Historia zapomnianego ludobójstwa* [Armenians. The History of a Forgotten Genocide]. Translated by Wawrzyniec Brzozowski. Kraków, Poland: Uniwersytet Jagielloński, 2005.

Wipszycka, Ewa. *Kościół w świecie późnego antyku* [The Church in the World of Late Antiquity]. Warsaw: PIW, 1994.

ANNEX 1

On the fate of the inhabitants of other Assyrian localities in 1895 mentioned in the book of A. Gōrgīs (1986)[1]

Ar-Ruha (Urfa) [Urhoy, Edessa][2] (p. 15)

Shaltael was a Christian blacksmith quite well known in the region. One day Muslims found the way to him, one by one, with orders for him to sharpen their swords, spears and other weapons. The craftsman was on the one hand happy, but on the other hand he feared that his customers might be up to something. He was not wrong in this. Soon, hordes of Muslims assaulted Christians; they would kill anyone they met in the street with daggers, they would plunder stores and flats, later burning them. The Christians fled to the roofs of their houses but they could not find refuge there either. Whoever could manage took shelter in the Great Cathedral that could hold several thousand people. And the angry mob of attackers found its way to them, like wild beasts. They destroyed the gates and entered the structure. All were

[1] Locality names used by A. Gōrgīs in Arabic were kept in original forms.

[2] According to a report by Edward Lewes Cutts, *The Assyrian Christians. Report of the Journey, Undertaken by Desire of His Grace the Archbishop of Canterbury and His Grace the Archbishop of York*, pp. 4–6, in 1876 the city counted 29,210 inhabitants, including 1,520 Assyrians.

slaughtered. The bodies lay in layers, in the streets and squares, in the houses and courtyards, but the most lay in the Cathedral. Armenians were the prime victims.

Weran Shahr[3] (Goran, Tella, Tel Mauzal[t]) (p. 23)

It is a city that was once razed as a result of an earthquake, but it was rebuilt by Emperor Constantine the Great in 357.[4] Before 1895 about three thousand Christian families resided here. On 3 November 1895 the city was attacked by Kurdish gangs, which began looting the Christians' stores. Hearing about this, the Turkish officer Ibrahim Pasha led his military and chased the Kurds out of the city. But the second day, the Kurds attacked the city again. This time Ibrahim Pasha, himself leading the actions of his men, destroyed six fortresses belonging to Kurds, confiscated their weapons, and thus dispelled the Kurds.

At this time, a caravan with a grand volume of goods belonging to Christian traders arrived from Aleppo. The goods were to be delivered to Mardin. However, Ibrahim Pasha advised the travellers against continuing: 'I fear the Kurds will attack you, kill you, and take all your goods!'

Pasha unloaded the goods in the courtyard of his palace and for twenty days the traders were his guests. Subsequently, he transported the goods to Mardin under heavy military escort.

Dereke (p. 25)

Dereke is an old and picturesque Assyrian locality, often mentioned by chroniclers, even if I were to name only Dionysius of Tel-Mahre from the 8th century.[5] It is located close to Mardin and is rich in sources of clean and healthy water, surrounded by olive trees and pistachio gardens. The ruins of an old monastery can be found not too far from it. The modern inhabitants are Assyrians and Armenians, among whom one can find Catholics and Protestants. On the morning of 20 November 1895 Kurds from nearby vil-

[3] Current name: Viranşehir.

[4] Wrong date; Constantine the Great died on 22 May 337.

[5] To this chronicle, ascribed to a patriarch of the Syrian Orthodox Church, the already mentioned Witold Witakowski had devoted a scientific paper, *The Syriac Chronicle of Pseudo-Dionysius of Tel-Maḥrē. A Study in the History of Historiography.*

lages mobilised their forces to attack the people of Dereke. However, a military unit of 150 soldiers, commanded by Osman Agha Rashsho, stationed nearby, reacted on time; they prevented the Kurds from executing their plan, dispelled them, and the Christians went unharmed.

Tel Arman[6] (p. 26)

This village lies a three-hour walk away from Mardin and is inhabited by Assyrians and Armenians. Feeling danger from the Kurds the inhabitants agreed with Reshid Agha, leader of the Kikiyye, and with the deputy commander of the units of Hamidiyye that for protection they shall pay them ninety gold lira. However, the units demanded 400 lira and a mare of noble breed. The inhabitants collected the money and gave it to these men, together with the mare. As it turned out, the persons whom they trusted betrayed them. In secret, they gave their countrymen, the Kurds, the green light to storm the village. As usual in such cases, the Christians hid in the church.[7]

The bandits surrounded the church and promised that if those inside surrendered they could hope for their mercy. This was a further despicable ruse, but the Christians had no choice. When all were out, the Kurds started stripping them and murdering further people in cold blood. This occurred before the eyes of these men, who stood on the roof of a house located opposite, laughing sarcastically. One of the Muslims entered the church and tore away an icon depicting St John, tearing it up, but when he proceeded to burn it he dropped dead on the spot. The wife of the leader of the city of Kerboran told this to me, as she was there together with her mother. It was exactly her who taught me spoken Turkish, and her husband, Reshid Bey, who taught me to write in Turkish.[8]

[6] The village is now known as Kızıltepe (Gaunt, D., *Massacres*, p. 261).

[7] See also Gaunt, *Massacres*, pp. 262–3.

[8] One of the reports informs about what happened in this village in 1915: 'Abrahameeya and Tel Armin. The first is wholly Assyrians – some fifty houses and out-station of ours, and the second a Papal Armenian and Assyrian village of more than 300 houses.' Report of Ḥannā Sheikhi, a Protestant brother, who escaped massacre by being taken for a Koord [sic]. 'When the Koords came down the mountains and attacked and plundered the village of Abrahameeya, I was in Mardin on business. Learning of what was going on, I started to return to my village, but found that when it was attacked, so many of the villagers who were able had fled to Tel Ermin, and had taken refuge in the large church and yard of the

Goliyye (Al-Qusur) (p. 27)

What can I say of Goliyye, this large Assyrian village of more than five hundred families, located on a plateau, a three-hour walk away to the south of Mardin?

When its inhabitants heard of what happened at Tel Arman, they turned to the leader (*mutasarrif*)[9] with a plea to protect them from Kurds. He provided them with a military unit of 150 soldiers, which he referred to as the 'rescue party', commanded by Fuad Efendi and Sadik Bey, deputy to the Hamidiyye army stationed there. When the soldiers reached the village, they noticed that the Christians had gathered in churches. They entered the houses of the inhabitants, took all weapons they found, and left, promising that they shall watch the situation carefully and, should danger arise, they would quickly arrive to defend the inhabitants.

That same night Kurds from the south started arriving at the surrounding villages, in order to jointly attack Goliyye and its inhabitants. The attack took place on Friday morning. Over fifty people were killed in less than an hour. Some of the victims fled, the rest climbed onto the roof of a church. The Kurds surrounded the site and also started climbing to the roof of the church. At that moment one of the Christians threw himself off the roof, falling straight onto a spear impaled in the earth. The spear pierced him through. A different Christian managed to pull this spear out of the ground and flee. The owner of this spear ran after him, shouting: 'A Christian stole my spear!'

From among the women and children who did not manage to escape

Papal Armenians where, along with those who had been left in Tel Armin, the Koords were making their second dab at the defenceless christians. I at once armed myself with a big stick and rushed into the churchyard to look for the members of my family and other relatives. Meantime I was shooting and swinging my big stick to prevent attracting the attention of the Koords to myself while I went around the yard and over the church building in my hunt. As I had let my beard grow and was wearing a Koordish headgear, the Koords took me to be one of them, and so I escaped being killed. My search was fruitless, since they probably had all been killed at Abrahameeya. I accordingly returned to Mardin and went straight to the Armenian Boys' High School, where I met Mr Andrus and told him the story before I sought much needed rest'. (Barton, J. L. and Sarafian, A., *Turkish Atrocities*, p. 101. See also Gaunt, D., *Massacres*, pp. 262–3.)

9 Head of a sanjak (district); during the Ottoman rule vilayets were divided into sanjaks.

the Muslims collected those they liked. The rest were murdered on the spot, whereafter the village was set on fire; the Muslims left with their booty.

Qal'at Mara [Ḥesnō d-Attō] (p. 29)

A famous and large Assyrian village on a mountaintop, close to the blessed Za'farān monastery to its east. Having found out about the Christian massacres, some inhabitants went to the monastery, from which they took all the [lead] printing forms used by the monastery printing house and melted them into shells. Thanks to these shells, there were able to ward off subsequent Kurdish attacks for five days, losing only four men, including one very old person. However, officer Abd Efendi was able manage what the Kurds were not able to do. He commanded a sniper unit. He surrounded the village from all sides, killing seventy people over the course of a week. During the siege, some of the inhabitants managed to flee to the monastery but the thirty-soldier unit sent away by the authorities brought them back to the village.

ANNEX 2

On the fate of Christians in 1915 in other localities mentioned in the book by A. Gōrgīs.

Ar-Ruha[1] [Urhoy, Edessa] (pp. 21–2)

Twenty years after the massacres of 1895, the time came for another slaughter, this time carried out with much more barbarism. Not all citizens reacted positively to the call of the state authorities concerning the necessity of surrendering any and all weapons. Without undertaking any sort of persuasive actions, the Turkish military, commanded by two German officers, suddenly attacked Edessa; the fortress was pounded using heavy cannons until it was razed to the ground, with scores of people dying inside. Afterwards, the military entered the town and started rounding up Armenians, murdering them in their own homes. An Armenian provost was dragged out of one of the churches, subjected to torture and then hanged. When he was being led to the gallows, he screamed: 'May I die as an offering to Christ and in love for Armenia!' They also killed many other Christians who could not enjoy amnesty, which was announced too late.

[1] Here the author does not give the parallel Turkish name in brackets, as he did earlier.

I came into possession of the memoirs of Salih Salim Pasha, the *wali* of Edessa, whose son studied with us for thirty years. Below are the interesting contents of one of the pages:

> During World War I a serious conflict between the Kurds on the one hand and the Armenians and Assyrians on the other hand emerged in Edessa. The former would gather in mosques, the latter in churches. Feeling rising tensions, I have drawn up a *firman* and ascribed it to the sultan. Its contents were as follows: 'Anyone who would be looking for a reason to kill, shall himself be killed'. The *firman* was posted at the gates of both churches as well as mosques. This was a grave risk on my part. Somebody might have accused me of seeking to replace the sultan. This is rewarded with capital punishment. However, having found out about what I have done, the sultan did not become angry, but instead he awarded me a medal. When I found out that the Kurds had illegally appropriated many precious items and much property belonging to Christians, I ordered them to return it all. And to the Christians, not seeing any changes of survival in their city, and who decided to emigrate to Aleppo, I granted protection along the entire march route.[2]

Waran Shahr (Goran, Tella, Tel Mauzal[t]) (p. 24)

In 1915 the Turkish army was stationed in force in the region between the border with Russia and the border with Persia. Everywhere, in cities such as Amida [Diyarbakır], Mardin, Si'irt, Bitlis, Rondan, Edessa, Midyat, Gziro and Nisibis, and the villages belonging to these, weapons were searched for, particularly those possessed by Christians. Before 1915 Weran Shahr was home to about 600 Christian families belonging to various churches.[3] At

[2] Gōrgīs continues: 'The simplicity of the Pasha was appreciated by the patriarchal emissary of the Syrian Orthodox Church in Edessa, who sent him a letter of gratitude. The Pasha was transferred first to Bitlis and then to Adana, where he was appointed minister of internal affairs of Turkey. In all the places that he would be posted, the Christians felt safe, and he would harm nobody. He spent his final years in Beirut. Many Assyrians participated in his funeral, particularly those stemming from Edessa.' Sadly, the author does not indicate the date of death of this good man.

[3] The name of the place is more typically spelled Virenshehir in English or Viranşehir in Turkish. Tel-Mawzal may be another name for it. The Assyrian population estimates range from 1,000 to 2,000. (Gaunt, D., *Massacres*, p. 267.)

the beginning of May the army initiated its procedure of searching to collect arms. Despite the fact that nothing was found among the Christians here a messenger of the *wali* of Amida came to the town and arrested the Christian leaders, threatening to kill them. He implemented his threats on 11 May, killing some of them. On 20 May one of the arrested men, named Abd al-Ahad, felt that he was soon to die, due to the ordeal he had to endure. He asked to see his mother and sister, with whom he would like to exchange farewells. The guards consented to this plea but on 8 June he died, together with eight others who were with him. On 15 June, in turn, the Armenian priest Isaac was killed; on 17 June the army and the Kurds filled the streets and squares of the city like locusts. All males aged between 12 and 70 were caught, 475 in total. All were bound in chains, in groups of four persons, and thrown in jail, to be led outside the city the following morning to be murdered. They subsequently collected the remaining youths as well as women and girls, 1,500 persons in total. They stripped them, divided them into three groups and treated them just like they did before. Father Gabriel Ahmar Dakno was among those who died. One of the brutals, named Ayyub Hamza Agha, confessed to the murder, having heard in the streets the call: ‘Christians are dogs that should be killed’.

Dereke (pp. 25–6)

In June of 1915 the ruthless Reshid despatched two officers to the house of Osman, where a meeting with the priests of all churches was taking place. Following the meeting the priests were released home, to be arrested moments later, with the demand that all the weapons in possession of Christians be handed over. A few days later, another officer appeared, this time with the pleasant news of the sultan’s amnesty for Christians. At the same time this officer had met in the night with the Muslim leaders and sheikhs, including Ibrahim Khalil and Alias Hajji Osman. He told them: ‘Anyone who would help the Christians will be killed.’ That same night, the authorities arrested many Christians and threw them into jail. Nobody knew what the deal was in this case.

But, as a few days passed, more important Muslim fanatics gathered before the prison. Together with the delegate of Reshid, they first hung the priests in the prison and subsequently they led out one group of Christians after another. They proceeded in the same manner with the Christians residing in their houses, irrespective of age or gender. However, they took the prettiest women and girls for themselves as slaves.[4]

Sha'bin (Kara Hasan) (pp. 33–4)

This village is located in the vilayet of Amida, and it was inhabited mostly by Armenians. However, Muslims lived there as well. When news about the Christian massacres reached the Armenian citizens, they decided to attack Muslims before they would attack them. And they proceeded this way: they exterminated them and burned down their houses.

Muslims from the surrounding villages heard of this and they mobilised a great army and executed a crushing attack on Armenians. Not being able to stand up to such a grand army the Armenians fled to a castle not far from Shabin. Fifteen days earlier, two Armenians of Erzurum hid in this castle, as in their city no single Armenian citizen was left alive. When one hid in a well with his rifle, the other one would go to Shabin to listen to news and beg for some bread.

When walking to the village of Shabin one day he met along the road its Armenian inhabitants. They were running away to the same castle, where he resided with his colleague. He did not continue his trip but returned to the castle with them.

The refugees had no time to rest. They were attacked. It was only after three days the one who was getting the bread previously remembered his colleague. He went and pulled him from the well; the colleague was almost exhausted.

After fifteen days of effective defence, the Armenian chieftain, Murad, summoned his people and said: 'This continued fight has no sense. The army, that will aid the Kurds, is approaching. We have to leave this place. Only women and children should remain in the castle. May God have mercy with them and spare their lives!'

These men, numbering about a hundred, emerged and escaped to the

[4] The author concludes this paragraph with the words: 'Volumes could be written on this. It suffices to remember that a total of 620,000 people were killed in the city of Amida and its surroundings.'

nearby tree-covered mountain. And the Kurds, in turn, entered the castle, murdering everyone that resided there.

These men, who were being hunted in the forest, defended themselves with all the resources they had. Most would be killed or die of hunger; a week later, fifteen were still alive. When they were fleeing to a different forest they encountered a group of Muslims from Erzurum. During their conversation they pretended to be Muslims hunting Christians. When the Armenians heard each of them boasting of the number of Christians they had killed in Erzurum, they opened fire on them and killed them on the spot.

Night fell. The closest village was Muslim. Music and singing could be heard from it. They came closer and saw a crowd of men watching two young Christian women dance at the centre. They were completely naked. The Armenians could not tolerate such humiliation. They opened fire again, killed many of the onlookers, and fled. They were planning on making it to the Armenian-Assyrian village of Kfardis. However, before entering the village, they stopped and randomly selected one who would venture ahead into the village. Fate decided it was to be Sergius. When he entered the village, he stopped in front of a store owned by a Christian acquaintance of his. A soldier passing by arrested him and took him to his commander.

'Who are you?' asked the commander.

'I am Kurdish!' replied Sergius.

The commander hit him in the face, shouting: 'Speak the truth!'

'I am Armenian. I served in the military, but when I heard that Christians were being murdered I came to check whether any one of them was left alive'.

Sergius was sentenced to prison in the night and forced labour during the day.

> On the first day, I received bread and yoghurt, but in the following days I did not get anything to eat. I feared I might die of hunger. One day, an unknown Agha reported to the commander, telling him: 'Release this Christian to me. Contrary to others, I have not killed a single one yet.'
>
> The commander agreed to this. The Agha took me to his home. He fed me, and asked: 'Would you like me to bring your wife here? I took her from the castle. She was wounded, but she is alive.'

As it turned out, the Agha came from the same village as I did. But I did not recognise him.

My wife was alone, without any of our three children. They died at the castle.

We spent a few years with the Agha. And when the situation calmed down, we travelled to Aleppo.

I have no knowledge of the fate of my colleagues, whom I have left on the outskirts of Kfardis.

Kfardis (pp. 36–7)

During the state-run operation of collecting weapons from the citizens the Christians of the village released their weapons but the Muslims did not. This caused uneasiness among the Christians, even more so as the authorities knew about this. In truth, only Armenians were supposed to be the target of this ethnic cleansing, but how many times have the Christians heard: 'A Christian is a Christian – Assyrian or Armenian!' And abuse and curses such as *giaour* (infidel) were a daily ritual. Was the conversion to Islam, as it happened elsewhere, the only choice for the local Christians?

Sadly, the Muslims of Kfardis would start to use the weapons they held against Christians.

One of the citizens, named George, knew that his wife and children were killed. He was left alone and was of old age. And as he resisted, the commander ordered two soldiers to take him far away from the village and for him to be shot there. The soldiers bound his feet and hands and told him to jump while they watched. He could not stand this. Knowing the soldiers can be bribed, he told them: 'A former commander, who resided here, gave me ten small coins once!'

Hearing this, the soldiers unbound his rope and released his hands. He sat down, rested a while, and then said: 'I had 200 lira at home. If you release my legs as well the liras are yours!'

The soldiers freed his legs and gave him some food and water and, as the time for prayer came, they both ventured to a nearby source to cleanse themselves and pray. Utilising the situation, the old man grabbed one of the automatic rifles left behind and killed both these soldiers, whereupon he returned to the village and, using the same rifle, also killed the Muslim sheikh and his wife, whom he happened upon at their own home. George was able to flee to his vineyard. When he was picking grapes and figs to satiate his hunger, soldiers caught up with him and killed him.

Erzurum (pp. 72–4)

As told by Danho from the village of Bote:

> I served in the Turkish army for seven years, until 1915. There were seven Assyrians in my unit. One day the commander delegated our unit to a location which we did not know how to find. He only showed us the direction. We were escorted by merciless officers and were treated very badly. Many soldiers died of exhaustion and hunger and they did not even let us bury their bodies. They were left on the roads, as food for wild animals.
>
> One day, the seven of us were sitting outside a hanger. We were sad and worried. A man passed by. Noticing our sorrow, he paused and asked: 'Why are you sitting here lost in thought? Am I right that you are Christian?'
>
> 'Yes! We are Christian!' we replied.
>
> 'I can also see that you are exhausted! Tomorrow morning, go to the bishop of this city, Erzurum, and tell him about your fate!' he suggested.
>
> This we did.
>
> In the city, we were taken to the bishop. He was grey from old age and covered in tears. We asked him the reasons for his tears. He started telling us his story:
>
> 'According to the decree of the sultan the soldiers have confiscated all weapons in possession of Christians, saying that they need them more than we do. Subsequently, a decree was issued concerning the extermination of Armenians. Now our nation cannot defend itself and nobody will defend us.'
>
> After a brief moment of silence the bishop asked us where we came from. When he found out that we came from Ṭūr 'Abdīn he said that our homeland is to the south of Erzurum, whereupon he opened a door to the right of his desk and told us to enter with him. A great chest of jewellery lay there. He inserted his hand into it and gave each of us a handful, saying: 'Take this and cover your needs. Others will soon take it all anyway. And on Sunday, come to mass. Perhaps God will give us and you his mercy.'

On Sunday, early in the morning, we travelled to the church. The church was packed. The mass was celebrated by five priests at five altars. The faithful prayed, focused, confessed, accepted communion and cried: 'God, have mercy on us!'

Following mass, we returned to our camp.

On the following day we saw massive crowds of Muslims from the entire region. In the city they mixed with soldiers and started rounding up men and women, the old and the young. They bound all in rope and dragged them to nearby valleys outside the city. There, some were stoned, some shot. The city became desolated.

They continued [with this] on the following day. We saw the bishop, together with his provost and the priests, in chains, escorted by a mounted unit. They were hit with whips and shoes. The seven of us were also forced to join this death march. We were all taken up a mountain, to a large cave. The bound clergy were aligned in front of the cave and then shot. We were, in turn, ordered to push the bodies into the cave and block the entrance with stones. We never experienced so much fear. We thought that we would share the same fate. Walking towards the cave I must have fainted twice. I wanted to kiss the hands of the bloodied bishop. But I feared they might shoot me.

Following this scene, we returned to our camp. None of us could hold back tears. We decided together that this night shall be our last in the army. We never knew how long this pitiful service was to last.

On the following night, at midnight, we tricked the guards and escaped. We made our way south, where our homeland, Ṭūr 'Abdīn, was. How far was it? We did not know. We walked during the night, hiding in caves or shrubs during the day. Any green growing thing was our food.

It was only after a few days that we made it to the hill of 'Ayn Wardo.

Ḥiṣn Kīfā (pp. 83–5)

Ḥesnō d-Kīfō (today Hasankeyf in Turkey) was a large, fortified city on the banks of the Tigris.[5] Most houses were carved in hard mountain

[5] The place is also known as Hesno-d Kifo, Hasankeyf, Hassan-Kêf, *Ḥiṣn Kayfa'* (in Arabic), or simply *Ke'fa'* (Assyrian, for "rock"). One estimate put its population at 400, another at

Figure 7 The village of ʻAyn Wardo (photograph by M. Abdalla, 1999)

Figure 8 The fortified church of ʻAyn Wardo, where Assyrians preserved themselves during the genocide (photograph by J. Kaczmarek, 2003)

Figure 9 Abandoned graves – the village of ʻAyn Wardo (photograph by M. Abdalla, 1999)

Figure 10 The ruins of Ḥesnō d-Kīfō (the rock fortress) at the Tigris, northern borders of Ṭūr ʻAbdīn, with houses and temples carved in rock (photograph by M. Abdalla)

rock, which also has numerous caves serving as homes. The mountain is bisected by a picturesque, broad and twisting gorge. Fertile valleys and fields extend around the city. In certain times the city was capital both to Ṭūr ʻAbdīn as well as the Gharzan region, and the territories it ruled stretched all the way to the borders of the city of Amida. It was the seat of sultans and Ayyubid kings,[6] as well as a theatre for many wars. The emperor Constans, son to Constantine the Great, who built Amida, liked Ḥiṣn Kīfā more than any other city, and joined many localities with it, such as Ra's al-ʻAyn and even Nisibis, Maypherkat and Arzun; the end of his influence was marked by the gates of the city of Gzirto. He constructed two great fortified castles in the city, which served as shelter for the inhabitants of neighbouring villages that were constantly threatened by Persian attacks. One of the castles was located on a high mountain-side close to the Bet Arbaya border; another was by the river. It was also Constans who named it Ḥesnō d-Kīfō [7] and it was a pearl of the region. The long period of wealth and prosperity of the city was interrupted by the Ayyubid dynasty.

The slaughter of the Assyrians of Ḥesnō d-Kīfō

The Christians of Ḥiṣn Kīfā were, for the most part, craftsmen; the Muslims, in turn, dealt mostly with farming. The city commander and the leader of all inhabitants was the Christian Zacheus Gabriel Tuma. Beside his administrative duties he ran a wine cellar famous in the area, where he would process the grapes from his vineyards. He also sold sugar. The governor of the region was a frequent guest of Zacheus, both at home as well as at the vineyard;

500, which sounds much reduced from Roman times as portrayed by the author. (Gaunt, D., *Massacres*, pp. 224 and 427.)

6 The Ayyubids were a dynasty of Sunni rulers, which followed the Shiite Fatimid dynasty and ruled Egypt (1171–1250), Yemen (1173–1229), Syria (1174–1260) and Upper Mesopotamia (1185–1259). Its founder, and the most prominent representative, was Salah ad-Din (Saladin), however the dynasty took its name from his father, Ayyub. Following the death of Saladin (1193), the sultanate was divided among its heirs, who created local dynasties. In Egypt the Ayyubids were deposed by the Mamluk dynasty, in Syria and Mesopotamia by the Mongols.

7 The Greek name was ςαφιΚ (*Kiphas*), which appears to be a translation or transliteration of the Assyrian word.

they were friends, even more so as the governor was quite fond of the wine manufactured by the host.

When the Christians of Ḥiṣn Kīfā heard of the massacres perpetrated against their brothers in the Bsheriyye and Gharzan regions, Zacheus shared his fears about the fate of Christians of Ḥiṣn Kīfā with the governor. The governor assured him: 'The *firman* of the Sultan does not apply to Assyrians, but to Armenians who have risen up against the authorities, and even their deeds will be forgotten. Fear nothing!'

Calmed down by these declarations, Zacheus appealed to his countrymen not to fall in to panic, because the governor, as an old friend, hitherto hid nothing from him and there was no reason to doubt the truth of his words now.

The city walls were tall, thick and extraordinarily strong. When the robust gates were closed for the night, no power could be able to get inside. The gates were always closed for the night and only Christians guarded them. In order to dispel the fears of Zacheus and his men, the governor suggested strengthening the guards with a unit of the regular army under his command, of which Zacheus was supposed to take care.

Zacheus thanked his friend for his generosity!

Meanwhile, it turned out that the governor secretly agreed with the chieftain of the region, Amin Ahmad Abdullah, on a plan to exterminate the Christians; at the determined time the forces under the leadership of Amin were to stand at the gates, which the governor's soldiers would open, allowing them to enter the town.

At the set hour the governor was a guest of Zacheus; they were drinking wine at the winery. Suddenly, a voice could be heard: 'Amin's people are at the city gates and are trying to open them!' Hearing this, the governor calmed the host down: 'Have no fear. My soldiers will shoot anyone who will storm the gate if Amin's people open any gate at all'.

In a moment, fire was exchanged, not between the forces attacking the gate and the soldiers but between the Assyrian guards and the soldiers. The soldiers were better armed and more numerous – they managed to open the gates for the people under Amin.

At the moment they entered the city, they began to kill the Christian inhabitants and to burn their property with wild fury. Both men, women and children, irrespective of age, fell victim – more than 400 people. The remainder of the inhabitants surrendered, including the leader, Zacheus, and some members of his family.

One of the people to escape the massacre by chance was Abd al-Ahad Gabriel Tuma, brother to Zacheus. Together with his wife he had travelled to the village of Kafro a few days earlier, in the company of its Muslim village leader named Darbaso, who was visiting his daughter – a resident of Ḥiṣn Kīfā after her marriage. Hearing what happened to the Christians at Ḥiṣn Kīfā, Darbaso decided to take his company to Midyat. On the way they were attacked by a group of ten armed Muslims. They were hunting for escapees from Ḥiṣn Kīfā. Darbaso sensed their plan and said to them: 'You have already killed hundreds of Christians, and I have not killed even one yet. Leave these two for me!' In this way, Darbaso saved his friends and took them safely to Midyat.

Gabriel, the father of Zacheus, was also away during the massacre. Knowing that he had nothing to come back to he went to a Muslim friend of the family, Sheikh Salih, whose house was located in the upper part of the city. The sheikh was not home but his wife took the guest in and gave him shelter. However, the governor and Amin found out that Gabriel was at the sheikh's home. Not willing to betray his friend, the sheikh swore that he had not seen him. Four days later the sheikh equipped Gabriel with food supplies and tobacco and his nephew led him under cloak of night to a mountaintop, from which he descended on a rope. His destination was Midyat; he would walk at night and hide in caves during the day. He reached Midyat after three days. However, the city was deserted. It turned out that its Christian inhabitants, who survived the massacres, escaped and sheltered in the fortified Assyrian village of 'Ayn Wardo. Gabriel travelled to 'Ayn Wardo and there he met his son, Abd al-Ahad, and his daughter-in-law.

The Village of 'Arbaya (p. 109)

The fate of the Assyrians from this village was no milder than the fate of the village of Bnēbīl, located quite close to it to the east. It was surrounded by Kurds from villages such as Diwan, Sardaf, Hermes, Shebaniyye and others; they cut off its water supply, which was diverted to take a different course. After a few days the inhabitants had to surrender, which does not mean that

Figure 11 Ḥesnō d-Kīfō – the remains of a house (photograph by M. Abdalla, 1999)

they were spared by the barbarians. They entered the village like hungry wolves and started murdering, robbing and burning. When the violence tired them, they would bind the locals with rope, drag them outside and shoot them. Subsequently, they travelled to its rich gardens and vineyards and cut the fruit trees down. They took almost all of the young children for themselves and raised them in the spirit of Islam. Only the Minas family was left alive out of all the inhabitants. They ran a large forge in the village, which the Kurds used to make their weapons.

By 1918 the massacres in the vicinity had subsided and the state gave the locals assurances of safety. Only twenty villagers returned, less than a tenth of the previous population. They were cared for by a monk named Safar (1848–1954). However this did not last long. The local Kurds harassed them, forcing them to leave the village and emigrate, primarily to Germany and Sweden.

The Village of Dayrō da-Ṣlībō[8] (p. 111)

When signs of war and news of massacres could be seen on the horizon the inhabitants of Dayrō da-Ṣlībō gathered and discussed how they would be able to protect themselves from the rage of the Kurds. They came to the conclusion that they would only be able to stand up to the oncoming avalanche if they were to stand united. They immediately collected their household goods and supplies and placed them in the famed and fortified monastery of St Āhō, also called Bet Il,[9] located on a hilltop in the village. They barricaded themselves there.

Not much later the Kurds swarmed in like locusts from many nearby villages: Sardaf, Harmas, Der Kfono and others. The battle between the attackers and the villagers lasted more than two-and-a-half months, until the *firman* of the sultan arrived, obliging all forces laying siege to Assyrian villages and attacking their inhabitants to stand down. In order to implement the orders of the *firman* a unit of the Ottoman army came to aid the inhabitants. It was commanded by George, the son of priest Asmar, leader of ʻAyn Wardo. The Kurds left the village, but they went unpunished, and the inhabitants were able to breathe easy again, as their food supplies had been running out.

The village enjoyed peace until 1923. In that year the Kurdish Sheikh Said and his people started attacking Assyrian villages without reason. Somebody sent the authorities letters, the originator of which was Sheikh Said himself. From these letters the authorities understood that Sheikh Said had started an uprising. The inhabitants of the village of Dēr aṣ-Ṣalīb were not able to stand up to the vast numbers of the Sheikh's units, as he chose the monastery as a place to hide from the Turkish army following and attacking him. The army entered the village and, in course of the uprising, destroyed the monastery and killed many innocent Assyrian inhabitants. Corpses lay everywhere. This tragedy caused the majority of the inhabitants to gradually abandon their village.[10]

[8] Translated as The Monastery of the Cross.

[9] House of God (*Il/ilu* Akkadian for God) – this is also the name of the village, not just the monastery.

[10] In the summer of 2003 a few Assyrian families lived in the village, and the Feast of the Cross (14 September) was organised by the inhabitants of Ṭūr ʻAbdīn as a central mass together with a vigil. In 2004 the village leader, Gabriel, was murdered in mysterious circumstances.

Some Places of Deportation and Execution of the Rounded-up Christians (pp. 38–9)

Deir ez-Zor[11]

This is a large city, built on both sides of the Euphrates river, where an Assyrian monastery named Dayrō Zʿūrō – the Small Monastery – once stood. Today Christians make up a small percentage of the inhabitants and have three churches: Syrian Orthodox, Armenian Orthodox and Syrian Catholic.[12] All reports on the genocide, be it oral or written, local or foreign, indicate this city as one of the places where close to 160,000 Christians, mostly Armenians, were driven to, in the majority from historic sites such as Bursa, Sivas and Cilicia. Their fate was planned for them to perish here. The local governor showed mercy to the deported, which cost him his transfer to a different province. In his place, the Turks appointed a true bloodthirsty beast, who ordered the execution of all the deported without thinking twice. This was perpetrated by soldiers and Cherkess, mostly through beheadings at the riverside or by shootings.[13] Out of subsequent transports, only some of the earlier orphaned children were saved. They were brought from an orphanage from Mardin and set up by the United States.

Ra's al-ʿAyn [Rish ʿAyna]

A Mesopotamian city quite famous in ancient Christian times, thanks to the existence of twenty-one schools here, from which famed philosophers, medical doctors, translators and poets graduated. The sources of three rivers can be found

A former inhabitant of this village, Alexander Demiral, presently an immigrant in Sweden, wrote an elegy to him, publishing it in the magazine *Hujådå*.

[11] Today in Syria, on the Euphrates.

[12] The book was published in 1986.

[13] As stated by Jacques Rhétoré, the first governor was named Jalal ad-Din, and was transferred to Baghdad. He was replaced by Fiqri Bey, a Cherkess. The latter ordered the burning of the great number of 25,000 bodies of Armenians murdered in August and September of 1916 so that they would not cause the locals to be infected with typhus. Based on eyewitness accounts, Rhétoré estimates the number of children and women deported to Deir ez-Zor and its region to be 540,000, of which 360,000 were murdered. Save for a selected group of women and girls, picked by the locals for harems, the rest, or close to 180,000, died of hunger and exhaustion in the desert (Rhétoré, *Al-Masīḥiyyūn*, p. 219).

here, of which the River Khabur is the most important. After the Muslims conquered the city, science started to decline along with the number of Assyrian citizens. In the years of the genocide the Turkish authorities in Amida and Mardin drove close to 100,000 Christians to this city, among others.

The local governor was ready to spare the lives of these Christians and to defend them from the Cherkess. On one occasion he ordered three Cherkess flogged for their aggression [against Christians].

In 1915 a transport of about 1,500 women arrived from Sivas. They were completely naked and barefoot. They chanted 'water, water!' When they reached the river, all drank from it. More than 200 of them died on the river bank. A day later the remaining women were transferred to the military compound in Deir ez-Zor; all were killed.

Following this transport, one more came, this time from Izmir, Konia, Ankara, Marash, 'Ayntab, Mersin, Dörtyol and other localities. It counted more than 170,000 people. Those who converted to Islam and the women and young girls survived; from the latter any Muslim could take any number they wanted; the rest was slaughtered on the banks of the Khabur river. We were informed of this by those who managed to escape this transport.[14]

[14] When describing the methods of elimination of the tens of thousands of children and women in this locality, Rhétoré (*Al-Masīḥiyyūn*, pp. 213–18) quotes two accounts. They describe German responses to these crimes. The first one: 'At Res-el-Aïn [this is the name form the author uses] three German officers lived close to an Assyrian priest. Immediately after they moved in, the priest decided to pay the newcomers a visit. However, they reacted quite coolly to this gesture, and asked: "Who are you?" – "An Assyrian priest. Your neighbour. I wanted to greet you," he responded. The tenants, when they heard this, acted as if they were bitten by a scorpion. They expressed their surprise with one voice: "What? Are there any more priests here?" "Yes! The Sultan had issued an order not to kill any more Assyrian priests. However, this does not apply to Armenians," explained the priest. The officers were greatly shamed by this answer: "You all deserve the same fate as Armenians, meaning, total annihilation, as you are not loyal to the state, and you collaborate with the Russian enemy and its allies." This undiplomatic response of these Germans only proves one thing: the genocide was perpetrated with their highest authorities knowing about it, and it applied to all Christians, without exceptions. So, we should not be surprised by the silence of the Germans with respect to these massacres that occurred at Ras al 'Ayn,' concludes Jacques Rhétoré. The second account is: 'The German baron Oppenheim was freely travelling across the east in a cart pulled by an Armenian worker. Thinking that he was Muslim, the baron spoke to him: "Be happy, soon there will be no more Armenians here!"' Ras al 'Ayn was the location of the workshops serving the construction site of the German railway line as well as the German military vehicle headquarters.

ANNEX 3

Title page of the first issue of the paper *Al-Jihād* newspaper from 5 March 1915, published in Berlin in Arabic

The inscriptions on the right side, inside the graphics, from the top down:

Wa qātilūhum ḥatta lā takūna fitna – Fight them til no sedition/treason remain[1]

In tanṣuru, allāhu yanṣurkum – If you help Allah, He will help you[2]

'Issue 1'

Inscriptions on the left side, inside the graphics, from the top down:

Al-Ǧannatu taḥta ẓilāli as-suyūfi – Know that Paradise is under the shades of swords[3]

[1] The Qur'ān, surah 2 (The Cow), 193 (fragment); all English translations of the Qur'ān follow the website <http://al-quran.info> (last accessed 21 September 2018).

[2] The Qur'ān, surah 47 (Muhammad), 7 (fragment)

[3] This quote seems to mean to say he who dies during the *jihad* with sword in hand shall go to heaven. It may be an allusion to a statement ascribed to Muhammad, or a *hadith*, e.g., Al-Bukhari, Vol. 3, 2818; at <http://sunnah.com> (last accessed 21 September 2018).

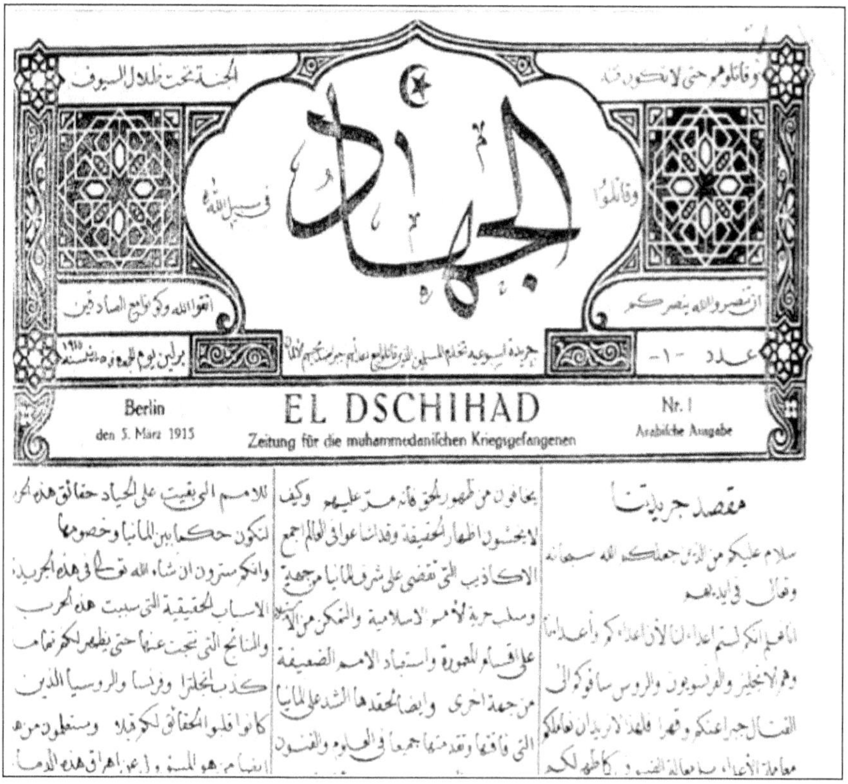
الجهاد

Berlin
den 5. März 1915

EL DSCHIHAD

Zeitung für die muhammedanifchen Kriegsgefangenen

Nr. 1
Arabifche Ausgabe

Figure 12 Title page of *Al-Jihād*, 1915

Ittaqū-l-lāha wa kūnū ma'a aṣ-ṣādiqīn – Be wary of God, and be with the truthful.[4]

'Berlin, Friday, 5 March 1915'.[5]

The large central area holds the title, *Al-Jihād*, in calligraphic script. In the centre, just above it, there is the crescent; presently, accompanied by a star, a like image serves as the emblem and flag of Turkey (on a red background) as well as of other Muslim states, including some post-Ottoman ones. The words on the right side of the title, *Wa qātilū* ('Fight'), form the beginning

4 *The Qur'ān*, surah 9 (Repentance), 199 (fragment).

5 As the intention of publishing the first issue of the paper on Friday, a weekday celebrated by Muslims, is clear, it is a mystery why the Christian calendar was used as a reference. The date 5 March 1915 corresponds to the Muslim calendar date of 18 April 1333.

of a sentence, the continuation of which, on the left side of the title, is *fi sabīli-l-lāhi* ('in the way of Allah').[6] Under the title, in turn, one finds the following sentence: *Jarīda usbū'iyya takhdumu al-muslimīna al-laḏīna qātalū ma'a a'dā'ihim ğabran ḍidda muḥibbīhim al-Almān* ('Weekly publication for Muslims forced to fight against their enemies beside the Germans, who love them').

The contents, spanning three columns:

The goal of our magazine.

Peace be with you, from those, whom God – may he be blessed and exonerated – bestowed with the task of caring for you.[7]

We know that you are not our enemies, but our and your enemies, meaning, the English, the French and the Russian, forced you to fight against your will. That is why we do not want to treat you as one treats their enemy, but like one treats their guests. As you have convinced yourself, they [the English, the French and the Russian] fear the truth, as they have missed it. They cannot reveal it, since all over the world they have published lies, the goal of which on the one hand is to tarnish the name of Germany, and on the other hand, to enslave Muslim nations. They want to rule the world and conquer the weak nations. For this, they hate the Germans, because the Germans exceed them and outdo them in science and art. In this paper, we want to convey the truth to these nations that stand at the side, so that they could themselves build an opinion as to the matter of the conflict between the Germans and their enemies. If God wants, you shall see in this magazine the true reasons for this war, and its effects; then you shall see the hypocrisy of the English, the French and Russians, who had been feeding you lies before. You shall find out who is responsible for the blood that was spilled.

[6] *The Qur'ān*, surah 2 (the Cow), 190 (fragment).

[7] Literally, this seems to say, 'under [or in] the arms of whom Allah had placed you'.

INDEX

Note: illustrations are indicated by page numbers in **bold**; place names are listed as predominantly used in the text with cross-references from alternative variants

Alsace, 53
'Amarke, 75–6, 108, 115
Amida (Diyarbakır), xvii, xviii, xxxi–xxxiii, **xxxii**, xliv, xlvi, 13, 37, 39–50, 61, 64, 65, 67–71, 75–6, 82, 83, 85, 96–117, 125, 131, 161–6, 169–70, 174
amputations, 29, 46, 110
Ananias, xxvii n.12, xxx, 9, 12n.17, 120n.8
Anastasiopolis *see* Dara
Anbarchay, 99, 115–17
Andrus, Alpheus N., 124n.13
Anhel, xxvii
Aniz Pasha, governor of Amida, 41–3, 45, 49n.29, 67
Anthimos, St, 21–2
Antioch, 9, 10, 17, 26–7
Antoninus Pius, 23
Antun, David, 71
Aphrahat, Abd al-Karim, 159
Aphrahat, Habib, 159
Aphrahat, Ya'qūb, 159
Al-Aqsa mosque, Jerusalem, 57n.12
Arab tribes, 36–7, 101, 122, 142, 145, 157, 159, 161, 174
Arabic language, xv, xvii, xxxi, xxxiii, xxxiv, xxxviii, 55n.7
Arabistan *see* Bēṭ Huzaie
Aramaic alphabet, xix
Arbela (Irbil), 13n.20, 33n.64
Arbo, xliv
Armenian language, xxviii, 90, 96
Armenians, xxxi, xxxii–xxxiii, xxxiv, 3n.1, 5n.5, 40n.5, 40n.7, 44, 46–8, 53n.2, 57n.13, 59, 65, 67, 78–9, 84–6, 98–9, 114, 118, 130n.21, 141–2, 150, 157, 162–5, 174–5
Arzu-Oghli, 48
Arzun (Garzan; Kortalan), 13, 134
asceticism, xxvi
al-Ashraf, Ali Naqib, 151–2
Ashur (city), 13n.20
Ashur (Yezidi leader), 140–1
Assyrian Church of the East (Nestorian), xxxi, xxxvi, 67, 138n.10
Assyrian Churches *see* Assyrian Church of the East (Nestorian); Chaldeans; Syrian Orthodox Church (Jacobite)
Assyrian Democratic Organization, xv
Assyrian New Testament, xxv–xxvi
Assyrian Orthodox Church *see* Syrian Orthodox Church
Assyrian schools, xviii, xix n.15, xxix, xxxi, xxxiii, 150, 152
Astal (Astil; Estel; Estil), xxxvii–xxxviii, 38
Aṭanāsiyyos, St, 14
Atatürk, Kemal, xxv n.3, xxxix
Athanasius of Alexandria, 32n.59
Athenogenes, 24–5
Augin, Mār (St Eugene), xxvi, 16n.32
Aurelian, 28
Austria, 52–3, 55, 57–8, 63, 66, 72
'Ayn Dalbe, 158n.24
'Ayn Wardo (Gülgöze), 155
'Aynshah, 48, 116
Aysho, Alike, 160
Azakh (Bēt Zabdāy; İdil), xxv, xxxiv, 13, 146n.1, 147

Babylas of Antioch, St, 26–7
Babylon, 32, 34
Badebe, **xliv**, xliv
Badger, George Percy, xxxii–xxxiii
Badlisi, Nuri, 157
Badr Khan, xliv–xlv, 8n.1
Bafawa, 123, 126, 127
Baghdad, 65, 70
Baghjachik, 116
Bahrain, xxxi
Bahram Pasha, 40
Bahzane, 138
Bajinne, 66
Bakale *see* Rishkalo
Baldwin of Jerusalem, 14n.24
Balis (Maskanah), 35
Balkans, 56n.12, 70
banishment, 22, 27, 28, 52, 73, 142
Bano, Barro Isa, 133
Banu Akil, 36–7
Banu Taghlib, 36–7
Bany Tanukh, 36–7
Banu Tayy, 36–7, 142, 145, 159, 161
baptism, xxvii, xxviii, 9, 11, 15
Bār Abe, George, 156
Bar Bshara, Salim, 84–5, 99, 107
Bār 'Ebrāyā (Bar Hebraeus), xxix, 29n.54, 36, 37, 119
Bār Eramia, ṣalībā, 71
Bar Faulos d-Bēṭ Raban, David, 135
Bār Garbo, Kadarsha, 71
Bār Hannush, Pheṭrus, 71–2
Bar Hebraeus (Bār 'Ebrāyā), xxix, 29n.54, 36, 37, 119
Bār 'Īsā, 'Abd an-Nūr, 71

Bār Malke Ya'qūb, Simon, 156
Bār Saliba, Michael, 174–5
Bār Ṣaumā, xxix,xxx
Bār Saydē, Asyā, 71
Bār Yaqin, Kadarsha, 71
Baran, Khashsho, 112
Barbat(i), St, 22
Bardaiṣān, 16
Barṣōm, Ighnāṭiyyos Aphrem I, xxiii n.2, xxxvii–xxxviii, xlii n.45, xlvi, 41n.12
Basebrino (Bsōrīnō; Hamerli), xliii, xliv, 68n.6, 155
Ba'shiqa, 138
Bashir, Abd al-Karim, 148n.9
Basil, bishop of Ancyra, 30
Basil, St, 31–2
Basilides, 24–5
Basra, 70, 136
Batte, Alike, 68
Bayyo, Muhammad, 175
beatings, 74–5, 77–8, 80, 81–2, 83, 85, 106, 132, 147n.7, 148
Bedouins, 36–7, 101, 122, 142, 145, 157, 159, 161, 174
beheading, 21n.11, 22, 33n.67, 49n.29, 99, 127, 130n.21, 150–1, 152n.13, 170, 172
Behnam, Fr (Qarabash), 99, 102–3
Beirut, xv, xviii, 9
Belgium, 53n.4, 58–9
Benedict XV, 54n.2
Beniamin (village leader, Qilleṭ), 131
Berlin, 55, 58
Berlin–Baghdad railway, 159n.28
Bes, Mhammade, 160
Beshar (road worker), 79
Bēṯ Garmaye, 32, 34
Bēṯ Huzaie (Khuzestan; Arabistan; Elam), 32
Bēṯ Lapat (Gundeshapur), 32n.62
Bēṯ Ramma, 174
Bēṯ-Ṣawoce, Jan, 46n.23, 47n.24, 147n.7, 153n.15, 154n.16
Bēt Zabdāy *see* Azakh; Gzirto
Bēṯ-Zabdōyō, Giwargis, xlv n.46
Bethlehem, xviii, xxxv, 11, 23
Bible
  Assyrian New Testament, xxv–xxvi
  in *estrangelo* script, 120n.4
  illustrated Gospels, xxvi
  translations, xxv–xxvi, xxviii
Bişeriyye *see* Bsheriyye
Bitlis, 61, 82–3, 150
Bkhere, 120, 123, 125, 127–8, 173
Bnēbīl (Bnabil; Bnāy-Īl; Bülbül), xli–xlii, 49, 120, 123–5, 127, 128, 172–3
Britain, 5n.5, 53–5, 59, 60, 63, 66, 70, 143, 145
Bsheriyye (Bişeriyye), 49, 114
Bshiroyo, Gabriel, 134
Bsōrīnō *see* Basebrino
Buknad, 13n.19
Bülbül *see* Bnēbīl
Bulgaria, 53, 109
burial customs, 137
burning
  of books, xlii, 29, 155
  of buildings and villages, xxix, xxxvii, xlii, xliii, xliv, 26, 29, 37, 40–1, 44–5, 46, 67, 73, 129, 130n.21, 150, 153
  of Christians, 21, 22, 25, 29, 127, 157n.23, 164
  of crops, warehouses and supplies, xlv, 67
Byzantine Empire, xxv

Callinicus (Ar-Raqqa), 35
Carrhae (Kirkuk), 32n.63
Carthage, 28
Catholicism, xviii n.10, xxxvi, 65, 90n.14, 130, 146, 147, 155
Chabakchur, 100
Chalabi, Hajji Assad, 159
Chalabi, Khalil, 109
Chalabi, Khider, 126, 149
Chalabi, Mahmad Ali, 126, 166
Chaldeans, xxxiii, 46n.23, 47, 65, 67, 112–13, 141, 146–7, 150, 151
Chanaqchi, 85–97, 116
Chan-Aqpenar, 48
Charukhiyye, 48, 112–13
Chatto, Jamile, 134
Chavish, Tawfiq, 154n.16
Cherkess, 75, 86, 108, 163
China, xxix, xxxi
Chirnak, 116
Christ, xxvii n.12, xxx, xxxv, 8–9, 10–12, 106
Christian academy, Edessa, xxv–xxvi, xxx, xxxi, 34n.71, 158n.24
Christian academy, Nisibis, xxiii, xxv–xxvi, 158
Christian property
  looting of *see* looting
  sale of, 166–7

Christianity, spread of, xxvi–xxix, 8–17, 18–19, 30, 119
Chronicles (Mōr Mīkhōyel Rābō), xxix
Chronography (anon.), xxix
Cizre *see* Gzirto
Claudius, 21n.9
Claudius Gothicus, 28
Code of Hammurabi, 6n.7
Committee of Union and Progress, 85n.10, 146n.3, 162
Constantine I (Constantine the Great), 15, 29–30
Constantine II, 15n.30
Constantinople (Istanbul), xxviii, xlv, 14n.24, 37–8, 43, 57n.13, 59, 124n.13
conversions, xxv, xxvii–xxviii, xxx, xxxvii–xxxviii, 9–11, 18, 24, 36–7, 60, 119, 171–2
Coptic Church, 14n.25
Council of Chalcedon, 14n.25
Courtois, Sébastien de, 40n.6, 40n.7, 44n.18, 45n.19, 56n.10, 99n.3, 164n.37
Cross of Christ, xxviii
crucifixion, 19n.6, 21, 22, 29, 30, 132
Crusades, xxx, xliii, 14n.24
Cutts, Edward Lewes, xxxi
Cyprian, St, 28
Cyprus, xxix, 10
Cyrene, 10
Cyril, St, 27

Dadushiyye, 159
Dagshuriyye tribe, 160
Damascus, xxix, 9, 17, 54n.5
Damkhiyya, xxviii–xxix
Danisor, 119
Dara (Oğuz; Anastasiopolis), 35, 37, 98, 119, 123, 125–6
Darakli, 100, 102
Dashi, Abd el-Aziz, 159
David, Abel, 133
David, Fr (Ḥesnō d-Aṭṭō), 155
David, Fr (Sa'diyye), 114–15
David, Zayno, 133
Davis, George, 158n.27
Dayr az-Za'farān monastery *see* Za'farān monastery
Dayro d-Kurkmo *see* Za'farān monastery
Dayro d-Mōr Gabriel *see* Mōr Gabriel monastery
Dayro d-Qartmīnōyō *see* Mōr Gabriel monastery
Dayro d-'Umro, 154–5
death marches, 73, 75–6, 83–4, 86–97, 100, 107–8, 110–13, 116, 133, 140, 148, 151, 163–5, 169, 172, 174
Deir ez-Zor, 141
deportations, 16n.31, 26, 28, 49n.33, 98–9, 130n.21
Der-Bashur, 116
Dērīk (Al-Malikiyye), xxxiv, 108, 110, 149n.9
Diocletian, 29, 87n.12
Dionosiyyos I Telmahroyo, 36n.85
Dionosiyyos Bar-Salibi, 42n.13
Dionysius of Alexandria, 27
Dionysius the Areopagite, St, 21, 36n.85
Dirscho, 151–2
disease, xliii, xliv, 4, 102, 140–1, 142, 165–6, 171
Divrha, Ibrahim Bahdi, 130n.21
Diyarbakır *see* Amida
Djemal Pasha, 40, 104
Dmō zlīḇō (Qarabashi)
  addition of critical apparatus, xv–xvi
  amendments and annotations, xx–xxi
  appearance and construction of manuscript, xix–xx
  content, xvi
  dedication, xix
  eyewitness accounts, xvi, 4, 77–97
  former users of manuscript, xxi
  pagination of manuscript, xix–xx
  title, xxi–xxii
  translations and editions, xv–xvi
d-Neṭfo monastery of the Holy Mother, 120
Dohuk, 158n.24
Dolabani, Yūḥānōn, xvii–xviii, xli
Dominican order, 150, 152
Domitian, 21–2
Domitian the Ascetic, 30
Dört-Yol, 59
drafting *see* miliatry service
Duhokgidi, 99
Dukar, 160
Dusfan, 139

earthquakes, 23, 31
Edesius, 13–14
Edessa (Ar-Ruhā; Urhoy; Urfa), xxv–xxvii, xxx–xxxi, xlvi, 10–13, 16, 34n.71, 37, 39, 71, 158n.24

Edict of Milan, 30
Eğlence, xl
Egypt, xxvi, 14, 17, 29, 54n.6
Ehwo (Ḥabāb), xliv
1895 massacres, xvi, xxxviii, xlvi, 35n.81, 39–50, 99
Elam *see* Bēṯ Huzaie
Elias, Fr (Gzirto), 147
Elias, Fr (Ḥesnō d-Aṭṭō), 155
Elias III Shakir, 10n.9, 126
Elyudo, Elias, 160
enslavement *see* slavery
Enver Pasha, 55–8, 70
Ephesus, 27
Ephrem, Fr (Si'irt), 151
Ephrem, St, xxv, xxxiv, 158
epidemics, xliii, 4, 165–6; *see also* disease
Erzincan, 87, 88, 91, 163
Erzurum, 61, 70, 139, 163, 171
Eskikale *see* Ḥesnō d-Aṭṭō
Estel *see* Astal
estrangelo (Syriac script), xlii, 120
Ethiopia, 10n.4, 13–14
Eugene, St (Mār Augin), xxvi, 16n.32
Euphrates, river, 16, 107
Eusebius of Caesaria, 12n.16, 23n.20, 23n.21, 25n.28, 28n.48, 29n.51
Eusebius of Nicomedia, 15n.30
Eustathius of Sebaste, 87n.12

Fabian, St, 26
Fakhr ad-Din, 136
famine *see* hunger
Farhan (officer), 121, 122
Farhan (village leader), 126
Fatih Pasha mosque, Amida, 164
Fayiz Beg, 85
Feṭrus, Mo (St Peter), 10, 11, 17, 18n.2, 21, 120
Fiji, 87
Firan, 123
First Council of Nicaea, xxv, 14n.24, 158, 165n.37
First World War, xxii, xxxiv, xlvi, 51–62, 63–73, 104, 124n.13, 150, 158–9
Flavius, Josephus, 19n.4
forced labour, 28, 74–5, 77–97, 116, 117, 157, 163; *see also* slavery
Forty Martyrs church, Mardin, 37, 119, 126
France, 24, 53, 55, 60, 63, 66, 70, 152n.13, 161n.32
Franz Ferdinand of Austria, 52–3
Fructuosus, bishop of Tarragona, 28n.44
Frumentius, 13–14

Gabbe, Alexander, 133
Gabriel, Fr (Si'irt), 151
Gabriel, Mōr (St Gabriel), xxxix, xliii, 154n.18
Gabriel, Peter, 131–2
Gabro, Malke, 131, 132
Galerius, 29
Galilee, 9, 19n.6
Gallienus, 28
Gamlin, 35
Garzan *see* Arzun
Gaunt, David, 99n.4
Gelinkaya *see* Kafr Ḥwārā
Geneva Conventions, 58
George (village leader, Bafawa), 127
George (village leader, Ka'biyye), 105
Georgia *see* Iberia
Gerke-Shamo, 160
Germany, xv, xxxviii, xxxix, xlvi, 5n.5, 53–60, 63, 66, 70, 72, 148, 159
Ger-Sheran, 160
Ghandūr, Ḥannā, xviii
Gharzan (Hazzo), 49
Gharzānī, Dāwūd, 49n.31
Ghazale, Khalil, 123, 124, 127–8
Ghirnak, 48
Gir, Ḥannush, 72
Givargis, Kirill, 67, 122, 126–7, 155
Goliyye *see* Qsur
Goranopolis *see* Tella
Gōrgīs, Asmar al-Qass, xxxvi–xxxvii, xli–xlii, 130, 157
Goze, Shakir Hajji, 159
Gozli, 77–8, 116
Greeks, xxxii–xxxiii, 3n.1, 10
Gregory I, 10n.8
Gülgöze *see* 'Ayn Wardo
Gulle, 113
Gundeshapur *see* Bēṯ Lapat
Güngören *see* Kafarbe
Gzirto (Cizre; Bēṯ Zabdāy), xxiii, 136, 146–9

Ḥabāb *see* Ehwo
Habashi, 81
Ḥabsnosoyo, Ya'qūb, 134
Haddad, Murad, 133
Hadrian, 23
Hag (road worker), 79

Hague Conventions, 58
Ḥāḥ, xxv, **xxxv**, xxxv–xxxvi
Hakkari, xlv n.47
Halluli, Ivannis Elias, 67, 122, 123
Hamerli *see* Basebrino
Hamidiyye, 43n.15
Hammo Sharro, 140, 141, 142–4, 161, 174–5
Ḥamza, Agha, xliv
hanging, 147n.7, 161n.32
Ḥannā, 'Īsā, xv–xvi, xxi
Ḥannā, Karim, 72
Ḥannā, Phaulos, 72
Hanne, Shamune, 68n.6
Hanno, Joseph, 157n.23
harems, xliii, 60, 87–92, 109, 128, 131, 148, 153, 161
Harin, 171
Harran, 36
Harris, Helen B., 47n.24, 48n.28
Al-Hasakah, xxxiv
Hasan, Aishe, 92
Hasan, Sofi, 89–92
Hasankeyf *see* Ḥesnō d-Kīfo
Havarchay, 85–6, 99, 113, 115–17
Havar-Dahle, 116
Havarkhase, 116
Hawerkiyye tribe, 160n.32
Hazzo *see* Gharzan
Helena (mother of Constantine), 29n.54
hermits, xvii n.9, xviii, 120, 136
Ḥesnō d-Aṭṭō (Eskikale), xxviii, 49, 69, 120, 121, 123, 155–7
Ḥesnō d-Kīfo (Hasankeyf), xxiii
Hippolytus of Rome, 26
Hirah (Al-Ḥīra), 15–16
Ḥisn Mansur, 49
History (Bār 'Ebrāyā), xxix
Hitti, Philip, 54
Hobur, 119
Holy Mother church, Amida, 42n.13, 43
Holy Mother church, Ḥāḥ, xxxvi
Holy Mother church, Kerboran, xxxvi
Homs, xxix
hospitals, xxix, 140, 141, 156
Hulagyu Khan, 136, 137
Hulan, 48
Hulva, 160
hunger, xliii, xliv, 4, 19, 23–4, 62, 63, 74, 77, 81, 82, 92, 102, 122, 141–2, 157

Iberia (Georgia), 15
Ibrahim (Arab chieftan), 159
Ibrahim (officer), 101–2
Ibrahim the Tall (officer), 79
Ibrim (village owner, Khezna), 160
İdil *see* Azakh
Ighnāṭiyyos Abed Mshiho II, 41–3, 45, 122–3
Ighnāṭiyyos of Antioch, St, 10n.8, 22
imprisonment, 19, 26–8, 52, 60, 62, 82, 131–3, 147, 150–1, 160, 164
India, xxix, 11, 34n.69, 56
Iraq *see individual locations*
Irbil *see* Arbela
Islam
  affluent Muslims living in Christian districts, 41
  churches converted to mosques, xxxiii n.31, xxxvii, 36, 37, 42n.13, 119
  conversion to, xxxvii–xxxviii, xli, 35–8, 60, 90n.13, 116, 133, 134
  and the 1895 massacres, 40–50
  emergence of, 35–8
  fanaticism, 33n.65, 41n.8, 153, 162
  German attitudes towards, 54–8, 70
  and military service, 65
  Muslim victims, 40n.7, 41
  Muslims providing help or shelter to Christians, 114, 126–7, 148
  and the 1914–18 massacres, 56–62, 71–177
  refusal to convert to, 16n.31, 36, 48n.24, 95–7, 113, 116, 151, 168–9
  resettlement of Bulgarian Muslims, 104, 109
  size of Muslim populations, xxxi–xxxv, xxxviii, xli–xlii, 116–17
Ismail Enver Pasha *see* Enver Pasha
Istanbul *see* Constantinople
Italy, xxvi, 53, 152n.13; *see also* Rome; Venice
'Iwās, Ighnāṭiyyos Zakkā I, 150n.12
Iwas family, 150
Iyawannis of Midyat, 39n.2
'Izzaddin Sher, xlv

Jacob Baradeus, St (Mōr Ya'qūb Bured'ōnō), 10n.4, 35n.81
Japan, 53
Jaqqi, Ḥannā Syrri, xxxiii
Jerusalem, xviii, 8–9, 10, 11–12, 19, 23, 30–1, 56n.12

Al-Jihad, 55n.7
John, Fr (Gzirto), 147
John Chrysostom, 26n.39
John '*Maqdeshyo*' (road worker), 80
John of Tella, St, 35n.81
John Paul II, 54n.5
John the Evangelist, St, 22, 24
Jordan, 54n.6
Jordan, river, 19
Joseph (Chaldean priest), 141
Judaism, xvi, xxxi, xxxii, xxxiv, xxxv, 9, 18–19, 21, 23, 24, 31, 34, 57n.12, 158
Judea, 9, 19
Julian the Apostate, xxxi, 30–2
Justinian I (Justininian the Great), 9n.4, 87n.12

Kabala, 38
Ka'biyye, 48, 78, 82–3, 105–12
Kachcha, Ahmad Agha, 150–1
Kadi, 48
Kafarbe (Kfarbo; Güngören), xxxviii–xxxix, 155
Kafarzo, xliii
Kafr Ḥwārā (Gelinkaya), xxxviii
Al-Kahtaniyya *see* Qabre Hewore
Kajjun, Baho, 133
Kalchu, 13n.20
Kankrat, 48
Karabahche, 83
Karakilisa, 48
Karkaisa, 36
Karko, Joseph, 172–3
Kartbart (Kharput), 49, 61, 71, 112, 161n.32
Karte, 48
Kartfort, 39
Kasre, 122, 165
Kefr Tuth *see* Kfar Tutha
Kerboran (Kfar Boran), xxxvi–xxxvii, 153–4
Kfar Mari, 158n.24
Kfar Tutha (Kefr Tuth), 35, 36, 119
Kfarbo *see* Kafarbe
Khaddo, Fahima Gabro, 148n.9
Khalaf, Abo Sheikh, 172
Khalaf Agha, 103
Khalil, Ahmad, 125
Khalil, Ibrahim, 160
Khalil Pasha, 102–3, 152
Kharput see Kartbart
Kharse, 144
Khave-Rashsh, Mhammade, 79
Khello (armed guard), 156
Khezna, 160
Khorasan, xxxi
Khoren (road worker), 79
Khurmiyye, 128
Khuro (road worker), 79
Khuzestan *see* Bēṯ Huzaie
Khwetla, 160
kidnappings *see* abductions
Kirkuk *see* Carrhae
Korekli Pasha, xlv
Kortalan *see* Arzun
Kozan, 45, 48
Kubayba, 160
Kufa, 136
Kurd Kaya, 108, 110
Kurds, xvi, xxii, xxxii, xxxiv, xxxviii, xxxix, xlii–xlvi, 3, 40–50, 72–6, 81, 83, 85–97, 99–104, 107–11, 114–16, 121–7, 129–32, 142, 146–7, 150–7, 160–1, 172–4

Laḥdō, Fr, xvi, 39
Lang, David Marshall, 57n.13
Lawrence, deacon of Rome, 28n.44
Layard, Henry Austen, xlv n.47, 8n.1
Lebanon, xvii, xxx–xxxi, 152n.13; *see also* Beirut
Leo X, 53
Leonidas, 25
Lice *see* Lije
Licinius Granianus, 23
Lije (Lice), 49
looting, xlii–xlv, 3, 37, 40–1, 43–4, 46, 60, 62, 67–8, 100, 107, 121, 123, 127, 130n.21, 148, 150, 152–3, 163
Lorraine, 53
Lulo, Amsih, 133
Lyons, 24

Mabbug (Manbij), 9
Al-Madine, 71, 114
Ma'esrōṯō, 123
Magi, xxv, xxxv–xxxvi, 11
Mahmud, Smail Ali, 156
Majdaddin, Sleman, 160
Malatya *see* Melitene
Al-Malikiyye *see* Dērīk
Malla-Chabre, 116
Malo, 107
Mamidha, 140–1, 144
Mansuriyye (Yalim), 49, 128–9

Manug (road worker), 78–9
Maqsi-Oghli, 92, 116
Marcus Aurelius, 23–4
Mardin, xviii, xxiii, xxxiv, xlvi, 35–7, 41, 43–4, 49, 64–71, 84, 96, 98, 110, 118–34, 139, 143, 155, 157, 159, 166, 168, 172, 174
Margan, Jezry, 165
Mark, Fr (Gzirto), 147
Marqus, Mōr (St Mark), 17
marriage customs, 137
Martianus (advisor to Valerian), 27
Martyropolis *see* Maypherkat
Mārūtā, St, xxxi, 34, 46
Mārūtā (*catholicos*), xxxi
Ma'sarte (Omerli), 126–7
Masjid Khalili mosque, Si'irt, 152
Maskanah *see* Balis
Mas'oud Beg, xlv
Masud, Fr (Qilleṭ), 131, 132
Mato (road worker), 79
Matraniyye, 102
Matthew, St, 14n.25, 120
Matto, Bakir, 172–3
Maximus II Daia, 29
Maximinus Thrax, 25–6
Mawid, 36
Maypherkat (Martyropolis), 34, 46
Mazdaism, 34
Media, 10–11, 16–17
Mehmed II, 87n.12
Mehmed V, 53
Mehyaddin Bey, 143
Melitene (Malatya), 39
Meropius, 13–14
Mesopotamia *see individual locations*
Mesrop Mashtots, St, xxviii
Metternich zur Gracht, Paul Graf Wolff, 57n.13
Meyrier, Gustave, 40n.6
Mghashniyye (Muhaşni), 38
Mḥalmaytō, xxxvii, 38n.88
Mḥalmōyē, xxxvii–xxxviii, 38n.96
Mhammad (tribal leader), 161
Mharka, 160
Michael (Catholic bishop, Gzirto), 147–8
Michael the Great *see* Mīkhōyel Rābō, Mōr
Midyat, xvi, xxx, xliii, 49n.29, 161n.32
Mīkhōyel of Nineveh, St, xxviii
Mīkhōyel Rābō, Mōr (Michael the Great), xxvii, xxix, 14n.23, 32n.59, 36n.85, 119
military provisioning, 66–7, 68, 69–70
military service, xviii, 61–2, 64–9, 71–2, 112, 117, 120, 125, 132, 139–40
military tribunals, 112
Milliyye, Shawkat, 126
Mirian, king of Iberia, 15
Mirzo, Ahmad, 156
Mnizal, 38
monasteries
  destruction of, xvi, xxix, 73
  founding of, xxvi–xxix, xxxix, 16, 135
  libraries, xxix, xlii, 150, 155
  looting and vandalism, xlii–xliii, 37, 62, 121
  seminaries and schools, xvi, xvii–xviii, xxix
  see also individual monasteries
Mongolia, xxix
Mongolian conquests, xliii
Montenegro, 53
Mopsuestia school, 158n.24
Mōr Gabriel monastery, xxvi–xxvii, xxxix–xl, xlii–xliii
Mōr Ya'qūb monastery, Nisibis, xliii
Mōr Ya'qūb monastery, Ṣaleḥ, xliii
Morgenthau, Henry, 57n.13
  Mosque of the Martyr (Sohdo Mosque), Mardin, 37, 119
Mosul, 75, 98, 138, 143, 145, 148, 149n.9, 152n.13, 175
Mother of Fortresses, Mardin, 118–19
Mousa Gorgis family, 150
Msafir Khane (House of the Traveller), Amida, 75, 100, 107, 112
Muawiyah, Caliph, 135–6
Mufti, Hasan, 166
Muhammad, Prophet, 16n.31, 33n.65
Muhammad Al-Fatih, 37
Muhammad bin Marwan, 36
Muhaşni *see* Mghashniyye
Mukhtar Pasha, 58
Muş, 30n.5
Mushe, Peter, 113
Mustafa, Hajji, 101

Naelband, Alexander, 133
Naelband, Sado, 133
Najmaddin, Razzo, 159
Najran, 16n.31
names *see* personal names; place names
Nāmiq, Yūsuf, xxx
Narsai, 158

Nazo, Muhammad, 149
Nero, 21
Nerva, 22n.16
Nesimi Bey, 49n.29
Nestorian Church *see* Assyrian Church of the East
Nestorius, 138
Neurath, Konstantin von, 57n.13
Netherlands, xv
newspapers, xlvi
Nicaea, xxv
Nina, St, 15
1914–18 massacres, xvi, xxii, xxxiv, xlvi, 3–4, 56–62, 71–177
Nineveh, 13n.20, 33n.64
Nishan (road worker), 79
Nisibis (Nusaybin; Ṣōbā), xxiii, xxv–xxvi, xxxi, xxxiv–xxxv, xliii, 37, 119, 125, 145, 158–61
Nizam ad-Din, Rafiq, 160
Nusaybin *see* Nisibis

Oğuz *see* Dara
Omar, Caliph, 16n.31
Omerli *see* Ma'sarte
Origen, 25, 27
Osman, Tharwat, 83, 105, 112
Osman Pasha, 47–8, 151–2
Ottoman Empire, xxi, xxxiii, 41n.8, 52–62, 63–73, 90n.14, 104, 143–5, 166

paganism, xxx, 16, 20, 24, 29, 30
Pal, 87, 114
Palestine, xviii, xxxv, 8–9, 54n.6, 56n.12; *see also* Jerusalem
Palmyra, 28
Paris Peace Conference, xlvi
Parthia, 11
Patrakiyye, 48
Paul, Fr (Gzirto), 147
Paul, Fr (Qarabash), 99, 102, 103
Paul, St, 9, 17, 21
Payran, 157
Peacock Angel, 136
Pella, 19
Persia, xxi, xxv, xxxi, 10–11, 16–17, 56
Persian Empire, 32–5, 158
Persians, xvi, xxviii, xxxi, xlii, 28, 31–5, 158n.24
personal names, xxv n.3
Peter, St (Mo Feṭrus), 10, 11, 17, 18n.2, 21, 120
Philip, St, 14n.25
Philoxenus, St, 9n.4
Phocas, St, 22
Phrygia, 25, 29
pigeon towers, 45, 46, 100
pilgrimage sites, xxviii, xxxi
Pirinjichi, Sidqi, 83–5, 99–100, 105
Pius X, 53n.2, 152n.13
place names, xxiii–xxv, xxxix
plague, 26, 165–6; *see also* disease
plunder *see* looting
Poland, xv
police, 107, 109, 154n.16
Polycarp (student of John the Evangelist), 24
Pontian, St, 26
Pozpenar, 116
Protestantism, xxxi, xxxv, xxxvi, xxxviii, 65, 67, 118, 124n.13, 130, 146, 155

Qabaskal, 116
Qabre Hewore (Al-Kahtaniyya), 159n.28
Qaddur Bey, 159–61
Qamishli, xviii, xxxix, 49n.31, 139n.12
Qara Kilise, 170
Qarabash, xvii, xxxix, 39, 44, 45–6, 71–2, 84, 85, 99–104
Qarabashi, Abed Mshiho Na'man
  in Amida, xviii
  in Bethlehem, xviii
  in Beirut, xviii
  birth, xvii
  diary manuscript *see Dmō zlīḥō* (Qarabashi)
  in Jerusalem, xviii
  orphaned, xvi, xvii
  poetry, tales and plays, xvii
  in Qamishli, xviii
  student at Zaʿfarān monastery, xvi, xvii–xviii, 4
  teaching, xvi–xvii, xviii–xix
  textbooks and treatises, xvii
  translations, xvii
Qarte, 116
  Qartmin (Yayvantepe), xxxix, xl, 154n.18
Qasemo (Kurdish raider), 151
Qasim Bey, 116
Qatrabel, 44–5, 112
Qawme (archdeacon, Qarabash), 99
Qilleṭ, xxxviii, 38, 130–2
Qōrō, Elias Malke, xvii
Qoshk, 116

Qur'an, 27n.42, 55n.7, 70, 120n.4, 172–3
Quriaqos (deacon, Ka'biyye), 108
Qsur (Goliyye), 49, 69, 129–30

Ragle, 116
railways, 159
Ramazan, Sheikh, 129–30
Rammo, Mustafa 'Ali, xxxvi–xxxvii, 153–4
rape, xlv, 6, 37, 46, 56n.12, 60, 73, 86, 106–7, 108, 110, 131, 132, 151
Ar-Raqqa *see* Callinicus
Ra's al-'Ayn *see* Rish 'Ayna
Rashdiyye (Raşidi), 38
Rasul, Mhammade, 149
relics, xxviii, xliii, 14n.24
religious holidays, 137–8
Resaina *see* Rish 'Ayna
Reshid Bey, governor of Amida, 75–6, 78, 101, 102, 107, 108, 111, 129–30, 146–7, 162–4
Reshmel, xli, 38
Rish 'Ayna (Ra's al-'Ayn; Resaina; Theodosiopolis), xxviii, 35, 36, 37, 119, 169, 172
Rishdi (officer), 162, 163
Rishkalo (Bakale), 87
Riza (officer), 159
road construction, 74–5, 77–85, 100, 107, 113, 117, 157, 163
Roman Empire, xvi, 11, 15, 17, 19, 20–32, 158
Rome, 17, 21, 25, 28, 152n.13
Ar-Ruhā *see* Edessa
Russia, 53, 63, 66, 70, 162

Sabbagh, Malko Bahhe, 133
Sabha, 160
Sabit-Bey es-Sueydi, 49n.29
Sa'diyye, 44, 83–4, 113–15
Sado, Hasane, 78–9
Safar, Malak Barson, 161n.32
Safna, 48
Sa'īd, Sheikh, xxxviii
St Āhō church, Damkhiyya, xxviii–xxix
St Āhō monastery, Arzun, 134
St 'Azazal monastery, Mardin, 120
St Behnam monastery, Mardin, 120
St Elias church, Qara Kilise, 170
St Ephrem seminary, Beirut, xviii
St George church, Ḥesnō d-Aṭṭō, 155
St George church, Kerboran, xxxvi
St John church, Amida, 37
St Michael church, Mardin, 71, 119
St Pachomius monastery, Egypt, xxvi
St Qawme church, Qarabash, 99
St Quriaqos and St Marqus church, Kerboran, xxxvi, xxxvii
St Quriaqos church, Bnēbīl, 123
St Sergius monastery, Sinjar, 135
St Sharbel church, Midyat, xxx
St Shmouni church, Bnēbīl, 123
St Shmouni church, Kerboran, xxxvi
St Shmouni church, Mardin, 119
St Thomas church, Qatrabel, 44
St Ya'qūb church, Nisibis, 158, 161
St Ya'qūb monastery, Mardin, 120
as-Sakakini, Khalil, 56n.12
Saladin, 54n.5
Ṣaleḥ, xliii
Ṣalībā, George, xv
Salim (villager, Gzirto), 148n.9
Salomon (Chaldean bishop, Amida), 113
Samaria, 9, 19
Samuel, Severius, 123
Sanders, Liman von, 57n.13
Sardinia, 26
Sare, 68
Sari Kamesh, 70
Sarri, Sadiq, 166
Sarsang, 81
Sasoun, 39
Satia, 48
Saul of Tarsus, 9; *see also* Paul, St
Sayde (villager, Dara), 125–6
Sayfo, use of term, xxi–xxii
Sayfuddin, xliv
Scher, Adday (Sliwa Sher), 150, 151–2
Sebastia (Sivas), 87, 91, 96, 124n.13
Segal, J. B., xxx
Seleucia, xxxi
Septimius Severus, 24–5
Serbia, 52–3
Sergius of Rishaina, 35n.76
Severus Alexander, 25
Shaddada, 141
Shaghule, Ḥannā, 72
Shakir, Elias, xvii
Shakir Bey, deputy governor of Amida, 75, 108, 115
Shammas, George, 133
Shams ad-Din, 136
Shapur I, 28
Shapur II, xxxi, 32–4
Sharabi, 100, 102

Sharaf ad-Din, 136
Sharbel, St, xxx, 22
Sharbel Makhlouf, St, xxxi
Sharkazoyo, Abdullah Bey, 159
Shauro, xxxvii, 38, 65, 114, 127, 131, 132, 133
Shawkat, Mahmud, 159
Shaytan Dare, 81, 83
Shemun, Abraham (village leader, Kerboran), 154n.16
Shem'un Qartmīnōyō, Mōr, xxvi, xxxix
Shendi (bandit), 126, 154–5
Sher, Sliwa *see* Scher, Adday
Shib al-Kasem, 144
Shkafto, 75
Shmalo, 36
Shmouni, Gawriyye, xxviii
Shmouwel Sauroyo, Mōr, xxvi
Sibaberk (Swirg), 39, 47–8, 83
as-Sida, Abd al-Hamid, 148n.9
Si'irt, 150–3
Sileme, 115
Simeon of Jerusalem, St, 19n.6, 22
Simon (bishop, Amida), 165n.37
Simon (*catholicos*), 33
Sinjar mountains, 61, 119, 135–45, 157, 159, 174–5
Sinjari, Khalaf, 144
Sirme, 79, 80, 116
Sivas *see* Sebastia
Sixtus, bishop of Rome, 28n.44
slavery, xliii, 21, 62, 87, 129; *see also* forced labour
sleepers of Ephesus, 27
Ṣōbā *see* Nisibis
Socrates of Constantinople, 32n.59
Sohdo Mosque *see* Mosque of the Martyr
Southgate, Horatio, xxxii, 35n.79, 37n.86, 87n.12
Sozomen, Hermiasz, 32n.59, 34n.69
Ṣṭayfō, 'Abd al-Aḥad Gallō, xix
Ṣṭēfānos, Mōr (St Stephen), 10, 18
Stephen, Fr (Nisibis), 158
stoning, 10, 18, 80, 148
suicides, xlvi, 60, 96–7, 128, 131, 153, 169–70
Surujiyye, 160
Sus, river, 148, 149n.9
Sweden, xxxvi, xxxviii, 153n.14
Swirg *see* Sibaberk
synod of Seleucia, xxxi
Syria *see individual locations*
Syriac language, xvi, xvii, xviii, xxxiii, xxxviii, 161
Syriac script (*estrangelo*), xlii, 120
Syrian Orthodox Church (Jacobite), xvii, xxix, xxxi, xxxv, xxxviii, xli, 4, 10, 47, 67, 71, 118

Aṭ-Ṭabarī, xxxi
Taffe, 114–15
Taleke, 165
Tamerlane, xliii, 87n.12
Tatars, xxxvi
taxation, xliii, xliv, 30, 33, 51–2, 65, 153n.15
Telhas, 48, 116
Tella (Viranşehir; Goranopolis), 35, 69, 98
Tertullian, 17
Thaddeus, St (Mōr Adday), xxv, 10, 12–13, 16, 119
Theodora, empress, 9n.4
Theodosiopolis *see* Rish 'Ayna
Theodosius the Younger, 27
Theophilus of India, 15n.30
Thom (American doctor), 124n.13, 156
Thomas, Fr (Qilleṭ), 131, 132, 133
Thomas the Apostle, St, 11–13, 14n.23
Tigris, river, xxiii, 13, 75–6, 100, 107n.8, 108, 110, 112, 114, 146, 163
Tikrit, xxxi
Titus, 19
torture, 21, 24, 28–9, 47n.24, 52, 75, 78, 102–3, 106–7, 112, 115–16, 131, 133, 147n.7, 151, 163–4
Trabzon (Trapezund), 70, 163
Trajan, 22
Trajan Decius, 26–7
Trapezund *see* Trabzon
Tuk, 38
Tumike, 172
Ṭūr 'Abdīn
  background of region, xxiii–xlvi
  key dates, xlii–xlvi
  key locations, xxx–xlii
  maps, **xiv**
  see also individual locations
Turkey
  engagement in First World War *see* Ottoman Empire
  locations in *see individual locations*
Turkish language, xvii, xxv, xxxiii
Turks, xxii, xxx, xxxii, xxxiv, xxxix, xlii–xliii,

xlv–xlvi, 3, 37–8, 72–3, 87, 108, 139, 143–5, 160
Tyre, 9, 13–14

'Umar ibn al-Khattāb, Caliph, 35, 154n.18
Uniate Church, xxxv, xxxviii, 47, 67, 112–13, 118, 146, 150
United States, 53n.2, 58, 104, 124n.13
Urfa *see* Edessa
Urhoy *see* Edessa
Us, Amar, 160
Usuf, Ahmade, 160

Valerian, 27–8
Västerås, xxxvi, 153n.14
Venice, 14n.24
Vettius, bishop of Lyons, 24
Vincenzo Maria di S. Caterina da Siena, xxx
Viranşehir *see* Tella

Al-Walid, Caliph, 36n.85
Al-Waliyy mosque, Amida, 37
Wangenheim, Hans Freiherr von, 57n.13
Warde, xxvii
weapon confiscations, 42–3, 60, 65, 74, 99–100, 105–6, 112, 124, 147–8
Western Aramaic Script, xxv
Wilhelm II, Kaiser, 53n.2, 54–5, 56–7
Wilson, Woodrow, 53n.2
women
  abduction of, xliii, xlv–xlvi, 44, 46, 60, 86–97, 103–4, 109, 128, 131, 148, 153, 161, 175
  and marriage customs, 137
  Muslim women providing shelter to Christians, 126–7, 148
  rape of, xlv, 6, 37, 46, 56n.12, 60, 73, 86, 106–7, 108, 110, 131, 132, 151
  sent into harems, xliii, 60, 87–92, 109, 128, 131, 148, 153, 161
World War I *see* First World War

Yalim *see* Mansuriyye
Ya'qūb (bishop, Kerboran), xxxvi, 153–4
Ya'qūb (Chaldean bishop, Gzirto), 147–8
Ya'qūb (road worker), 79
Ya'qūb, Gara bet, 72
Ya'qūb, Mōr (St Ya'qūb), xxv, 158n.26
Ya'qūb, Tūmā, xvii
Ya'qūb Bured'ōnō, Mōr (St Jacob Baradeus), 10n.4, 35n.81
Ya'qūb of Serugh, 42n.13
Yasin Agha, Yihia, 83, 99–100, 105, 112–13, 116, 171
Yayvantepe *see* Qartmin
Yazdegerd I, xxxi, 34
Yemen, 15–17
Yezid, 135–6
Yezidis, xxxiii, 66, 135–45, 157, 159, 161, 174–5
Yonan, Gabrielle, xlvi, 55n.7
Yūḥānōn d-Bēṭ Kofar, Fr, 44n.17

Zafar, 15n.30
Za'farān monastery, xvi, xvii–xviii, xxix, **xl**, xl–xli, 4, 50, **64**, 67, 111, 119–23, 125–8, 155–7, 158n.27, 170, 173
Zakiyya (villager, Gzirto), 148n.9
Zenobia, queen of Palmyra, 28
Zolfi (messenger of the governor), 146–7
Zorava, 116
Zoroastrianism, 34

EU representative:
Easy Access System Europe
Mustamäe tee 50, 10621 Tallinn, Estonia
Gpsr.requests@easproject.com

www.ingramcontent.com/pod-product-compliance
Lightning Source LLC
Chambersburg PA
CBHW071833230426
43671CB00012B/1954
* 9 7 8 1 4 7 4 4 4 7 5 1 5 *